Edna St. Vincent Millay
and Her Times

THE UNIVERSITY OF CHICAGO PRESS, CHICAGO
THE BAKER & TAYLOR COMPANY, NEW YORK; THE CAMBRIDGE UNIVERSITY
PRESS, LONDON; THE MARUZEN-KABUSHIKI-KAISHA, TOKYO, OSAKA,
KYOTO, FUKUOKA, SENDAI; THE COMMERCIAL PRESS, LIMITED, SHANGHAI

Edna St. Vincent Millay and Her Times

✼

By ELIZABETH ATKINS

THE UNIVERSITY OF CHICAGO PRESS
CHICAGO · ILLINOIS

TO
Elisabeth Wittmann
AND
Bruno Klinger

INTRODUCTION

CONTINUALLY in England and America one hears the question, "Who is our finest living poet?" God help me, I think I know the answer. But I am in no mood to divulge it, for I am pacific and vulnerable, and it is terrifying to be set upon by a mob of militant believers in divers other poets. This book grows out of the safer question, "Who is our most popular and representative poet?" At that question the most disputatious roomful calms into agreement in an instant. Everyone recognizes that Edna St. Vincent Millay represents our time to itself, much as Tennyson represented the period of Victoria to itself, or Byron the period of Romanticism. She is the only living poet who is casually quoted in philosophical treatises and in moving-picture magazines, in churches and in night clubs, in the rural schools of Oregon and in the Sorbonne of Paris. It is this character of Edna St. Vincent Millay as our representative-at-large—the incarnation of our *Zeitgeist*—which has set me wondering.

I used to assume that her distinction lay in her being such an artist as John Webster, whose ears drank in everything that others of the seventeenth century were saying and who then reuttered it with an effortless perfection which showed it never to have been quite said before. For whenever a new book by Miss Millay is published, one finds in it many things that had been recently said in England and America, only less articulately, less inevitably. But all my notions of her

vii

indebtedness to her contemporaries were changed when I followed the course of twentieth-century poetry by reading it chronologically. Many of Miss Millay's poems are not included in her collections for years after their first appearance in periodicals, but during those years they are echoed and re-echoed on both sides of the Atlantic—echoed slavishly by poetasters and echoed subtly by writers of eccentricity and by poets of original genius. A new mood, a fresh theme, a distinctive turn of phrase, a word strange to poetry (or else abandoned to prose ever since the seventeenth century) are likely to appear in the volumes of not one but a dozen other poets soon after each of her poems is first printed or read from manuscript. A resemblance which would pass as coincidence in a single poem following hers is revealed unmistakably as imitation when it appears in many. I once amused myself by listing chronologically some thousands of metaphors used in English literature. It showed me, among other things, how largely Miss Millay has set the tone for recent poetry. She has been the initiator, not the imitator.

I suppose we are all sometimes ashamed of devouring so much of our own day's expression, when we might be assimilating the riches of the past. Yet it seems that we cannot refrain; our appetite grows from a fundamental human need. I bruise my knees crawling about the orchard, the bag of my apron bulging and heavy with windfalls, and I eat them at random, spitting out seeds and rotten spots and little worms, when I might be supping decently indoors, at a table spread with the miraculously preserved fruits of former times. It is not that I am indifferent to that table. I wish that I knew more of Sophocles, and of

Lucretius, and of Racine, and of Goethe. But there is
no use in trying to subsist on them altogether. There
is a sunny, new flavor in the windfalls which I must
have, if I am to keep healthy enough to taste the
great poetry of earlier days. Even the crudest fresh
provender, even a handful of dandelion greens snatched
from the roadside by a Vachel Lindsay or a Jesse
Stuart, with sunflower sticks and thistles among the
edible weeds, may prevent literary scurvy and sharpen
one's appetite for Shakespeare.

Perhaps one's need of present-day writing comes
partly from the fact that one must approach poetry in
utter innocence, as a wild deer sniffs through the
forest for possible food. And complete innocence in approaching long-established poetry is possible only to
the most untutored, or else to the most mature, who
have traveled the long road through sophistication
and beyond. The average reader knows that the
Divine Comedy is "good," and he sits down to it with
a self-conscious smirk for his good taste that causes
Beauty to shudder and withdraw. But if a plagiarized
phrase of a heavenly beauty appears in a detective
story or some newspaper doggerel, and the reader
comes upon it all unknowingly, then, if he sees it in
any fashion, he sees it face to face, without his
pompous self-approval standing in the way. And so
it is with the occasional freshly inspired phrase in
newly published poetry books. Reading new poems,
as yet unjudged by the tribunal of time, one gradually
learns to read all poetry as if it were new, as if no one
had ever pronounced an opinion on it.

Then, too, our natures crave the assurance that
poetry can grow out of today's soil. We need to wit-
ness the miracle of new-springing growth in order to

know that our world is still the world that produced Aeschylus and Vergil and Dante and Shakespeare. Of course, it is the fashion today among critics and poets to shriek that it is not. Poetry, they feel, is a magnificent redwood tree, that throughout the history of man has been striking downward and upward and putting forth its tender green, but in our century year after year of drought and dust have cut its fresh needles, cracked its earth, and exposed to desolation its strongest roots. Future generations, if they come to birth, must languish in a desert, with only a deformed juniper, if anything, to shelter them. Well, it may be so, but reading similar complaints by Edmund Spenser and Gabriel Harvey and their circle, in the years when Shakespeare and Marlowe were almost grown and Elizabethan poetry already in powerful ferment, reminds one that there has seldom been an age that has not seemed to the poet a devil preventing him from being a greater poet, and to the cankered critic the cause of his literary indigestion. Just before the *Dialogues* of Plato appeared, literary people considered the times very bad indeed, with language so worm-eaten that the philosopher Cratylus was reduced to abandoning words and communicating by wagging his thumb.

I suppose my taste in centuries is execrable, for I would far rather live in our own time than in the time of Queen Elizabeth or of Pericles. What part of the past could one possibly give up? And living now we have the longer story—possibly, some say, the final chapter of the tragic and glorious human race. Bad our times certainly are, bad politically, bad morally; but are they so bad poetically? To be gnawed by the wild beasts of capitalism and revolution and speed and greed, to feel our kind in danger of extinction within a few years—is that bad at all, poetically speaking? How the artist in Christopher Marlowe would have gloried in the extremity of our danger! Where did people get the idea that poetry is a smoke-wraith blown from a calm cigarette, dissipated in the first draft of danger or horror? I believe that poetry is the toughest, most stubborn spirit in the world. When everything else that is human is battered back into the ground, I believe that spirit will go down last of all, flinging at heaven a curse that is a song.

To be sure, I have my moments of senseless cheer when I believe that the human race is not going to be strangled with mustard gas next year, or devoured by little bugs the year after; but that does not make me sorry that the most characteristic poetry of our day is tragic in temper, condemning the present, despairing of the future. For the cry that poetry evokes from the human heart is not "Alas!" And it is not "Hallelujah!" It is "Selah!"—that mysterious cry from farther within the soul than either pleasure or pain. Poetry is a deep, deep well, reaching the profound waters that are under the earth; and it matters little what the surface mood of the poet may be—delight, fear, disgust, horror, love—providing that he plumbs his mood so deeply that he reaches poetic ecstasy, a thing beyond joy or despair. Robert Nathan, in a sonnet written shortly after *Wine from These Grapes* appeared, admonished Edna St. Vincent Millay against the blackness of her present vision, saying there was danger that, in crying, " 'All ahead is death and dark,' " she would "miss the remoter heavens of the soul." Rather, it seems to me, her foreboding cry is an assurance that she is in those heavens already—in

that heavenly city which, Plato says, exists surely
whether it is ever realized upon earth or not, since it
is the standard by which we judge imperfection, and
by which, if we will, we may set our own house in
order.

The surface mood of epitomizing poetry is not particularly contagious. Each of us knows a representative portion of the human race for himself, as a tremendously diverse thing, speckled with good and evil;
and poetry will not change the spots of our daily lives
for us. Rather, a poet's unified vision of man, whether
in the major key of Dryden's symphony,

> The diapason closing full on man

or in the heavy minor of Edna St. Vincent Millay,
equally recalls to the hearer the magnificence and the
shame of man, in that he might be nobler than he is.

TABLE OF CONTENTS

I

RENASCENCE

Poetry of a Child's Certainties

LAST SPRING the newspapers reported that the manuscripts of all Edna St. Vincent Millay's unpublished poems had just been destroyed in a hotel fire. The report of the catastrophe underscores a fact that is likely to be obscured in a study like my present one, namely, that it is too soon to shut Miss Millay within the covers of any book. What the quality and nature of her future writing will be, no one knows. Even she herself can have no more than an inkling of her future inspirations, and I shall not commit the absurdity of a prophecy.

Edna St. Vincent Millay is now in her early forties—an age at which a minor poet is usually dead, whether he realizes it or not, and an age at which a major poet is usually discovering how complexly alive he is. At that age Chaucer was probably beginning the formal plan for his *Canterbury Tales;* Spenser was in the midst of his *Faerie Queene;* Milton was hoping for leisure to compose *Paradise Lost;* Goethe was perhaps seeing, far in the future, the completion of the first part of his *Faust.* The forties, for major poets, usually correspond to late summer. If Miss Millay nowadays is foretelling not her harvest month but dead midwinter, perhaps that is her way of wishing herself good luck, remembering how even Shakespeare bemoaned his stripped boughs that shook against the cold before he had

1

written many of the plays that make him Shakespeare. Miss Millay's own attitude toward her age is her own affair, but with unappeased vitality as visible as fire within her, it would be unwise for literary historians to carry her too precipitately into the cellar of the house of fame.

And yet the world seems to have lived a dozen lifetimes since the *St. Nicholas* magazine for children first printed a poem signed "E. St. Vincent Millay." Indeed, returning to those days is like pushing a weed-choked gate

> Into some long-forgot, enchanted, strange
> Sweet garden of a thousand years ago.

Perhaps every human being feels a certain superiority to all who are older or younger than himself, all who are, therefore, unable to see the world under that peculiar perspective of time which to one's own eyes seems patently to be truth *sub specie aeternitatis*. Still I insist that an especial vision accrues to folk born in the early 1890's, who in the sensitive years of their late adolescence were hurled into the churning chaos from 1914 onward, after growing up in a world steady as a millpond—that so slightly mechanized world at the turn of the century, free from premonition of terrestrial dangers and cosmic uncertainties. Perhaps that world was just a silly room, as Edith Sitwell describes it, with a ceiling of tinsel stars and a badly painted ancestral portrait of God. But it was a fine, safe world for children, and plenty big enough to allow for twenty years of uncramped growth.

About the time when other children of America were learning that Vincent (so she was called) was a poet, the presidency of the United States was passing from

the Rough-riding and Trust-busting national hero
with the Big Stick to a portly Santa Claus oddly interested in a world peace court, although everyone knew
that wars were the romantic prerogative of earlier
generations. Our times were too civilized and too
tame for them. When one's father talked of civilization in general, he might mention tiny sores like
tainted money and Negro lynchings and famine in
India and suffering among coal miners. But all these
things were very far away from a child in Rockport,
Maine. Farther away still, but in practically complete
control, was God. The reins had not yet tangled in his
frantic hands,[1] for Vincent or for anybody else.

Closer at hand was an asylum, where practically
every child was taken once to look at the "crazy"
people. Friendly and sociable enough they were with
a little girl, but still they were supposed to be fasci-
natingly and utterly different from ordinary people,
who understood just how everything really was. Also
on the fringe of life were a few events of intense
excitement, as when somebody's house burned down
and the children had to sleep the rest of the night at
a neighbor's, or when the incredible circus came to
town with its painted wagons,

Colored wagons creaking with wonder.

Very close at hand was a hard, hinged school bench
every day until four o'clock and humdrum teachers
who patiently presented gray pebbles of information:
dates, and rules for grammar, and problems in wall-
papering, and the news that James Whitcomb Riley
and Rudyard Kipling were the greatest living poets.
After four o'clock there was home with one's little

[1] Edna St. Vincent Millay was eighteen years old when she used this expression
in her poem *Interim*.

3

sisters, who played dominoes and spun tops and blew soap bubbles and gradually learned to sew and to iron the starched tucks and ruffles of the layers on layers of clothing they wore. And there was, of course, the cat, not a long-haired lazy darling lolling in an armchair, but a family servant, trim and precise, who knew her place around the back door and had a decent pride in getting rid of mice and keeping her white bib clean. Later the cat died.

Outdoors one helped to plant and weed radishes and onions and lettuce and marigolds and zinnias, patting with one's hands that black dirt that has an unforgettable feel different from anything else in the world. One played house under a tree with drooping branches, and one crawled among brambles, gathering plums in one's skirt. And one went with a small friend to deliver milk in a tin pail, at five cents a quart. Probably the friend was allowed to save the nickels for a college education, as all parents knew that thirst for higher learning was the noblest ambition of American youth.

And at least once during one's childhood, despite the code of sheltered innocence, there was a nameless horror, something that outraged the entire community and that a little girl must not know, but that in the middle of the night made her scream her way out of infinitely black and empty nightmares such as children of the 1930's, who clamber into bed replete with spinach and gangster movies, seem to know nothing of.

All this if one were almost any little girl. If one were a little girl with a boy's name and sharply cornered green witch eyes and red hair, all this was true with a thousand-fold intensity. Queen Elizabeth

4

had had red hair, and so had a notorious murderess or two; chances for glory or the gallows were about even. But whether for honor or dishonor, red-haired girl-children were different. Everyone knew it in those days, even teachers, who allowed for noisier explosions of temper from them. Also a girl whose mother would call her by a boy's name naturally had more leeway out of doors than other children. She could play outside her own yard, could, in fact, bring home sandburs on her legs from the whole countryside, could run far, far along the beach, could play out in the rain—sometimes after dark, even.

And if this daily life in Rockport and Camden, Maine, was tame, close at hand was something that was not tame, something with a look that answered the infinite sky, something that beat with the pulse of eternity, a pulse like anger and desire and agony and bliss.[2] Poets who grow up inland, knowing a sharply divided land and air, may choose between cloddy realism and airy idealism, but a poet who grows beside the ocean learns the meaning of rising on ecstasy without leaving tangible, sustaining reality. The Platonic picture of the sensuous world as a body restlessly molded by ideality seems to such a one only the most obvious truth. I cannot conceive of Edna St. Vincent Millay's poetry without the ocean tide "that treads the shifting shore," or without the powerful winds of the Maine seacoast, with Matinicus in the distance, that island where the tide

> Came pounding in, came running through the Gut,
> While from the Rock the warning whistle cried,
> And children whimpered, and the doors blew shut.

[2] Edna St. Vincent Millay first became acquainted with the ocean when she was eight years old, for then her parents moved from the inland town of Union, Maine, to Rockport, on the seacoast.

Perhaps those tides, with a restlessness as of conscious life in them, gave her the animistic attitude
toward nature that is still so evident in her poetry.
Toward the human race her poetry holds no maternal
gentleness, but to everything out of doors—a mullein
weed, a blue flag in a fire-seared bog, a single tree with
its leaves fluttering against the city traffic, a little hill
"that sits at home so many hundred years"—she has
always given passionate mothering. The world is
alive to her in a far simpler, less metaphysical way
than it was to Wordsworth; her feeling toward it is
such unreasoned child's tenderness as that of St.
Francis, who was gentle with the stones on which he
walked and the water with which he washed himself.

Yet for half of each year her outdoor world was
stern, and her home was poverty-stricken enough to
keep her aware of that sternness just beyond the
windowpane. In Maine winters the storms that make
the world a "whirling whiteness uniform" give poor
families keen awareness that tight roofs and steady
fires are the greatest of blessings. No child growing
up in rooms apparently warmed by a tiny heat regu-
lator on the wall can possibly develop Millay's feeling
for fire. Fire is always Promethean in her poetry,
something loved and lovely, coaxed into being with
one's own breath, and by it one's sight and hearing
and one's very bones are "warmed by all the wonders
of the earth." And the economy of her poetry, its
way of stripping life to its essentials, may be due
partly to her early life being so stripped, in a home
that meant chiefly a rooftree and a stove and house
plants and meals where the equivalent of "milk and
tarts and honey and white bread all in one day" represented a glorious rare extravagance.

As for her first reading, Mother Goose had sunk
into her heart early enough and deep enough to save
her from the anemic pulse of verse made on the prin-
ciple that a foot must be an iamb or a trochee, a
dactyl or an anapest. Probably a few ballads had
underscored this sense for freedom of pause and accent
and had taught her once and for always that true
poems are made to fit a tune in one's head, and not a
visual or arithmetical pattern. Some audiences, hearing Miss Millay read her poetry aloud, imagine that
it is the remarkable timbre of her voice that gives it
most of its music. But it is foolproof. I have heard it
read by the completely unpoetic, and it never quite
loses its intensely individual pause and flow.

The fairy tales she read were not the exotic ones.
Among the little sons and daughters of university professors, I have found a tendency to parade fondness for
the fairy tales and legends of Oscar Wilde and Laf-
cadio Hearn, but to enjoy only furtively, with a conscious condescension, the old homely ones. But the
tales that color Millay's poetry are those threadbare
old democrats, *Jack and the Beanstalk, Red Riding Hood
and the Wolf, Snowwhite and the Dwarfs,* and the *Sleeping
Beauty.*

From Mother Goose and fairy tales, she turned immediately to Shakespeare. But though she had read
all the plays of Shakespeare before she was nine years
old, she seems to have escaped the misfortune of pre-
cocity. At fourteen she was still contributing verse to
St. Nicholas, and it was still a child's poetry—not so
lovely as some of little Hilda Conkling's poetry of a
dozen years later (no doubt the editors would have
refused it if it had been such an unstraitened utterance), but clear and musical and right, and in Edna

7

St. Vincent Millay's own voice, albeit in a small and childish treble. She listens to the silken rustle of the grass, searches for the world of romance out in the fields with her little sister, and prays with touching simplicity that nature may lend her calm "until I have more calmness of my own." It is good to have childhood last a long time. I have seen children of ten sniffing and sneering at what they should be laying to their roots as manure against the coming years. Everyone's genuine standards of beauty come from the shapes and sounds and colors and textures that his curious senses touched with most delight before he knew sophistication. Wagner, Baudelaire—many artists have testified that genius is childhood recovered at will. Those who are in a hurry to abandon childhood have too thin a soil for poetry to flourish in. They spend their later years worrying whether they have the proper taste in sunsets and garden flowers and breakfast foods.

At fifteen, however, Vincent seems to have felt that childhood was definitely ending; and, aware that a period of uncertainty was upon her, she wrote a farewell—or au revoir—to poetry. More consistent than so many older poets who insist upon the world's hearing that they have resolved to hold their tongues, she did not send it to *St. Nicholas*, and it now sees the light of print for the first time:

> Let me not shout into the world's great ear
> Ere I have something for the world to hear;
> Then let my message like an arrow dart,
> And pierce a way into the world's great heart.

She went on with her high-school studies and waited, with what patience she possessed, for the fire from heaven to fall. Eventually she reached graduation; and every young person feels a great faith that that event will mark an end and a beginning. But still nothing happened outwardly, and there ensued those days of frustration when the world—the glamorous, real world—seems to be everywhere except within the circle of horizon of which one is the center, and it seems of tragic importance to reach it before one is completely grown. And then one day there came the terrifying and ecstatic hour when she knew that the time had come, that there was no use in waiting to get away, that, prisoner in an ordinary Maine town though she still was, she was no longer a child; she was older than Chatterton ever became, older than Bryant when he wrote *Thanatopsis;* almost as old as Milton when he wrote *On the Morning of Christ's Nativity* or Keats when he wrote *On First Looking into Chapman's Homer.* There was no evading the issue; she must find out whether she too was a poet.

And so *Renascence* was made. The spring gushed and failed and gushed again, but at the third flowing the poem became complete, with a beginning and a middle and an end. A fair copy was made and sent to the judges of the Lyric Year contest for 1912. Now that the poem had proved to her own satisfaction what spiritual company she belonged in, she figured that it might as well be earning five hundred dollars for her, too. She certainly needed it. Or perhaps, since she was so very young, she needed even more the assurance that the poem was truly as astonishing as it seemed to her.

It is, of course, poetry's scandal of the century that *Renascence* did not win the Lyric Year prize. Its very length, one would suppose, would have saved it from being overlooked, would have shown it shimmering and rippling like a lake in the desert of conscientious

verses surrounding it. But, after all, the poem was not
what the judges were looking for, and nothing blinds
like a single-minded search. They were instructed to
give the prize to a poem revealing the time spirit, and
the young Edna St. Vincent Millay was the time spirit
of 1798, or of 1590, or of 1380, rather than of 1912.
Their ears were cocked for novelty, and these limpid
octosyllabic couplets were no more novel than Chaucer's *Book of Blanche the Duchess* or Milton's poems to
joy and pensiveness, or Coleridge's *Christabel*. As for
the subject, what was it but Chaucer's Springtide and
Milton's Mirth, with a dash of Wordsworth's burden
of the mystery? All it amounted to was that an unknown young girl (though by Milton yclept Eu-
phrosyne) was cast down by loathed Melancholy as
she considered human suffering, and then leaped up
more ecstatic than ever as she felt the wonder of April.
So the judges argued, perhaps. However they argued,
one should be slow about scorning them, remembering, "There but for the grace of God go I." Besides,
one of the three did vote for *Renascence*. Mr. Ferdinand
Pinney Earle is probably still glowing with pride.

Nor was the poem wholly without competition. It
is the fashion to shrug at those years when Irving
Babbitt, taking up the mantle of Lessing, had in his
New Laocoön supposedly settled all poetic problems for
another two hundred years, and when public taste,
liking its art at the same time dashing and slick, was
acclaiming Sargent as its greatest painter, Kipling as
its greatest poet, and Pinero as its greatest dramatist.
And it is true that some of the best living poets were
silent just then. In England A. E. Housman had not
spoken since the *Shropshire Lad*, long before, and
George Santayana had turned away from poetry; but

Walter de la Mare was singing a silvery trickling song, and Thomas Hardy (who was later to say that America had just two great works of art to its credit: recessive architecture and the poetry of Edna St. Vincent Millay) had recently completed his tremendous poetic drama, *The Dynasts*. In America Edwin Arlington Robinson was keeping silence. Theodore Roosevelt, years before, had discovered him and characteristically had tried to "push" him. But Robinson, refusing to be a perambulator, had gone back to his shabby New York bedroom, and in 1912 was presumably sitting there, wondering "where he was going, that man against the sky." Another poet had been silent so long that most people had forgotten her existence: Lizette Woodworth Reese, a gray little schoolteacher in Baltimore, who after writing a perennially appealing sonnet in her youth had apparently dried up in the classroom. Yet she was to burst into bloom again, in her sixties and seventies, in verses unexpected and freshly lovely as hawthorn blossoms in November.

But though none of these poets contributed to the *Lyric Year*, almost everyone else of any importance did, and there are more than a score of very respectable literary names in the volume. Sara Teasdale has a lyric there, and if it is less poetic than *Renascence* it is only because a sudden fluttering gauze of spring rain, gone in a breath, is less than the gust and gleam and freshness of all April. Poetry gained something when Sara Teasdale saw bright April shake out her rain-drenched hair. For the rest, the volume is filled with apostrophes to the emasculated Victorian Pan who haunted minor poetry books so long, and with appreciations of Robert Browning (it was his centenary) and with

11

meditations on abstract beauty and on social injustice. It is all honést-enough stuff in intention, but Matthew Arnold would have shaken his head over it with the sigh, "'Tis well, 'tis eloquent, but 'tis not true."

Yet the table of contents, as I have said, is very respectable. Among the contributors were a few survivors of the London *fin de siècle*. Most notably there was Richard Le Gallienne, still weaving his golden filigree. And there was Bliss Carman, that forerunner of the Boy Scout, to whose marching feet all color was fluttering flag. And then there was Professor George Woodberry, with knees creaking a little in his obeisances to a sedentary marble goddess, but with a passionate sincerity in his austere adoration of intellectual beauty that would redeem paler and stiffer stanzas. In the same tradition there were a few poets who had been protégés of George Santayana at Harvard, and who were now trying to grow up to him, though they were still rather wobbly on their poetic legs. Also there was Edwin Markham, who, after his voice had reverberated boldly in *The Man with the Hoe*, was spending the rest of his life trying to strike a ringing note again. And of course some future prose writers were, in accordance with tradition, forming their style with the warming-up exercises of verse; John Erskine, Ludwig Lewisohn, Donne Byrne are in the volume. And, what was of most importance, there was the flock of young poets who were soon to be appearing in the magazine *Poetry*, which Harriet Monroe was launching this year, and with it, she hoped, a renaissance of poetry in America. There were Vachel Lindsay, Louis Untermeyer, William Rose Benét, Joyce Kilmer, Arthur Davison Ficke, John Hall Wheelock, Witter Bynner, and half a hundred others, all panting with impatience to put twentieth-century America on the poetic map.

Oh, yes, and there was also included in the book the forgotten man, the man-who-took-the-prize. Developing later into a person of charming humor, who looked at his baby and

> laughed like a lord
> To see a human being that was not yet bored,

Orrick Johns is probably properly ashamed of carrying off the prize, though one can scarcely contend that it was his fault. His *Second Avenue* attempts to "express" New York City and to make human greed despise itself. It is just the sort of heavily admonitory verse that Miss Millay herself would probably be turning out by the ton if she did not happen to be a poet. But it does not touch the outermost fringe of poetry.

The girl up in Maine who failed to win the prize knew next to nothing of all these people and of the state of art in America. She was living in another world (scarcely less young than ancient Lesbos) wherein poetry was still a direct and innocent thing. It meant to her, quite simply, playing noble chords and melodies, and trying to fit her passionate apprehensions of life to the sounds of her instrument, regardless of all literary fashions. And yet, since she was studying music at the piano rather than the lyre, she could not be wholly unswayed by literary tradition. In the music of Mozart and Bach and Beethoven, she inevitably heard the measures of past poetry. For, in spite of having spent most of her years in an American public school, she had discovered a few great books, and they had become a part of her.

Chiefly, there was the *Aeneid*. The great rock of of-

fense or of triumph in the inflexible high-school course of the day was Vergil. To untutored young minds that intensely civilized man in complex Roman society stood for almost the beginning of the world, and his serenely sad hexameters, heavy with the tears of things, seemed dampened only by the dews of the world's dawn. Many a young person read him with a touch of that marvel which William Ellery Leonard recalls:

There in the homestead at Hilton I sat by the window with Vergil:
Under the morning star, words like woods to explore.
Tityre, tu patulae . . . . O eery quest in the silence!
Magic of dawn on the earth, magic of dawn in the boy!
Thrilling from letter to letter, and every word an enchantment:
Silvestrem tenui . . . . even ere meaning was known. . . . .
Then, as the words became phrases and phrases grew into verses,
(Change as subtle and vast, even as cell into flower!)
. . . .
There, with the mist on the meadow, I sat by the window with
    Vergil,
Sat with the soul of the dead, living again in my own.

There is evidence that Vergil sank as deeply into Edna St. Vincent Millay's young heart. Indeed, she felt him from a long way off, and read all of Caesar's *Gallic Wars* by herself during the summer when she was fourteen, in order that she might take up Cicero's orations the next fall and so reach Vergil's *Aeneid* the sooner. And to this day, if Vergil does not haunt her poetry in bodily form as he does Dante's, he is there nonetheless, touching the metaphor, teaching the grave, far vision, swaying the music.[3]

    [3] Before Edna St. Vincent Millay entered Vassar as a Freshman she had read not only Vergil but Ovid and Catullus. At Vassar she continued her study with always increasing enthusiasm, and learned many Latin poems by heart. Her husband reports that her love of Latin poetry remains undiminished. He says, "I have noticed that whenever she is very much distressed

For the rest, in the high-school English courses she, who before she was twelve years old had read almost all of Tennyson and Milton and much of Elizabethan poetry, was "taught" Tennyson's *Elaine* and Milton's *L'Allegro* and *Il Penseroso* and also Coleridge's *Ancient Mariner* and a little Shakespeare. It was a narrow well of water, but undefiled. And perhaps it is just as well that she did not receive much encouragement to read extensively. At the same age Floyd Dell was nervously gulping everything that had been said and thought in the world, and was thrown into a literary colic that killed the poet in him. It is of decidedly doubtful benefit to a very young person of great sensitiveness to read fast and widely.

Of these poets that she knew, Coleridge touched *Renascence* more than the others. John Livingston Lowes, who in *The Road to Xanadu* has so uncannily traced the subterranean course of almost every word in *The Ancient Mariner* back to its source in Coleridge's encyclopedic reading, must enjoy seeing bits of *The Ancient Mariner* itself glimmering through the stream of this poetry of a later century. Of course it would not be enjoyable or interesting at all save for the fact that *Renascence*, like *The Ancient Mariner*, is pure poetry, original as all pure poetry must be. It is trans-

---

over something, she will either sit down at the piano and play Bach or Beethoven, or take up a book of Latin poetry. This winter after she had finished eight months of hard work on the Baudelaire translations, she said, 'Now I will have an absolute rest from all this,' and proceeded to reread almost all of Vergil. For years she has not travelled anywhere without a book of Latin poetry in her suitcase; this goes in as automatically as her tooth brush. In the hotel fire, a month ago, which burned up not only her manuscripts, but many precious things, only one thing was lost for which she mourns: a tiny, scrubby, little leather-bound edition, published in the sixteenth century, of the poems of Catullus, Propertius, and Tibullus. This book was always on the night table beside her bed." (Letter to the author, June 15, 1936.)

parent brook water from Helicon, flowing over the brown stones of the author's reading. True, one or two stones stand above the surface of the stream:

> A sound as of some joyous elf
> Singing sweet songs to please himself,

is Coleridge's

> A little child, a limber elf,
> Singing, dancing to itself.

This stone is only splashed a bit about the base by the wave of her thought. But by a subtle transmutation another line becomes wholly her own. Coleridge's

> The rain poured down from one black cloud

changes into

> And the big rain in one black wave
> Fell from the sky.

The blackness of the waterspout belongs to Coleridge, but that "big" lies between Millay and Shakespeare. In another instance she changes something that is fine in Coleridge into something finer. The mariner is haunted by the stare of the dead sailors, for, he says,

> The look with which they looked at me
> Had never passed away.

That look passed into Millay's poetry with a difference. In her vision of universal human woe, she sees a man dying of hunger on the other side of the world, and she says,

> He *moved his eyes* and looked at me.

Few poets since Homer have succeeded in writing with such simple literalness as that, as she tells in three words the gruesomeness of seeing a last conscious

16

muscular effort (so weak and slight!) after life seemed
to have ebbed beyond the possibility of any further
sign.

The other influences are farther under the wave.
Millay's supernatural experience of being weighed
into her grave by a horrible compression of the universe is very different, superficially, from Coleridge's
supernatural voyage with his ancient mariner, but
both poets have the experience of seeing their whole
world become putrescent. For Coleridge "the very
deep did rot"; for Millay's probing sense,

> The universe, cleft to the core
> Lay open,

though its disease sickened her. The suffering of each
is given in terms of weight. Coleridge's mariner says,

> The sky and the sea and the sea and the sky
> Lay like a load on my weary eye.

It is the sky that weighs on Millay, too, but how
much heavier it is! It is the universe itself, focused
upon her unenduring consciousness.

> Ah, awful weight! Infinity
> Pressed down upon the finite me!

But in the end both victims are released from their
ordeal and return to the sweet pastoral air of an April
countryside. To the mariner it is fragrant "like a
meadow-gale in spring." To Millay it is "a miracle
of orchard breath." And both poets close their poems
with a moral admonition. Millay's is characteristically far more muscular than that of the fat and lethargic
Coleridge, who thinks it quite enough for men to sit
still and love all things both great and small. But to
the young, eager, untried girl, it seems that people
ought to *do* something:

17

The heart can push the sea and land
Farther away on either hand;
The soul can split the sky in two
And let the face of God shine through.
But East and West will pinch the heart
That cannot keep them pushed apart;
And he whose soul is flat, the sky
Will cave in on him by and by.

In spite of all these parallels, I doubt that Coleridge
was in her mind for an instant, from the beginning to
the end of the making of *Renascence*. He could not have
been, or she could never have skirted the edge of servile
imitation so surely, like a sleepwalker gliding lightly
along the edge of a precipice.

The seventeenth century seems at this time not to
have sunk so deeply into her feelings as the nineteenth,
though there is one apparently accidental resemblance
to Andrew Marvell in *Renascence*. Although she read
none of Marvell's poetry until her freshman year at
college, still his

The grave's a fine and private place

is half-echoed in her

A grave is such a quiet place!

And in spite of her eager reading and re-reading of
Shakespeare ever since infancy, his touch, if it is on
the poem at all, is very slight. Her expression "All sin
was of my sinning" recalls Shylock's turn of phrase in
"No tears but of my shedding." And in *Richard III*,
Clarence's terrible nightmare of drowning, and yet
being unable to free his soul, smothered within his
panting hulk

That almost burst to belch it in the sea,

18

may have been transmuted into Millay's image,

> My anguished spirit, like a bird,
> Beating against my lips I heard;
> Yet lay the weight so close about
> There was no room for it without.

Perhaps the most significant touch of all upon the poem was Sappho's. No young girl who aspires to poetic genius refrains long from looking up the fragments of Sappho, and Sappho's line, "I do not think to touch the sky with my two arms,"

> Ψαύην δ' οὐ δοκίμωμ' ὀράνω δύσι πάχεσι

must have suggested Millay's nightmare of actually touching the sky. Did she also know Baudelaire's

> *Quand le ciel bas et lourd pèse comme un couvercle?*

I doubt it, though she was affected by the music of Baudelaire later on. I think it was stories of medieval torture by a weight slowly descending from the ceiling that, blending with the memory of Sappho's sentence, grew in her mind into those lines that describe the sky mercilessly descending upon her, in the beginning so unaware of her impending doom that she expresses her first consciousness of its nearness with a childish, slangy flippancy:

> The sky, I thought, is not so grand;
> I 'most could touch it with my hand!

But then the realization of the horror comes all at once:

> And reaching up my hand to try,
> I screamed to feel it touch the sky.

Down, down, down it pressed her, till she had sunk six feet underground,

> And sank no more—there is no weight
> Can follow here, however great.

19

In this list of influences—Sappho, Shakespeare, Coleridge, Keats—we have, so far as I can see, all her literary sources, no more, no fewer than enter into any powerfully original poem. One other sort of influence I feel in the poem, however, and that is a musical one. Can anyone read *Renascence* without feeling that the music of Haydn, with its clear beat of one-two-three-four, is behind the verse, like a light, steady wind blowing it onward? Even the single crash of Haydn's *Surprise Symphony* is there, startling without breaking the rhythm. Perhaps I am only fancying that influence, but Edna St. Vincent Millay was very fond of Haydn in those days. The poem is even divided into movements of varying emotional tempo, like a Haydn piano concerto.

The philosophy of the poem, when one analyzes it, is a rather intimidating blend of Berkeleyan idealism and Jamesian pragmatism. Both philosophies were very much in the air at the time, and a young girl could easily have imbibed them without reading a word of either James or Berkeley. I should be very much surprised, in fact, to learn that she had read them at that age. *Renascence* holds a good philosophy; but of course it might have held good philosophy without being of any worth at all as a poem.

The secret of the poetic power of *Renascence* is not its philosophy but its language—a truism as obvious as that musical power is a matter of notes, though a surprising number of people feel it is belittling to think that a poem's magic is "just a matter of words." Despite what a few reviewers have said, Millay's great secret is that she never, at any stage of her growth, has repudiated her heritage of natural English speech. Yet in a public school the pressure upon

20

her to do so must have been terrific. Little girls in her grade-school days were taught that it was a mark of refinement to say "large" rather than "big," "strong," rather than "stout," "beautiful" rather than "pretty," "happy" rather than "glad," "thin" rather than "lean." The list was endless, and the idea seemed to be that everything that a child said naturally was vulgar. Adjectives ending in *y* especially were taboo. How the small Vincent must have had to fight to keep her "mouthy," "skinny," "throaty," "bony," "fussy," "rooty"! And her natural turn of a phrase: "to take my mind up," or "hush with your knocking," or "he heard me my Latin," or "his face went pale"—all were quite, quite uneducated, according to the notions of teachers in the early 1900's. (Edna St. Vincent Millay talks like the farmer wife who was my mother. And such a time as her college-bred daughters had with her, trying to break her of talking like a poet!)

Robert Frost is the only other living American poet who has that essential thing—a speech rooted in his earliest life and intertwined with all his natural instincts. But Frost, unlike Millay, lost confidence in that speech as he grew up, possibly because the idioms of his Californian and New England homes jangled together in his mind. His first poetry (which he was writing at the time *Renascence* was being made) is in the stiffest of poetic dictions. Awkwardly, slowly, but at last triumphantly he has worked his way back into his natural speech idiom, until today every sentence that he publishes has the signature "Robert Frost" woven through it like a rune. But most other poets nowadays lack that most essential thing. Some of them painstakingly preserve a shoddy and intrusive

21

dialect of their childhood as a means of securing an individual style. And some of them weave a picturesque slang idiom for themselves (like Sandburg's) or an ironically intellectualistic one (like Marianne Moore's) or a God-knows-what one (like Ezra Pound's), but they never find a speech that stretches, running or sitting, like their own skin. A sudden new thought to express, a strange emotion, and pop! A seam has burst, and a patch from a different vocabulary has to be inserted. But most of them have learned to sit without squirming in one corner of the universe, murmuring of what comes easily within their artificial range of words.

Edna St. Vincent Millay has no such problems. The words she spoke at three and the ones she learned at thirty all grow together in her heart, equally her children, beloved members of one family, and so they can live together in one course of thought. Her mother talked a natural Shakespearian and Chaucerian English, a folk speech, and so Vincent, almost as soon as she learned to read, moved into the vast vocabulary and ample phrase of Shakespeare with no sense at all of moving out of her own speech.

An instance of the flexibility and unity of her speech is in the change from the first movement of *Renascence* to the second. The first movement, in which there is scarcely a word which is not a child's monosyllable, reaches its climax and its sudden chilling turn of mood in

I screamed to feel it touch the sky.

Then the second movement, with its grave ponderability of mood, changes to a heavier, more abstract vocabulary:

22

> I screamed—and lo!—Infinity
> Came down and settled over me
> . . . .
> And pressing of the undefined
> The definition on my mind. . . . .

Then, finally, with the joyous relief of the third movement, simplicity returns, and continues to the child-
wise expressiveness of the close:

> And he whose soul is flat—the sky
> Will cave in on him by and by.

Cave in, by the way, was not considered a possible
expression for poetry until Millay used it. But before
long one found it in the poetry of the sophisticated
Dial magazine, and then it was in vogue. A good
many of her words and expressions have such a later
history. An amusing example of other poets' suggesti-
bility followed her use of the word "creaking" in
Renascence. Poetry had been well oiled for centuries;
if it had creaked at all before *Renascence*, it had done
so in some literal and prosaic connection. But the
child Vincent had apparently attended the circus on a
windy day and had been impressed by the incessant
straining and tugging of the great tent overhead.
Therefore, in *Renascence*, Millay imagines

> The creaking of the tented sky.

The word seems to me to be used with its literal meaning. But in 1917, when the poem was reprinted,
"synaesthesia," or the description of one sense in
terms of the others, was very much under discussion
in sophisticated circles, and this "creak," by persons
who knew little of open-air circuses, was praised as an
example of transposition into auditory terms of a

visual impression. The next creak I heard, though I was probably deaf to a few, was in Aldous Huxley's *Leda*, wherein the swan had a "creaking flight." Since the swan was Zeus, there is no earthly reason why it should have been rheumatic; the word seems to have some relation to the creaking sky from which the swan was descending. Soon afterward, in *Soles Occidere*, Huxley had Truth creaking, though I admit that he here gave it intellectual legs to account for its condition. Then in 1924 Edith Sitwell, synaesthesiast extraordinary, described "creaking light." Since then poetry has creaked on and on; the last instance I have noticed is Stephen Spender's "creaking of dusty day" in 1934.

But the influence of *Renascence* on other poetry has not been confined to imitation of its diction and metaphors. The whole framework of it, as an allegory in octosyllabic couplets giving a poet's world-vision of grief and his eventual reconcilement with the universe, has been imitated a good deal. Its most comely poetic offspring are Elder Olson's *Thus Revealed*, Mary Ogilvie's *For This Have Poets Died*, Mabel Simpson's *Prayer*, and George Dillon's *Anatomy of Death*, with its

> Then from the solid home of breath,
> The world of dust that wished me death,
> The granite ridges risen in greed,
> I retched and panted to be freed,
> And it may be I died indeed.
>
> . . . .
>
> Yet April comes, and here am I.

But the strongest of its offspring, I think, is Joseph Auslander's *An Eye*, a poem in which, after struggling with the paradox of the world's cruelty and its pastoral beauty, Auslander wins a "desperate peace" in the conclusion,

> You have stared into your heart
> And found your brother's counterpart:
> For every stain upon his head
> You shall bleed as he has bled,
> And the dead shall bury the dead.

This poem, indeed, has inherited from its young poetic mother a strain of bleak courage which was not apparent in her features for some years to come.

II

THE LAMP AND THE BELL

In Vassar College during the War

WITH the poem *Renascence* the brief and gold-
en months of creative infancy ended, when
Edna St. Vincent Millay's poetry had been
as high and clear and young as the music of a thrush,
or of Gluck, or of William Blake. Blake's *Book of Thel*
and Millay's *Renascence* belong to that strange "poetry
of innocence" which seems as if the poet were a visi-
tant from a purer world, looking at earthly beauty
and corruption and death with the puzzled brow and
clear eyes of a diviner sort of child. It is not the greatest kind of poetry, but of all sustained poetry it is the
rarest.

Everyone in the small group which became acquainted with *Renascence* in 1913 realized that this
golden age could not continue—or could it? One en-
thusiast became so exercised over the future of this
young sibyl in crass twentieth-century America that
she offered to cloister her for four years. Sarcastic comments have been made on the point of view that regarded it as a kindness to send a poet to a girls' college,
but in so far as one can judge of anything in an infinitely complex and unpredictable universe, going to
Vassar seems the best thing that could have happened
to Millay in the cataclysmic year of 1914.

What ought she to have done instead—have gone

26

popping into New York or Chicago in one of the new
T-model Fords, as so many talented young people were
doing, shouting some variant of the popular cry, "The
past is a bucket of ashes," or "History is the bunk"?
I should have hated to see her thrown into a raucous
crowd of iconoclasts and experimenters and agonists
after originality at a time when she had only a
young girl's random readings as a balance wheel. If
there ever was a time in the world's history when it
was important to learn the past sorrows and endur-
ances of the human race before facing its future, it
surely was during the World War. Vassar, with its
courses in history and philosophy, in ancient poetry
and French and Elizabethan literatures, gave the girl
a chance to imagine the great human woes and endure
them in spirit before she actually met them. It made
it possible for her to say as Aeneas said of the prophe-
cies of the sibyl:

Omnia praecepi atque animo mecum ante peregi.

One must acknowledge that too much cloistering
has mildewed most of the poetesses of the past.
Elizabeth Barrett saw her danger clearly when she
commented on her secluded life in Wimpole Street: "I
am, in a manner, a blind poet . . . . I make great
guesses at human nature." But four years are not a
lifetime, nor, for that matter, is a college an invalid's
bedroom. Human nature is to be found even on a campus, and if it is usually human nature at its freshest
and best, it is not altogether so. Insanity, abortion,
perversion, suicide, murder have not been totally unknown in the history of women's colleges, although
they are far less common than a certain type of

sweet girl graduate would have one believe. Millay's
Humoresque, with its beginning,

> "Heaven bless the babe," they said;
> "What queer books she must have read!"

pronounces flatly that life can be tragic and criminal,
even among the young and sheltered.

    Still, on the whole, the air of a college like Vassar
was of an Arcadian sunniness that was unreal as a
dream to the hysterical and prejudice-ridden people
outside it, in the years of the World War. Nowhere on
the planet was a saner, more detached understanding of
that slaughter obtainable than in the women's colleges
of America. This was at the time when Calvin Cool-
idge was qualifying himself for the vice-presidency by
exposing their radicalism. It is not an accident that
one of the few poems inspired by the World War (out
of the countless thousands of pages of verse written
about it) came from the campus of Vassar. There are
catastrophes so deafening that they cannot be heard
at all unless one is very far away. Millay's sonnet *Not
in This Chamber* is on a plane above Rupert Brooke's
Nineteen-Fourteen, even; for Millay wrote not as a
patriot, but simply as a human being, and she was
able to see all the countries in the war with the same
pitying vision with which later, in *Epitaph for the Race
of Man*, she was to look upon all human history. The
war meant to her simply the impending desolation of
a lost civilization, and she mused:

> So is no warmth for me at any fire
> Today, when the world's fire has burned so low;
> I kneel, spending my breath in vain desire,
> At that cold hearth which one time roared so strong,
> And straighten back in weariness, and long
> To gather up my little gods and go.

There was no taking-sides possible for her, who even in her college days was aware of herself not as an American but as

> Child of all mothers, native of the earth.

Until June of 1917, then, she lived the life of any college girl, rising for eight-thirty classes, wandering along the leafy paths until the clock of Taylor Hall tower called her back, joining in the singing of hymns at evening chapel and of "Gaudeamus Igitur" at outdoor pageants, and having the Philalethian literary and dramatic society for her theater and the young daughters of clergymen and bankers at first for her very dubious critics and then for her friends, and their admiration for her incense when her poems began to be published, not merely in the college *Miscellany*, but in the very print of life, in the *Forum* and *Century* magazines and in *Poetry*.

Those poems reflect her as being no less entirely a girl than she had been a child in the mood which had inspired *Renascence*. Whether the theme of her college poems was gay or sad, dresses and shoes and pretty hands and feet were of importance in them. The incongruous red gown she wished to be buried in is the theme of *Shroud*, a poem somewhat reminiscent of the old ballad of *The Queen's Marie*, in which Marie was directed to wear a gold gown at her hanging:

> You must not put on your robes of black
> Nor yet your robes of brown,
> But you must put on your yellow gold stuffs
> To shine through Edinburgh town.

In another poem, *Sorrow*, the depth of the young poet's grief is measured by her not caring what gown or what shoes she wears. She was as "noticing" a girl

29

about shoes as Sappho had been; indeed a very short time later, in one of her little elegies, the sharpness of her grief at the sight of her dead friend's narrow shoes on the closet floor reminds one of Sappho's poignant memory of another friend: "A broidered strap of fair Lydian work covered her feet." And hands were noticed no less. Though her own must have been the most delicate pair in Vassar, she wrote of her friend,

> She learned her hands in a fairy-tale.

In fact, hands continue to touch her thought and shape her imagery throughout the whole course of her poetry. The "ugly claws" of a woman who is losing her youth appear in *The Lamp and the Bell*. And in her sonnets Millay has brooded on the time when her own hands will be "withered," and again on the "wrinkled hands" she will have in old age. And the awkward and ugly hands of an artist, clasped about his knee, jarred on her admiration for him and made her wonder "why I love you as I do." In another sonnet she envisioned God, not in full figure, but as the sculptor's thumb that pressed the hollow in her lover's temple. And later, as the cosmos fell apart for her and its director lost all intelligence, instead of God she saw Doom with a "swart thumb" on which mankind is set in a ring of brass.

No less girl-like than her intense interest in dress and hands and feet was the delight of her college mates and herself in the woodland about Vassar. At no other age, probably, could Millay have written *God's World*. It is not exactly a poem to be ashamed of, but one wonders if she has not sometimes felt like disowning it because of the degree to which it has set the tone for what is known among pedagogues as the Oh-God-the-pain-girls school of poetry. Under the influence of *God's World* a hundred poetesses have developed a yearning to be Semeles, with mortal bodies that cannot sustain the onrush of heavenly power. Reading the effusions of these thin-waisted girl poets, thrown into violent cramps by the beautifulness of beauty, one turns back with relief to Mrs. Browning's *Aurora Leigh*. Mrs. Browning may have been an invalid weighing less than a hundred pounds, but she could take her beauty neat, without whimpering.

Of course, it would not have been good form for Edna St. Vincent Millay as a young poet to be wholly contented in college. She was true to the Shelleyan tradition, and, like some of her brothers in Harvard, she felt that bullying a well-meaning college into expelling her was a necessary part of testing her poetic nature. But her instinct for thrift showed itself here, and she did not seriously court expulsion until her four-year course was complete and she had only the formalities of graduation to forfeit. One cannot take her chafing against the restrictions too seriously. Obviously she has always belonged to that fragment of the human race which conforms to the Aristotelian definition of man as one who desires to know; and a certain docility toward education is evident in her poetry. "Instruct" and "teach" are verbs that she uses very kindly, and

> all the little books
> That went to school with me

are loved with passionate tenderness. From the beginning she must have been at times a stubborn student—obedient dislikes she would have nothing of,

31

ever; but she has never scorned the most prosaic road that has promised a fresh revelation of beauty. No one has ever been more receptive in the classroom to "immortal page after page conceived in a mortal mind." If these daily classroom lectures did not invariably assume more importance than the skimpiness of butter at meals or the restrictions against rising and walking out into the moonlight at three o'clock in the morning, they have nonetheless left their mark on her poetry.

Mathematics, philosophy, Latin, French, and English seem to have been the subjects that sank deepest into her nature, though the grades in the registrar's books may not always have tallied with the depth of her perception. There is a legend that she grew so enamored of her Freshman course in mathematics that she spent the night before the final examination writing a sonnet about it instead of cramming, and consequently failed to pass; but that anecdote is a bit too polished to be plausible. A member of the mathematics department of Vassar was winning world-acclaim with a new theorem in 1914, and very likely it was partly this achievement that brought home to Millay the consciousness that the mathematician, as well as the word-wielder, may be a poet. Indeed, with the hot generosity of youth she avowed that only the mathematician may become pure poet:

> Euclid alone has looked on Beauty bare.
> Let all who prate of Beauty hold their peace. . . . .

Perhaps she had been reading Bertrand Russell, who in 1910 had held somewhat the same point of view. Russell had written:

To reconcile us, by the exhibition of its awful beauty, to the reign of fate is the task of tragedy. But mathematics takes us still farther from what is human, into the reign of absolute necessity, to which not only the actual world but every possible world must conform. . . . . The true spirit of delight, the exaltation, the sense of being more than man, which is the touchstone of the highest excellence, is to be found in mathematics as surely as in poetry.

Whatever its immediate inspiration, the Euclid sonnet is among the most elevated ones in the English language, and the impulse that created it goes beyond the single sonnet into the whole texture of Millay's work, for it is her relentless quest of the clear, high vision, her quest of an austere and simple design in human life and in the universe that still, in 1936, gives her poetry its distinction. And in her eager youth this adoration of Euclid must have been imperiously demanded by her nature, like Goethe's similar devotion to the mathematical precisions of the philosopher Spinoza. Recalling a youth not unlike Millay's in spirit, Goethe wrote, "The all-composing calmness of Spinoza was in strong contrast with my all-disturbing activity. Reading him, the air of peace floated over me."

The young Edna St. Vincent Millay needed the peace of abstract Euclidean mathematics to counteract the horrors of astronomy, of which she knew little and surmised much. Even before she went to Vassar, she had looked deeply enough into space to make forever impossible for her the placid inspection of the starry heavens that had been habitual with poets in the nineteenth century. For her the steadfast stars to which Victorian lovers had aspired to ascend were all unfixed, and the heavens became a roaring whirlpool, an unrolling scroll of spiral nebulae, a horrible blizzard of falling suns. In her teens she would start out of nightmares in which, she writes, she saw

> the universe unrolled
> Before me like a scroll and read thereon
> Chaos and Doom, where helpless planets whirl
> Dizzily round and round and round and round
> Like tops across a table, gathering speed
> With every spin, to waver on the edge
> One instant—looking over—and the next
> To shudder and lurch forward out of sight.[1]

Years afterward her reading of Eddington and Jeans and then her independent study of astronomy were to reinforce this old feeling of cosmic terror, so that in her *Epitaph for the Race of Man* she was to muse on astronomical space:

> Now for the void sets forth, and farther still
> The questioning mind of Man . . . . that by and by
> From the void's rim returns with swooning eye,
> Having seen himself into the maelstrom spill.

Yet her first studies in philosophy half-reassured her that there might be an entelechy even in a bottomless and stormy physical universe, and in *The Suicide*, written before she went to Vassar, she had worked out a pragmatic belief for herself. She had decided that one should live as though this life were a task which one had undertaken in some forgotten prenatal paradise, a task whose purpose will be clear when one returns to the world of ideality. And she reinforced her pragmatism with memories of readings in logic, which had taught her how little pure reason can be counted on to govern life, since logical proofs cannot be strictly

[1] This poem, *Interim*, was written in the same year as *The Suicide* and *Renascence*. Its theme is purely imaginary. No one whom she knew at all intimately had died before she was eighteen, at the time when she wrote her description of wild and inconsolable mourning.

34

applied to the future. Naïvely, in *Interim*, she repeated her lesson in logic:

> Not truth but faith it is
> That keeps the world alive. If all at once
> Faith were to slacken—that unconscious faith
> Which must, I know, yet be the cornerstone
> Of all believing—birds now flying fearless
> Across would drop in terror to the earth;
> Fishes would drown. . . . .

But there is neither such good philosophy nor such good poetry in these pieces as in that less reasoned poem, *Renascence*. That had held the best philosophy in the world, albeit a purely mystical and nontransferable one, the philosophy that life is good because the taste of it is good on the lips of a strong spirit.

It was inevitable that she should stagger a bit in making the transition from the firm ground of ignorance to the escalator of higher education. The cramming of books faster than one can digest them, which is so inevitable a concomitant of college life, confused her for a year or two, and made her forget, in a few of her lines, the distinction between her own voice and the echo of another's. In *Ashes of Life* her

> Tomorrow and tomorrow and tomorrow and tomorrow

is an unfortunate prolongation of Macbeth's cry of tedium. And again her "Dark, dark," is spoiled by recalling the cry of Milton's Samson, "Oh dark, dark, dark!" But this sort of thing she never does again, after her first years in college. As soon as she catches her balance, she moves as independently as Webster's Bosola, with his motto:

> I will not imitate things glorious
> No more than base. I'll be my own example.

She soon became too profoundly affected by the literature of the past ever to imitate it servilely.

During the war years the department of English was
perhaps the strongest one in Vassar, since the college
president, Henry McCracken, was himself a scholar
of English; and, having been trained under Professor
Kittredge, he had brought to Vassar the Harvard mode
of teaching English literature. The chief value of
Millay's course in English lay in its deepening her acquaintance with the Elizabethan period, in which she
already knew Shakespeare and Marlowe and Fletcher.
Probably there are many people now living in England and America with a more scholarly grasp of
sixteenth- and seventeenth-century England than Millay possesses, but I am sure that no one else in the
twentieth century—not Rupert Brooke, not T. S. Eliot
—has become attuned to the physical and emotional
temper of that period as Millay has done. If it were
not a gross sentimentalism and a denial of the inexorable onrush of time to say so, one would almost
aver that in her girlhood she became in spirit a veri-
table Elizabethan, for her plays and sonnets henceforth
were to be, not mimicry of the works of Elizabethan
times, but such writing as one may fancy that Drayton and Webster and Middleton and Beaumont and
Fletcher might have done if they had known twentieth-century New England as well as their own time.

Millay's first poetic drama, *The Lamp and the Bell*,
is not her best one. *The King's Henchman*, written in
1926, will stand up beside any play of the seventeenth
century, excluding Shakespeare's. One never believes
that until he reads it while he is absorbed in seventeenth-century drama. But read *The Duchess of Malfi*
and *The White Devil* and then reread *The King's Hench-*

36

man. There it still stands, untarnished, bold and beautiful as ever. Her college play, *The Lamp and the Bell*, is much slighter, but it, too, can be read among seventeenth-century plays without ceasing to be beautiful. The worst that one can say of it in that company is that it looks like Dido in the world of spirits, or like Piccarda in Paradise, like a mere splinter of moonlight in the dawn. But when one considers it as the work of a girl just graduated from college it becomes amazing. I doubt that Marlowe did anything half so good at Cambridge University. Certainly it is, in my opinion, far superior to his *Queen Dido*. But of course it is fairer to compare it with the work of Webster and Middleton and their contemporaries, because they had the work of Shakespeare as a model, even as Millay had.

It is true that *The Lamp and the Bell* was formally composed in Paris, after Millay left Vassar, and that it was not acted on the Vassar campus until 1921, four years after her graduation. But all the spirit of it, the atmosphere and the theme, came from her undergraduate days. The kingdom of Fiori is Poughkeepsie-on-the-Hudson, and college students and faculty keep looking straight through their Italian veils, very much as Elizabethan Londoners keep lifting their masks in Shakespeare's Illyria and Verona and Messina.

The theme is that one of burning concern to students in any girls' school—the theme of friendship; and the play takes up their endless arguments as to whether an ardent feminine friendship is healthy and whether it will last. Octavia, the very mildly wicked stepmother in the play, supposedly a queen but essentially a dean of women, avers that the friendship of the princess and her own daughter is not healthy and will not last. Of course, the girls prove her wrong. The princess, without a murmur, gives up her lover to her friend; and long afterward she consents to violation by her most loathed enemy, in order to be permitted to reach her friend as she lies dying.

The theme is surely Elizabethan. From Lyly to Beaumont and Fletcher, Elizabethan literature is filled with asseverations that friendship is a stronger thing than sexual love. In the words of Lyly's Endymion: "When adversities flow, then love ebbs; but friendship standeth stiffly in storms." The only novelty is that this twentieth-century play deals with the friendship of women instead of men; and *Much Ado about Nothing* is the only Elizabethan precedent for that which I can call to mind, unless one counts *Two Noble Kinsmen* because of Emilia's memory of her love for Flavina.

But of course it is not the theme or the plot that matters. The excellencies of *The Lamp and the Bell* lie in its dramatic movement, its interwoven moods, its characterization, its fluid blank verse, its lyrics, its imagery.

In its dramatic components *The Lamp and the Bell* is as like late Elizabethan tragi-comedies as they are like one another. There are a law-court scene and a wedding scene, as in *Much Ado*. There are a hunting scene and singing in the twilight, as in *Two Noble Kinsmen*. There is a play within a play as in *The Tempest*, an uprising of the common people as in *Philaster*, a dying for love as in *The Maid's Tragedy*, a compact that the heroine shall give up her chastity to the villain, as in *The Changeling*. There is a scene in which the daughter keeps on dancing at the ball after her father has died, as in *The Broken Heart*. There is a delicate, tuneful fool as in *Twelfth Night*, a plotting stepmother as in *Cymbeline*, a child unaware of the significance of death, as in *The White Devil*. But it is hardly worth while to attach titles to these dramatic elements and situations; all late Elizabethan plays are a pastiche of them. All that matters is that in *The Lamp and the Bell*, as in the seventeenth-century plays I have mentioned, there is a current of life flowing through the action that makes all the stock situations fresh and real.

Stage tactics are handled with the daring of a beginner. When a character appears on the stage without an excuse, she simply announces that she cannot think why she is there and goes away to remember. It is far more plausible than many of the ingenious excuses for their presence that some more experienced playwrights have given their characters. Whenever an action is especially meaningful and difficult to present, it takes place off stage. This arrangement would seem to be all wrong, but as a matter of fact it underscores the most effective qualities of the play: its suspense and its foreboding. The audience is kept in the dark as to what has already happened in a way that is almost without parallel. Thus, after the scene in which the princess learns that her friend is in love with the same man as herself, there follows a gay scene in a flowery meadow, where all the court are gathering flowers for the wedding, but there is no hint to the wondering audience as to the identity of the bride. The waiting heightens the effectiveness of the next scene, in which we discover the princess overseeing the final touches being given the bridal toilet of a her friend. Again the suspense is very effective after a mysteriously tragic scene in the dark forest, at the close of which some children find the princess' sword stained with blood. Not till two scenes later do we learn that the princess' tragic melancholy is due to her having been the unwitting slayer of her friend's husband.

Along with this suspense as to what has already happened runs a continual premonition of future action. Over the sunny content of the child princess and her friend drifts the wistfulness of the fool's song:

> Oh, little rose-tree, bloom!
> . . . .
> Summer, for all your guile,
> Will brown in a week to autumn.

Over the joy of the princess in her betrothal comes the mist of tears because her friend is so far away, the friend who is to return and win away the lover's affections. The gaiety of the wedding party is interfused with melancholy for the audience, because of its foreseeing the grief of Beatrice when she discovers that her father has died. The gay account of the royal hunting party riding forth in the morning sunlight is overtinged by the onlookers' dark speculations about great folk riding back

> At times, of a rainy night, to such a burden
> Of cares as simple folk have little mind of.

And at the end of the play the pathos of the princess' grief for her dead friend is overshot with sunlight because her friend's children are to be hers, and her fool foresees summer picnics with supper

> On a flat rock behind a mulberry bush
> Of milk and tarts and honey and white bread
> All in one day.

The effect of the three interwoven interests of the audience—their suspense as to the past, their observation of the present, their forewarning of the future—is to make the play deeply musical in feeling, like a symphony in which the dominant melody is associated with brief echoes of the melody that is gone and little murmurs of the one that is to come. Musical in effect, also, is the trick of the repeated phrase, especially as it is used in the scene where the princess and the bridegroom, both loving Bianca so tenderly, keep responding, "Did she say that?" to each other's accounts of Bianca's messages. And later there is the repetition of Bianca's last words, which we hear first from her own lips as she lies dying, and then hear again in the hesitant and subtly varied recital of the messenger to the princess. Most musical of all is the repetition of the key metaphor of the play, the one which gives the title of *The Lamp and the Bell*. First at the preparations for Bianca's bridal the princess is moved by Bianca's happy voice to exclaim,

> You are to me a silver bell in a tower,
> And when it rings I know I am near home.

This first giving out of the metaphor augments its meaning at the close of the play, when the princess, hearing the message of reconciliation from her dead friend, muses,

> She is not gone from me. Oh, there be places
> Farther away than death! She is returned
> From her long silence, and rings out above me
> Like a silver bell!—Let us go back, Fidelio,
> And gather up the fallen stones, and build us
> Another tower!

These things, even more than the actual melodies heard in the songs of the fool, make the play as essentially musical as *The King's Henchman*, which, in the opera by Deems Taylor, has been set to music throughout.

There is not a wooden character in *The Lamp and the Bell;* all are alive, but all, with the exception of the king of Fiori, are girls. The king, with his self-characterization, "I am a tractable old fellow," is like an especially kindly head of a girls' college, keeping his humor and his dignity under the onslaughts of a bustling female faculty. Who but a weary old college president, grown patient under harassment, could with such brilliant irony reassure a mother who is fearful lest her daughter may "have ideas put into her head":

> Fear not. . . . . Your daughter's head will doubtless,
> In its good time, put up its pretty hair,
> Chatter, fall dumb, go moping in the rain,
> Be turned by flattery, be bowed with weeping,
> Grow gray, and shake with palsy over a staff—
> All this . . . . as empty of ideas
> As even the fondest mother's heart could wish.

There speaks a man. But of the other ostensibly male characters, Fidelio is masculine only in name; he is the most girlish of fools, with his wistful, idealistic "crush" on the princess. And even Guido, the villain, for all his big talk of civil war and rape, is really that peculiarly trying type of college girl, the malicious and envious one who is never happy except where she is not wanted. Guido's friend Giovanni sums up his femininely feline nature,

> You are like a cat . . . .
> There never was a woman yet that feared you
> And shunned you, but you leaped upon her shoulder.

As for the characters with girls' names, each one is a college type. There is the flirtatious fat and lazy one, pretty in spite of too much candy, who would "as lief open a vein as a book," and who is always teasing a boy to wait on her. There is the vixenish, clever one, who at whatever danger to herself cannot restrain a *bon mot* at the expense of the authorities. And there is the tragic older one, Francesca, a very real and developing character, too softly abandoned in her love, too given to sentimental harping on one string to be able to hold her lover's interest, and too single-minded to dream of giving him up after she has lost him, who therefore pursues him with a brine-soaked relentlessness that drives him to hate and brutality, and who grows reckless of her life as her hope wanes, so that she at first seeks death through some semi-accident, but finally, out of her brooding jealousy which reaches the proportions of insanity, evolves a strength of will enabling her to kill her faithless lover and herself. Not many strokes are given to unfolding Francesca before us, but there is not a false stroke among them.

And then there are the princess, Beatrice, and her friend, Bianca, as full of bubbling schoolgirl laughter, at the beginning of the play, as the princess and her maidens in *Love's Labour's Lost*, but more closely resembling Shakespeare's Beatrice and Hero in *Much Ado*. Like Shakespeare's Beatrice, the Beatrice of *The Lamp and the Bell* is taller than her friend, more given to initiative, quicker to jest, cleverer at sports, and cleverer with her brain, too; whereas Bianca has a docility and fragility even as a young girl that make her early death dramatically plausible, just as Hero's fragility made her deathlike swoon in the marriage scene what was to be expected. As Shakespeare's Hero

43

"crept sweetly into the study of imagination" of Claudio, so Bianca's gentleness creeps into Mario's heart. But the girls are not mere reflections of the heroines of *Much Ado*, for all that. Rather each is a dramatization of one side of the nature of that girl revealed in all Millay's elegies. Bianca has the beautiful voice of the dead girl of whom it was said,

> But your singing days are done:
> But the music of your talk
> Never shall the chemistry
> Of the secret earth restore.
> All your lovely words are spoken.
> Once the ivory box is broken,
> Beats the golden bird no more.

And Beatrice, who could outrun her lover, has the other side of the nature of that girl who used to go on her

> exultant feet
> Up paths that only mist and morning knew,

the girl who was so "proud and wild," so "flippant, arrogant, and free" that she seemed to have no need of love, even as Mario imagines that Beatrice has none.

Possibly the most important lesson that Edna St. Vincent Millay learned from the Elizabethans was that passion and exaltation are not divorced from one's bodily condition, and that dramatic poetry is most convincing when it makes us share the physical states of the characters. Most characters in modern poetic dramas are like shadows on a cinema screen, mere shape and sound, but Millay's people, like the Elizabethans, impress us as being able to eat and to smell. It is curious how intense a feeling of reality is given by odors. No other sense actually confuses illusion and reality as the sense of smell can do, if the artist appeals to it subtly enough. And as the breeze blowing through Webster's and Massinger's plays is always bringing us whiffs of garlic and sweat and medicine, or of spices and roses and herbs, or of roasting meats and pastries, so Millay's plays bring us stenches and fragrances. Even her imagery is sometimes based on odor. Never was there a more concise characterization of a debauchee than the characterization of Guido, when, upon his remarking that he has "opened up" his mind to the princess, his friend exclaims in olfactory stupefaction, "That is the last thing you should have done!"

Cookery metaphors appear in the talk of the women of the play, and it makes them seem at once more human and more feminine. Thus when Carlotta vents her irritation with the queen, she shouts,

> The woman stirs me to that point
> I feel like a carrot in a stew—I boil so
> I bump the kettle on all sides.

That is Shakespearian imagery, as in his "my business seethes," but it is also very much Millay's own, in its homeliness and vigor. And, like most of Millay's vigorous characteristics, it has set a fashion in poetry. Only the other day I ran across the comparison, in a poem by Donald Paquette,

> She bubbles with the bitterness of the times
> Like a kettle of mission soup.

Perhaps the most effective use of culinary imagery is in that scene, psychologically as sound as anything in Webster, wherein Bianca and her mother behave, as Bianca says, like "two strange, unhappy women."

Both being lonely widows, spending long, empty days together, they drive each other to helpless tears by their needlelike probing for subtle motives. Finally Bianca, taunted beyond endurance by her mother's insinuations, cries out,

> Oh, do not be so proud! Let us speak truth
> At length, a little! We are so garnished up
> With courtesies, so over-sauced and seasoned,
> We cannot taste each other!

That sort of homely cookery image goes back as far as the *Iliad*, wherein the wounds of Ares are healed as swiftly "as fig juice thickens white milk, that curdles as one stirs it." And in English poetry it goes back at least as far as Chaucer, with his

> So thrive I, this night shal I make it wele,
> Or casten al the gruel in the fire.

But after the seventeenth century imagery associated with food was dropped as unpoetic. So unpoetic, indeed, did food come to seem, that nineteenth-century novelists seldom allowed their heroines to appear at mealtime, and George Meredith felt obliged to submit a lengthy apology for allowing his Lucy to eat berries in sight of the reader. But Millay's Bianca is able to speak of food without lessening our sense of the pathos in her dying. And food becomes one of the important resources for imagery to many of Millay's admirers, notably Elinor Wylie.

As domestic in tone as the cookery metaphors is the sewing imagery in the play. For example, one of the women, after speaking of the old nurse's absent-mindedness, adds,

46

> And yet
> You may be sure 'tis nothing more than the thimble
> Of the matter she's forgotten. I never knew her
> Mislay the thread or needle of a thing.

This type of imagery, too, is caught from the Eliza-bethans, and to them it did not seem trivial. Lyly could speak of his thoughts being "stitched to the stars" and Shakespeare of the "ravelled sleave of care" or the "pleats of majesty." But after the seventeenth century it, also, dropped into disuse until Millay and Marcel Proust and Hazel Hall brought it back into favor.

The blank verse of the play is suited to all these feminine characters. It is not the mighty line of Mar-lowe, by any means; it walks with a light, swift, girlish tread. Millay has written only one bad line of blank verse in her life. In one of the poems written when she was eighteen, the line

> To effigy its incorporeal bulk

slips under the reader like loose sand. But there is no skidding on the blank verse of *The Lamp and the Bell*. Its movement is reminiscent of Fletcher rather than of Shakespeare, for there are many light extra syllables in the line, especially where it is charged with emo-tion, as in Beatrice's

> But my quick blood
> Went suddenly quiet in my veins, and I felt
> Years older than Bianca. I drew her head
> Down to my shoulder, that she might not see my face,
> And she spoke on and on.

And the swift extra syllables are used even more effec-tively to give a rush of warm young feeling to the lines in Bianca's speech of farewell on her wedding day, where the hurried *v* and *r* sounds in the "whenever's" are like a vibrato:

> And I shall think of you
> Whenever I am most happy, whenever I am
> Most sad, whenever I see a beautiful thing.
> You are a burning lamp to me, a flame
> The wind cannot blow out, and I shall hold you
> High in my hand against whatever darkness.

A very feminine play it is, in subject matter and in style. Indeed, it is almost a childlike play, scarcely more than a fairy tale. But it has subtle qualities of greatness.

III

THE REEDY'S MIRROR SONNETS
In a Time of Free Verse

VERY likely *The Lamp and the Bell*, along with many respected but infrequently acted plays of other centuries, may please some future generation more than it pleases us today, for nowadays we have little taste for poetic drama. Indeed most of us, most of the time, would rather see a New York "box-office" play than a performance of *Hamlet*, for our taste in action is so crude that verse seems to get in the way of a play's movement. When we hanker after *Hamlet* we usually are craving not the onward sweep of drama, but isolated examples of psychological insight and verbal felicity. We wish to be moved by a single phrase lighting up some unsuspected depth in the cavern of a human soul or, in a sudden gust, blowing clear some trivial but precious sight or sound long hidden in a sand dune of our memory. In our impatient day, therefore, it is natural that Millay's plays are little known, and that her reputation as a belated Elizabethan is based chiefly on her sonnets. Fourteen lines are about as much poetry as most of us can see at one time. A larger light dazzles our sight black.

The same Elizabethan qualities are in Millay's first sonnets as in *The Lamp and the Bell*, especially the impression they give us of being with someone alive in all five senses, someone with "that tingling sensation all

49

over," as Herman Melville once expressed it, which accompanies a strong feeling of personal identity. And in addition the sonnets have, to a greater degree than *The Lamp and the Bell*, the fluent pentameter line that had seemed to belong to Shakespeare alone, a line in which the syllables are like leaves springing from a twig, so subtly are their vowels and consonants varied and repeated. Such a line as the dying Hamlet's

> Absent thee from felicity awhile,

with its panting *f*'s, its languid *l*'s, and its darker vowels around the three short *i*'s together in the climactic word, so that "felicity" seems lifted into a glimmer of sunlight in a gloom—such a line seems to have as much living oneness as a green branch has. It almost moves one to exclaim in the phrase of *Interim*, "Oh, little words, how can you fall apart . . . . and hereafter aid in trivial expressions?" Millay's closest approach to the Elizabethans, and to Shakespeare himself, lies in her power to create the same sort of magic in fitting the sound of a line to its sense, so that the words seem to have said themselves, or to have grown together without artifice.

Like all the Elizabethans, but especially like the young Shakespeare and Greene, Millay is not afraid of very bold effects in alliteration. In twentieth-century verse, alliteration of the same letter on all five beats of the line ordinarily slays the poetry by reminding the reader of an advertising billboard, yet in the lines,

> Loving you less than life, a little less
> Than bittersweet upon a broken wall,

Millay somehow comes off safely with those five accented *l*'s, probably because they run on so swiftly to the *b*'s and *w*'s of the next line, where a sixth, more lingering *l* brings the phrase to a close. No less bold are the effects in

> No rose that in a garden ever grew,
> In Homer's or in Omar's or in mine,

where the second line not only holds the daring echo: "Homer—Omar," but underscores the consonants of those words with another *m* and two more *r*'s within the line, in which the repetitive sounds *in—in—in— ine* make up the remainder of the ten syllables. In a line where the meaning progresses, repetition could hardly go farther.

But her best effects are far more subtle than these, as in those lines in which she muses on children dancing:

> I know how lost forever, and at length
> How still these lovely, tossing limbs shall lie,
> And the bright laughter, and the panting breath.

There the eight *l*'s subtly link the phrases, and in the last line the four short *a*'s and the *br*'s accent the impression of color and energy. Even finer is the sound of the line,

> And you as well must die, beloved dust.

There the diphthongal *i* rings out like a solemn bell from the dull short *u* sounds around it; the inner rhyme of "must" and "dust" is unobtrusive but potent, and the second and third *d*'s of the line, in "beloved dust," give a little stammer of emotion to the phrase of endearment. That line is very characteristic of Millay's handling of sounds.

In this same sonnet, foretelling the death of the beloved one, is one of her greatest and simplest lines:

> Nor shall my love avail you in your hour.

The most moving word in the line, "your," is sounded the more strongly because of the "you" just before it, and the three *r*'s of "nor"—"your"—"hour" give the line a musing slowness. And in addition there is the effect of balance given by the *l—v* followed by *v—l*, in the central words. Such a line, if it were meaningless, might rival that so excessively admired line of the 1890's:

<blockquote>The vine, the viol, and the violet.</blockquote>

The dilettante in verse loves to fit syllables together, seeking such effects, and when he achieves them, the sounds are pretty and silly as glass wind-bells. Such experiments move some critics to ignore the sound of great and noble lines of poetry, insisting that whatever oral felicity they may possess comes by accident, since a poet moved by overwhelming emotion is obviously in no mood to tinker aimlessly with pretty sounds. But such critics, I believe, do not realize exactly what an overwhelming poetic emotion is. Everyone has had the experience of hearing a tune in his head which he cannot sing correctly, and he has been very uncomfortable until he has at last succeeded in getting hold of the tune with his throat muscles and actually sounding the notes that make it up. A poetic emotion is like that, and it is not really experienced as an emotion until it is expressed in all the perfection of sound that one has been vaguely conscious of as belonging to it. A poetaster, of course, gives up after a few trials and makes up a line "something like" the emotion that he seemed about to feel, or he loses track of the feeling altogether and simply fits some euphonious sounds together to take its place. But the true poet cannot get rid of his unrealized emotion so easily. It torments and strangles him, until at last, after hours or days, it comes right. There is all the difference in the world between a line shaped from without, such as

> The vine, the viol, and the violet,

and a line shaped from within, such as

> Nor shall my love avail you in your hour.

There is many a line of this sort in Millay's sonnets, that one can sound over and over endlessly, as the hero of Proust's *Swann's Way* used to play a single phrase from the Vintiell sonata, constantly finding a new subtlety in its simplicity.

Edna St. Vincent Millay was not, it is interesting to see, born knowing how to write a perfect sonnet. Her first sonnet in her initial volume betrays the awkwardness of inexperience. As she is flying along, she suddenly finds her wings striking against the glass walls of the sonnet's small inclosure, and she tumbles precipitately to the floor. Nothing but the embarrassment of a novice in having to come to a conclusion with only ten syllables left unoccupied can excuse the solecism of throwing in a parenthesis between a verb and its object, as in that last line:

> I drink—and live—what has destroyed some men.

At this very moment hundreds of thousands of men and women and children are attaching better concluding lines to sonnets than that one, I fancy. And yet even this first sonnet reveals her not as a sonneteer, but as a poet. Consider the steady succession of six *d*'s in the lines,

> Like him who day by day unto his draught
> Of delicate poison adds him one drop more.

That effect of stillicide, echoing the thought of the sentence, belongs in the same world as the succession of *k*'s in Sappho's lines imitating the roll of funeral drums:

Κατθναίσκει, Κυθέρή, ἁβρος ῎Αδωμις, τί κε θεῖμεν
Καττύπτεσθε κόραι καί κατερείκεσθε χίτωνας

Sonneteers never do such simple and inevitable things with sounds. Sapphic is the mood also; in fact, I know of no English rendering of Sappho that is so faithful to the spirit of her *Ode to Anactoria* as this sonnet is. All Sappho's troubled sense of physical tumult in the presence of the beloved is in Millay's breathless lines:

Though I bend before thee, though
From left to right, not knowing where to go,
I turn my troubled eyes, nor here nor there
Find any refuge from thee, yet I swear
So it has been with mist—with moonlight so.

If one can point to a nick in the final line of this first sonnet, it would be a carping critic who could find any technical flaw in the immediately following sonnets. However, in the quaint academic world where Millay was still living, there was a strange superstition, handed down through Oxford and Cambridge and Harvard and Yale, that the incomparably finest sonnet sequence in the language—Shakespeare's —was noble in spite of being all wrong in rhyme scheme, and the veriest tyro in rhyming was urged to struggle with the quadruple rhymes of the Petrarchan form lest his reader imagine that he was sluttishly shirking the clean sweep of perfection. Nobody in the professorial world seemed to mind, or indeed to notice, that in English the average Petrarchan sonnet resembled nothing so much as a very elaborate cast-iron grill. But Millay, from the beginning, used the Shakespearian rhyme scheme whenever the spirit moved her. If the mood was like a Niagara, then she was likely to use the Shakespearian form, sweeping straight on the forceful close; if the mood was brooding and still, like a spring rising and spreading in a pool, then she used the Petrarchan form. It is due to Millay, chiefly, that the prejudice against the Shakespearian rhyme scheme has come to seem archaic and absurd. By the time her *Fatal Interview* came out, a dozen years later, its Shakespearian form excited only a very few perfunctory or stubborn "Tut-tut's" from the professors.

But if Millay had not been shut away among the professors when she began to write her sonnets, she would have encountered a far more serious opposition to them, striking at their very roots. From 1912 to 1922 one might have supposed that the sonnet was a kind of quack grass, judging by the intensive campaign to stamp it out of American poetry altogether. The threefold prohibition of Harriet Monroe's *Poetry* editors was: no poetic diction; no classical references; no sonnets. Nor was less vitriol poured on the sonnet form by Miss Monroe's rejected suitors, who were organizing rival groups and trying to beat her to that renaissance of poetry that she saw in the immediate future. Among the new poets there were right-wing and left-wing radicals, but all had as one plank in their platform the slogan: "The sonnet must go."

One has a good deal of sympathy for this campaign. The sonnet, in the early 1900's, *was* a kind of quack grass, cropping up in all the interstices between essays and stories in the magazines. The fourteen lines were such a convenient space-filler that editors allowed for poems of that length even before they read them, and there was so little variation among them that they might almost as well have been printed before they were read, also. Perhaps they were. Certainly they were not much read afterward. The reader's eye took them in merely as the expected tailpiece design at the close of a piece of prose. By temporarily stamping out this obnoxious jointed weed, the agitators made room for the rare sonnet that is real, a small poem but an upward-shooting one, like that young sapling of a palm tree which Odysseus saw at Delos, springing by an altar to Apollo.

One grave injustice was done by the campaign, however. Arthur Davison Ficke wrote a fresh and genuine sonnet sequence during the worst years of the sonnet's depression, and because his sequence failed to override this initial prejudice, his *Sonnets of a Portrait Painter* did not win the admiration they deserve. That failure dissuaded a number of his friends from publishing sonnet sequences. Rupert Brooke's *Nineteen-Fourteen* sonnets were written in this time, too, but their form was excused by the poetic radicals because they had four counts to their credit. In the first place, Brooke showed an irreverent carelessness in his rhyme scheme; in the second, he was an Englishman and could hardly be expected to keep abreast of the poetic times; in the third place, the war theme gave the sonnets a strong journalistic interest; and, in the fourth place, his early death seemed to the romantic a seal set upon poetic excellence. But his sonnets were regarded as a literary freak, and were emphatically advertised as not setting a precedent for young poets.

There is little doubt, however, that to Millay they

did set a precedent. The influence of Brooke on her poetry is very slight, but it is there. She could not have failed to be astonished and exhilarated by Brooke's freedom. The sonnet, which for a century had been mincing along in black taffeta "thee's" and "thou's" and carefully skirting the square fence corners of rhyme, suddenly began to move like an athlete, in speech stripped of affectation and archaisms. Brooke's sonnets,

> Heart, you are restless as a paper scrap,

And

> I said I splendidly loved you; 'tis not true,

begin like a boy suddenly springing up with a cry of honest exasperation. Of course, Brooke had caught that accent of honesty from the late Elizabethans; Donne, in his opening lines, has the same air of starting up from prolonged reverie into spontaneous speech, to give some brusque direction, perhaps, as in

> Whoever comes to shroud me, do not harm
> Nor question much
> That subtle wreath of hair which crowns my arm.

But Brooke's sonnets, being in twentieth-century idiom, were more noticeably colloquial than the speech of Webster and of Donne, and so had a special influence of their own.

By the time she wrote her second sonnet, Millay had learned everything Brooke had to teach, and more. Her

> Time does not bring relief; you all have lied
> Who told me time would ease me of my pain!

has enough vehemence for twenty old-fashioned sonnets, and it runs on to its swift close as fast as her unruly thoughts wheeled back to the one from whom she would escape, causing her to "stand stricken, so remembering him." But whereas Brooke's running feet spurned rhymes like pebbles out of his way, letting them sting whom they might, Millay has here written a perfect Petrarchan sonnet, with a swift naturalness that almost gives the illusion of its being free verse. Not only that, but the ticking of the *t*'s and *d*'s in the opening lines about time, the misty drip of the short *i*'s in the line about the rain, the steady fall of the *v*'s and *f*'s among the recurrent short *e*'s in "where never fell his foot"—all this and much more reveals her as a perfectionist in almost microscopic detail, without losing for an instant the broad, free sweep of thought and phrase which mark the major poet. The best way to see the scope of that sonnet, I think, is to place it beside an admirable Elizabethan sonnet on the same theme—one of Daniel's sonnets to Delia, that has the closing lines:

> Seek out some place, and see if any place
> Can give the least release unto thy grief;
> Convey thee from the thought of thy disgrace;
> Steal from thyself and be thy care's own thief.
> But yet what comforts shall I hereby gain?
> Bearing the wound, I needs must feel the pain.

That is fine, but it lacks not only the richly crowding images of Millay's sonnet, but also its lithe, springing movement, which gives the impression that she could down any other sonneteer with one hand tied behind her.

The same youthful litheness is in the loveliest, if not the greatest, sonnet in her first volume, the one beginning,

> Mindful of you the sodden earth in spring.

That poem is filled with a sense of thrusting life extending even to the movement of the four seasons of the year, as if the eagerness of youth were speeding the year through its cycle. In spite of its being an elegy, it walks with the springing elasticity of girlhood, recalling Montaigne's remark, "In early youth the joy of life lies in the feet," or Catullus' *Iam laeti studio pedes vigescunt*. And Catullus himself does not hold, for me at least, the loveliness of those lines:

> You go no more on your exultant feet
> Up paths that only mist or morning knew,
> Or watch the wind, or listen to the beat
> Of a bird's wings too high in air to view. . . . .

If ever youth was tiptoe for flight, it is there.

Only a few sonnets are hidden away in the back of Millay's first volume of poetry, published in the year that she was graduated from Vassar. The revulsion against the sonnet was still too strong for a publisher to deem it wise for an untried poet to flaunt many in the face of the public. It was not until 1920 that her sonnet sequence appeared in print, and then it was in the comparatively obscure pages of *Reedy's Mirror* of St. Louis. And even after the sequence appeared there, she was reluctant to print it as a solid block in her next volume. Instead, she dribbled the sonnets out in the volumes that appeared during the next three years. But she need not have worried. Even a prejudiced public could not resist the magnificence of those poems. Critics broke out in a storm of approval. If Millay had never written anything but those twenty sonnets, her place in literature would be secure.

Merely making beautiful reflections and echoes of earlier poems does not, of course, make great poetry.

Of the hundreds of sonnet sequences in the libraries, only those are great which cannot be confused with one another in style and turn of thought. Judged by this standard there are not many great sequences of love sonnets in the English language. In the sixteenth century, besides Shakespeare's, there are Daniel's and Drayton's and Sidney's which are immediately distinguishable from one another; in the nineteenth century there are Christina Rossetti's *Monna Innominata* and Mrs. Browning's *Sonnets from the Portuguese*, Dante Gabriel Rossetti's *The House of Life* and Meredith's stretched sonnets, *Modern Love*. Are there any other sequences of love sonnets in the language in which there is a sturdy and flourishing individual life, rooted deep enough to reach abiding beauty? Well, there is Elinor Wylie's *Angels and Earthly Creatures*, and there are the *Reedy's Mirror* sonnets and *Fatal Interview*.

Of course, Millay's intensely feminine point of view distinguishes her from all the men who have written of love and gives her sonnets a marked individuality. Yet these sonnets in *Reedy's Mirror* are even less like any sequences by women. Her difference is not, I think, the one that has often been attributed to her, that she is more honest than the other women. The difference, as I see it, is merely that she is temperamentally much stronger, much more complex and imperious. Christina Rossetti's patient tone of abnegation is not Millay's; Christina Rossetti moves with deep feeling but with a weary, middle-aged step through her faultless octaves and sestets. And Mrs. Browning is just Mrs. Browning. I don't believe that anyone could imitate her even if anyone should ever want to try. Her sonnets are so atrocious and so unexpectedly glorious for a line or two at a time, seeming to snatch one up to heaven's gate by the hair of the head and then to drop one in a tin-can dump. Nor is either of Millay's sequences to be confused with one by Elinor Wylie, who in her *Angels and Earthly Creatures* reminds us of the child Jesus among the doctors, as in her pure phrases she expounds a philosophy of love. Millay never reminds one of Jesus at any age. No, when Millay begins to speak in this first sequence, it is not in Elinor Wylie's or Shakespeare's or Rossetti's or Meredith's or any other voice but her own— a voice at the same time musing and throbbing with eagerness for flight, like a thrush's call to another far across the dusky field.

> Once more into my arid days like dew,
> Like wind from an oasis . . . .

How the eager, springing movement toward a goal catches one up immediately into her stride! She walks through her phrases as Willa Cather's Lucy Gayheart walked, "as if she were catching step with the wind."

In one sense the *Reedy's Mirror* sequence is not a sequence at all, for it does not deal throughout with a passion for one person, as all former sequences of love sonnets, at least ostensibly, had done. But it is precisely this fact that gives the sonnets their individuality and peculiar unity. For they all deal with the bewilderment of a girl strangled with a passion for intellectual beauty and for physical vitality, which refuse to sit at opposite ends of a bench, like Titian's "Sacred and Profane Love" (if that is really his subject) coolly appraising each other's separate identity. Instead they shift in and out of each other's forms confusingly, so that she is continually crying with desperate earnestness, "No, this is not you," or "You are not this!" It is not that, like many poets of the past, she wants to sublimate a physical passion into a spiritual one (far from it!), but that she wants to see clearly what is what. It is this baffled pouncing upon a distinction before it can get away from her that gives the vehemence and singleness of intention to all the sonnets, whether she is speaking of her love for the mathematics of Euclid or for a beautiful boy, or for a discouraged middle-aged artist, or for her mother, or for something that seems to her for the moment the very essence of physical life—the reckless leaping of a line of dancing children. Sometimes it seems to her that her love of the earth has a permanence and roothold that distinguish it from her other passions:

> I shall return again to the bleak shore
> . . . .
> I shall be gone to what I understand,
> And happier than I ever was before.

Sometimes, on the other hand, it seems that she can be swiftly satisfied with the myriad flashes of beauty in the ugly kaleidoscope of headlong city life:

> Her the inhabiter of divers places,
> Surmising at all doors, I push them all.

Sometimes she is sure that the distinctions among her feelings are clear at last:

> Learned from earliest youth am I
> In loveliness, and cannot so erase
> Its letters from my mind, that I may trace
> You faultless, I must love until I die.

Sometimes she hurriedly collects herself as a new gust of love seems about to take her, and thinks that this

time she will keep her sense of direction and discrimi-
nation in spite of becoming enraptured

> Till all the world, and I, and surely you
> Will know I love you, whether or not I do.

But only one central truth is unshakably hers throughout, like the lantern by whose light she so desperately
struggles on among these distinctions, and that is the
conviction that the inalienable passion of her life is
for this quest, for the torment of loving life not as a
mere girl but as a poet. All the sonnets hold, in essence, the same cry:

> Cherish you then the hope I shall forget
> At length, my lord, Pieria?—put away
> For your so passing sake, this mouth of clay,
> These mortal bones against my body set,
> For all the puny fever and frail sweat
> Of human love—renounce for these, I say
> The Singing Mountain's memory . . . . ?

It is the "sternness of her soul's chastity," as she calls
it, that gives these headlong struggling sonnets their
shape; and it has given them an outline austere and
perfect as that of the Singing Mountain itself.

IV

A FEW FIGS FROM THISTLES

In the Palmy Days of Greenwich Village

MOVING from Vassar into Greenwich Village was a bit like stepping off from a level meadow into the Grand Canyon. And it was a good deal like moving from the age of Sappho into the age of Napoleon. The war was working to its close; London and Paris were running high temperatures; New York was in the first hysteria of the same fever. To the very young people who were flocking around Washington Square all the hectic racket seemed normal and inspiring. The world was their drum, not yet perished in the west end. The coming armistice was in the air, and as soon as that was declared, the younger generation, with the help of the *Liberator* and the *Nation* and the *New Republic*, and especially of Max Eastman and Floyd Dell and John Reed, was going to make a clean sweep of all the injustices that had ever afflicted the earth, and everybody was going to be gloriously abandoned to happiness. Edna St. Vincent Millay's pulses swung into the tempo without hesitation. On the date of New York's celebration of the armistice (appropriately enough the false armistice, a few nights before the real one) she celebrated all night in the fashion recorded in the gayest of all the victory poems:

> We were very tired; we were very merry—
> We had gone back and forth all night on the ferry.

64

It was bare and bright, and smelled like a stable,
But we looked into a fire; we leaned across a table,
We lay on the hill-top underneath the moon;
And the whistles kept blowing, and the dawn came soon.

The more tired the world grew, the merrier it insisted upon trying to be. But as boatloads of returning soldiers began to dock in the New York Harbor, something began to ring false in the cheer. There were too many laconic reports that some girl in nurse's uniform or some man in khaki had quietly slipped over the rail into the mid-Atlantic, or had stirred into a drink a sleeping potion guaranteed to have permanent effect. As the others marched down Fifth Avenue, their faces did not properly reflect the onlookers' broad grins of pride that Uncle Sam had so truculently stepped across the Atlantic and cleaned up that little mess in Europe. Evidently such an attitude was old-fashioned. Very soon it was beginning to be generally said that the war had been a mistake, fought, as Ezra Pound put it,

> For an old bitch gone in the teeth,
> For a botched civilization.

The idea seemed a bit out of key with the celebration. But nothing kills a false note so well as a louder noise. New York blew its saxophones and slide trombones fortissimo and swung into the jazz age.

The credo of the jazz age was that all was for the best in that best of all possible times. Everything that had been lost was contemptible. Security, kindliness, faith in other people's good intentions, self-discipline in living up to a long-established code, patient devotion to an intricate intellectual problem, shame and piety before an unattainable ideal of beauty or of goodness—all these notions had been the silliest of frauds, with which the human race had crippled itself for many generations. The human animal was, as a matter of fact, simply a lump of tingling flesh capable of feeling surprise and anger and fear and sex, at least up to the age of thirty or thereabout. There was only one heaven: being dead-drunk with novelty and excitement; there was only one hell: the Tophet of uncommitted sin. On with the dance!

All the arts swung into line. Henri Bergson already had worked out a philosophy of aesthetics adaptable to the needs of the hour. If, as Bergson asserted, reason was merely a crusting ice on the banks of onrushing human impulse, then art, which belonged at the tip of on-thrusting life, must have no intellectual content. Only such art as seemed to be under tremendous pressure or in the act of violent explosion was acceptable. The aim of art was to be invasive, to pierce through callous cuticle and jaded areas to a nerve that could still jump. In music this meant an orchestra weighted with trumpets and drums; the dream of critics and of serious young composers was to get rid of "caressing" strings altogether. It meant the percussions and syncopations of Stravinsky, the discordant intervals of Schoenberg. In painting it meant a palette of scarlet and orange and poison green, and a line that bulged and sagged in vain contortion toward a third dimension. In sculpture it meant (oddly enough in a time when women were winding themselves in adhesive tape to achieve a "boyish form") the ballooning buttocks and breasts of Gaston Lachaise's statues, the pock-marked surface and agonized expressions of Epstein's. In the ballet it meant the brutal and violent grace of Nijinsky. In the cinema it meant the farces of Chaplin. In literary criticism it meant Mencken and Van Wyck Brooks, the latter with his credo, "All the past of American art has been vitiated by the vice of prudence." In the novel it meant Scott Fitzgerald and Sinclair Lewis and James Joyce, stirring the mud of the college campus and of Main Street and of the stream of consciousness. In poetry it meant Vachel Lindsay and Carl Sandburg and Amy Lowell and Ezra Pound.

But that last hardly touches the flying skirt of poetry in 1920, the year in which *A Few Figs from Thistles* appeared. Vachel Lindsay had been beating the big bass drum and Carl Sandburg had been "going whisha-whisha" with the sandpaper all through the war years. Both were losing their novelty. Ezra Pound, however, was at the height of his power, and if he was little loved, he was admired for his carrying voice. As E. E. Cummings tolerantly expressed it, "Pound is, whatever you may say, the riveter announcing the erection of a sky-scraper." And Amy Lowell was in full career.

I like Amy Lowell. If she was not a real poet, she was that next best thing—a writer who stimulates a sharp appetite for poetry. And from 1912 onward no one had done better service than she in house-cleaning American verse. All the lint of verbiage, all the cobwebs of vagueness, all the mold of secondhand emotion had vanished before her energetic scorn. To be sure, a good deal else vanished before her brisk broom, a good deal that one would not wish to be long without. But then the house of life never stays house-cleaned long. Her orders to young poets were: "Don't reason. Don't remember. Don't anticipate. Don't experience emotion. Simply drink in the nowness of now. Smell it. Taste it. Touch it. Listen to it. Look at it." And it had been a welcome relief, during the war years, to have the soft sighs after the unutterable shut off, and instead of them to hear her poems and those of the other imagists—poems sharply limited to some single sensation, such as soaking oneself in sunny bath water, or listening to raindrops on a silk umbrella, or breathing the wind of speed in an automobile. But she reached her apogee in 1919, when her *Pictures of the Floating World* appeared, for by that time the restless post-war world was ready to declare that her latest metier alone constituted poetry, that drinking in an immediate sensation was all that a man had been born into the world for, that drinking in a poet's reflected image of a sensation was the next best thing to experiencing it directly. Imagism, then, was in the saddle—or rather, at the steering wheel. Life was a joy ride, and poetry was disconnected toots of the automobile horn.

To be sure, by 1920, so swiftly did the jazz age run through its novelties, the innocent sensations in *Pictures of the Floating World* were beginning to seem too tame. But Amy Lowell was attending to that in her plans for treating of the gruesome in her next volume, and most of her disciples were limiting their imagistic moments to the heavily erotic. In fact, the very newest philosophy, Freudianism (which means Freud as interpreted by the literary), taught that there were no moments except sex moments. Truth was sex; sex, truth. That was all one needed to know, back in 1920. Truth, said Jean Cocteau, points to her sex. Nature, said Mina Loy, is an irate pornographist. Therefore, the newest poems did not deal merely with the sexuality of people or of other mammals, nor did they stop with the obscene exhibitionism of the moon and the lasciviousness of worms in the earth and of birds in the air; they went on to detect the concupiscence of custards, the hermaphroditism of telephones, the—but one may as well stop there. Let no unabashed reader of an unexpurgated Shakespeare or Chaucer imagine that he can turn back to the periodicals of 1920 and reread Alfred Kreymborg, Evelyn Scott, D. H. Lawrence, Mina Loy, E. E. Cummings, *et al.*, without a blush.

Yet, bluster as the literary might, their super-colossal sexual vitality was seldom convincing, and they were continually slipping on into the next stage of drunkenness, with the helpless and babyish wail, "I wanna go home!"—home to the prenatal security of the womb, of course. As Robinson Jeffers was to express the feeling more articulately a little later:

> We came from a purer peace
> And a more perfect heaven, where there was nothing
> But calm delight, no cold, no sickness, no sharp hail.
> The haven of neither hunger nor sorrow,
> But all enfolding love and unchangeable joy
> Near the heart of life.
>
> . . . .
>
> The nine months are better than the ninety years.

The nearest one could come to regaining this felicity, it was felt, was to live in imagination in an infant's world. Deliberate infantilism, or Dadaism, as it was called, had already swept like wildfire through the literary circles of Paris and Rome and Vienna and Berlin. Dadaism forbade a poet ever to carry an idea intact throughout a sentence; in fact, it was far better to start without any idea in the first place. Merely to do things with one's mouth was the intention; and there was a genuine conviction behind Dadaism that

•this was the way back to the irresponsibility and un-jaded sensations of childhood and of primitive races. In 1920 Dadaism had scarcely reached America as yet, and on our shores it was never to attain the perfection of utter idiocy, but the impulse toward it was strong enough that the magazines were eagerly publishing the "poems" of children of three or four years of age, and men of thirty were trying their best to emulate them. Wise old George Santayana looked on with a tolerant smile, speaking up once, however, to remind poets that savages are not rudimentary on purpose and that children are not aware that they are childlike. And indeed poets were soon to be disconcerted by their child models. They proved bewilderingly unlike one another, at least after they reached the age of six or eight. In England the playmates of Bertrand Russell's small son were using all the conventions of the Scottish ballad; near Boston the small daughter of a Wellesley professor was composing in the manner of Amy Lowell; in New York the tot of a journalist was spattering the dictionary over couplets in the best newspaper tempo. This refusal of children to show the road back to blissful infantile irrationality was crush-ing. Poets did not know what to do about it. Most of them took another drink and wrote a little more wildly and obscenely.

In this world *A Few Figs from Thistles* appeared. To say that it became popular conveys but a faint idea of the truth. Edna St. Vincent Millay became, in effect, the unrivaled embodiment of sex appeal, the It-girl of the hour, the Miss America of 1920. It seemed there was hardly a literate young person in all the English-speaking world who was not soon repeating, *ad nauseam:*

70

My candle burns at both ends,
   It will not last the night;
But ah, my foes, and oh, my friends,
   It gives a lovely light!

Of course the gay and reckless little verses were not
great poetry. Indeed, these inverted proverbs were
scarcely poetry at all, scarcely original, even; for Oscar
Wilde had started the fashion of turning proverbs inside out thirty years earlier. But the novelty was that
here were no lily languors in velvet breeches, reminiscent of Wilde. And yet here was none of the synthetic
"pep" that was the last word in post-war literature.
Here was, instead, the bubbling, irresistible laughter
of a girl at her first wild party, catching up the smart
sayings of her dancing partners, nodding her head to
their vehement remarks, but too busy dancing her
stockings through to notice the fetid air and the jaded
nerves about her. New York felt about these poems
much as the court of Louis XVI must have felt in the
presence of an actual giggling dairymaid, or as the
audience of John Dryden's plays must have felt when
a young girl with a child's fresh mouth appeared before the curtain to speak the very naughty lines of his
prologues.

Not that these *Figs* are naughty at all, but they
owed part of their popularity to the supposition that
they were. It seems odd, considering the tone of current literature, that they were even noticeable for their
unconventional sentiments. But out in the states the
post-war mood had not traveled so fast as in New
York, and these poems were among the pioneers of the
youth movement. And they had Millay's inalienable
quality of clarity. The writers of the ultra-sexual
poetry of the time not only were incoherent, but many

71

of them amused themselves by standing off and shoot-
ing the punctuation at their poems through a pea-
shooter, doubling up in helpless convulsions when a
semicolon lit in the middle of a syllable. It was good
fun, but it interfered with their shocking the bour-
geoisie as thoroughly as they longed to do. On the
other hand, when Millay's merry and innocent little
Singing Woman from the Wood's Edge appeared, all the
sentences were perfectly intelligible, and when unsophisticated readers came to

> After all's said and after all's done,
> What should I be but a harlot and a nun?

they jumped in joy or horror, according to their temperament. "She says she is a harlot!" the whisper buzzed
from one end of the United States to the other and
back again. By the time it reached Nebraska, rumor
had fathered two bastard daughters on her.

But the more jaundiced part of the world found the
girl pictured in *A Few Figs from Thistles* very different
from the post-war flapper celebrated in most of the
poetry of the year. Louis Untermeyer, for instance,
had just written a poem to a girl "white and young,
and hard as nails." And Stewart Mitchell had expressed the infatuation men felt for the fashionable
girl of the time—a girl who

> follows men with calm sagacious eyes,
> Watching them falter, looking on her smile;
> Gazes as there were never thought so vile
> Or lust so strange that she could not surmise.

Queen Victoria herself was scarcely less like this type
of girl, blunted with sensual experience, than was the
childlike Singing Woman with her naïve boast,

> Oh, the things I haven't seen and the things I haven't known!

A FEW FIGS FROM THISTLES

The line holds the same young world-wonder which gives charm to many of the early folk ballads. And the same zest was in her feeling for the romance of geography, her thirst for the unknown, expressed in

> How shall I know, unless I go
> To Cairo or Cathay,
> Whether or not this blessed spot
> Is blest in every way?

Here was no sophisticate, but the most credulous and wide-eyed of adventurers in life.

Yet here were all the fads of the hour. Here were its childishness and its wish to be shocking:

> "And one thing there's no getting by—
> I've been a wicked girl," said I;
> "But if I can't be sorry, why,
> I might as well be glad!"

Here was its contempt for maturity, its recklessness with the future:

> The years that Time takes off *my* life,
> He'll take from off the other end!

Here was its restless quest of novelty:

> And if I loved you Wednesday,
> Well, what is that to you?
> I do not love you Thursday—
> So much is true.

Here was scorn for the old virtues, in the boast,

> But my true love is false!

And here was acceptance of the doctrine that romantic love is only an illusion:

> Whether or not we find what we are seeking
> Is idle, biologically speaking.

73

Here were the hampering conventions of the hour, even; for of course 1920, like every time, had its own conventions. Millay is obliged to apologize for a seeming violation of the code of infidelity:

> Oh, think not I am faithful to a vow!
>
> . . . .
>
> So wanton, light and false, my love, are you,
> I am most faithless when I most am true.

Yes, these poems spoke the speech of the hour, but with a freshness that made the gluttons of experience, who were almost beginning to wonder about indigestion, turn back with renewed appetite to the fruits of the tree of knowledge.

Probably the main reason that Millay was able to swing so lightly into this new dance step, after the earnestness of her Vassar poetry, was that the mode was not so novel to her as to most young New Yorkers. She was aware that the world had felt this flippant recklessness before, and she had made its acquaintance in Donne and Marvell, and possibly the Earl of Rochester—poets not yet reintroduced to society by T. S. Eliot and his disciples. Not even Marvell's *To His Coy Mistress*, later to be casually quoted even in the movies, was as yet much known, though it expressed the spirit of 1920 perfectly with its persuasion,

> Let us roll all our strength and all
> Our sweetness up into one ball,
> And tear our pleasures with rough strife
> Thorough the iron gates of life.

And Millay knew Donne as well as Marvell—had very likely read his version of the candle image that was to make her so notorious. In *The Canonization*, Donne had said,

> For God's sake, hold your tongue and let me love!
> . . . .
> We are tapers too, and at our own cost die.

And with middle age Donne had made a bargain comparable to the one implied in Millay's *Midnight Oil*, for in *Love's Usury* he had said,

> For every hour that thou wilt spare me now,
> I will allow,
> Usurious God of Love, twenty to thee
> When with my brown my gray hairs equal be!

And in the same spirit that animates Millay's *Thursday* Donne had complained, in *The Indifferent:*

> Alas, some two or three
> Poor heretics in love there be
> Which think to stablish dangerous constancy;

and again,

> Must I, who came to travel through you,
> Grow your fixt subject because you are true?

And in *Love's Alchemy* he had expressed his disillusionment with love,

> Oh, 'tis imposture all.

Fletcher, too, has an echo in *A Few Figs from Thistles*. In *The Two Noble Kinsmen* the gaoler's daughter, in love with Palamon, had complained, "In the next world will Dido see Palamon, and then she will be out of love with Aeneas." Millay's foreboding of her lover's irresistibility, even beyond the grave, is expressed in much the same terms:

> I am not willing you should go
> Into the earth, where Helen went:
> . . . .

EDNA ST. VINCENT MILLAY

Cressid could love again; Dido,
Rotted in state, is restless still.
You leave me much against my will.

No, the little poems are not especially original or especially noteworthy. Edna St. Vincent Millay would not have lost a great deal if she had signed them with her pseudonym, Nancy Boyd. But how original they seemed to other poets! And how they were flattered by imitation!

Mary Austin set the fashion of echoing or quarreling with Millay's *First Fig*, by writing, in 1921:

When I was young, my son,
I dreamed of a life exempted as yours is today
From the claims of the past and the future,
A tiny, two-penny candle to burn on the altar of now.

Edith Sitwell echoed the *Second Fig*, Max Eastman imitated *I Think I Should Have Loved You*, Maxwell Bodenheim imitated *She Is Overheard Singing*, Rose O'Neill imitated *The Penitent*, Virginia Moore imitated *The Merry Maid*, Louis Untermeyer imitated *O Think Not I Am Faithful*, and Louise Bogan imitated *I Shall Forget You Presently*. Of course, I am naming only poets of originality, who did more than make a blurred carbon copy of the original. In addition, carbon copies enough were made and printed. It would be a thankless task to count them.

V

ARIA DA CAPO
Tragedy in the Jazz Age

BUT *Figs from Thistles* revealed only one mood of
the poet. What Proust has called "the inter-
mittences of the heart" made it possible for
Edna St. Vincent Millay to be a light-hearted girl, ac-
cepting a mad and merry world, during lyric intervals
of the same year when she was writing the maturest
of ironical dramas and was staring at the life of her
century with eyes as disillusioned as Jonathan Swift's.
Her *Aria da Capo* is a bitterly hopeless analysis of the
logic of all wars and of the irreversible machinery of
tragic human history. And yet on the surface it is
farce.

Aria da Capo is a most original play, in style, in
theme, and in mood. It was written at the time when
Belasco's lavish and slavish realism in the theater was
beginning to pall, but before any of the commercial
theaters were willing to go far in sponsoring symbolic
drama. But eager young experimenters in Greenwich
Village had formed the Provincetown group and were
writing and producing their own plays, going as far
as they liked in stylized drama. Most of the plays
went very far indeed, and amounted to very little.
On the other hand, some of the plays were the early
experiments of Eugene O'Neill, and one was Millay's
Aria da Capo. No one need be reminded that O'Neill's
early experiments radically affected the twentieth-

century theater, reviving the soliloquy and the aside and introducing a stylized representation of split personality. But I doubt that O'Neill's effect on the theater has been any more incisive than the effect of *Aria da Capo* upon twentieth-century poetry. For in this play Edna St. Vincent Millay inaugurated a type of poetry that is usually thought of as stemming from T. S. Eliot's *The Waste Land* (composed in the following year), a complex poetry which telescopes time by presenting several historical periods simultaneously, and which, in the second place, uses a new method of writing tragedy, presenting it with deliberate reticence, under a surface of bitter jest. And, in the third place, it makes use of symbolism.

Millay solved the problem of telescoped time, or relativity, with a lucidity which accounts, I suppose, for the public's scarcely noticing how difficult her task had been. She represented her two courses of time as separate plays, acted in the same theater. In other words, *Aria da Capo* is deliberately removed one degree from reality by being played as two plays within a framing play. A sophisticated farce of the twentieth century and a prehistoric pastoral tragedy are dovetailed to make a complex allegorical drama.

Pierrot and Columbine come on the stage to play a brittle drawing-room farce. Pierrot represents a talented young New Yorker, catching up all the fads of the moment—futuristic painting, modernistic music, mathematical relativity, socialism, patronage of the theater, dress-designing, drinking, scientific love-making—but he is really overwhelmed by the futility of existence and diverted by nothing but the sound of his own voice. Columbine represents the typical "flapper," a stupid young woman trying desperately to

78

please Pierrot by affecting violence and fickleness of
feeling. In the midst of their play the stage manager
abruptly orders them off and calls two primitive shepherds to play a pastoral tragedy. The shepherds begin
reluctantly and falter at crucial points in the action,
but with prompting from the stage manager they succeed in acting out the story of two Arcadian shepherds
who in the midst of a joyous afternoon think of a
new game—the game of private property and na-
tionalism. By the use of theatrical symbolism their
game is represented by stretching a tissue-paper wall
across the stage. Soon a real wall of distrust and envy
rises between them and makes it impossible for either
one to stop playing. Trivial as each act is, they find
that it can never be recanted or ignored. Trade is in-
stituted; it is agreed to exchange a bowl of water for
some colored stones (really confetti), but by this time
murderous hate has reached a climax, so that while
one is holding poisoned water to the other's lips, he
is strangled by a necklace of jewels. As the two die,
the stage manager calls back Pierrot and Columbine
(whose off-stage bickering has been interrupting the
shepherd's play), and they, after a momentary shudder
at the dead men underfoot, take up their parts, and
history begins to repeat itself with the silly opening
words of their farce.

The play of the two shepherds is as stark as Chaucer's *Pardoner's Tale*, which it resembles in its outcome, but it differs from Chaucer's tale in the essential gentleness and innocence of its two characters,
both of them bewildered and frightened as they dimly
see where the logic of history is carrying them. Once
caught in the movement of events, they must go on
automatically to the tragic end, symbolizing the

World War. Very moving is the breaking of the tissue-paper wall, as Corydon, blinded and dying, staggers through it unknowing, crying, "Where is the wall? There isn't any wall, I think," and huddles under a corner of the other shepherd's cloak, to die. But perhaps more tragic is the matter-of-fact bang with which the stage manager closes the promptbook and recalls the harlequins—replying to their objection that the audience will not tolerate a banquet scene in the presence of dead bodies,

> What makes you think so?
> Pull down the table-cloth
> On the other side, and hide them from the house
> And play the farce. The audience will forget.

There are people whose horror at a tragic event is in direct proportion to the size of newspaper type used to report it. To such people Millay's *Aria da Capo* is either utterly meaningless or it is a trivial farce, burlesquing the World War and capitalistic civilization by reducing the human race to stage puppets, and the causes of its tragedies to the insignificance of confetti and paper ribbons. In 1920 such people yawned over a performance of *Aria da Capo* at the little Provincetown Theater and went back to Broadway, where they suffered eagerly through St. John Ervine's *John Ferguson*, because it was plainly marked "Tragedy."

There are other people whose reverence for catastrophe is of a religious solemnity, and who impute to doom an Aristotelian or Hebraic sense of decorum. To such people a laugh, however sardonic, at the workings of fate is like shaking a tambourine during an organ fugue. Such people looked with nausea at the "gay black and white" and "somber flame" of *Aria da Capo* and heard in its wit only the ultimate

80

cynicism of the damned. They went back to Broadway to laugh at George M. Cohan in his latest musical comedy, comfortably insulated from a tragic universe by an impervious wall of hokum.

There were, however, a few people in 1920—and there was to be an important poetic school of them later—who felt that a fusion of farce and tragedy into what one may call "tragic humor" was destined to be the most meaningful, and therefore the most richly poetic, expression of the twentieth century. Santayana, above all others the poet's philosopher of our time, was saying, "A pompous idealist who does not see the ridiculous in *all* things is the dupe of his sympathy and abstraction; and a clown who does not see that these ridiculous creatures are quite in earnest is the dupe of his egotism." And Santayana felt that man's capacity for smiling in the midst of tragedy, far from being an evidence of cynicism, was the happiest evidence of human dignity and freedom, even of hope —for, as he said, "a world which lets us laugh at it and go free is after all a friendly world. We have no need to bear that serious grudge against it which we should be justified in bearing if it fooled us altogether."

One must not overestimate the novelty of this mood of tragic laughter as it appeared after the World War in American poetry. Some appreciation of the universe as a tragic joke has been expressed here and there throughout world-literature. In Greece there were traces of it in the irony of Aristophanes and Lucian. In Rome it appeared in Catullus, in Tacitus, in Lucretius. In modern Europe something of it appeared in German literature, flashing out most keenly in Heine, but revealing itself also in Goethe, who commented on the irony of a poet's tragic fate: "It is not customary to respect a poet who shows himself rebellious at his fate; rather he must wear the pleasanter smile, the bitterer his cup is, so that the composed spectator may not be offended by any kind of grimace." In France tragic humor appeared later, in Baudelaire, and also in Corbière and Rimbaud and Jules Laforgue, for whom Baudelaire had set the fashion of jesting about one's misery by "lying like a dentist," as he put it, about the degree of suffering revealed in *Les fleurs du mal*.[1] And in twentieth-century French literature tragic humor was, about 1920, appearing in such sarcasms as that of Paul Morand, who in a poem called *A Fine Day* commented on the early-morning smile of the British ambassador:

> In order not to spoil the success of the day for him,
> The wounded are going to promise not to suffer any more.

And something of it was in the Russian Andreyev.

But in spite of such flashes of irony in the literatures of all nations, Englishmen and Americans like to believe that a capacity for jibing at disaster is an especially Anglo-Saxon trait. Even in the earliest literature of England it appears in the one indubitable joke of *Beowulf*, when the hero tells his host at the feast that if Grendel eats him, then "no thu ymb mines ne thearft lices feorme leng sorgian" (the food of my body need not worry you), it being the same joke as Hamlet's about the supper of the dead Polonius, "not where he eats but where he is eaten." The mood of tragic humor appears in Chaucer, most plainly perhaps in his Pardoner and throughout the story of

---

[1] After Edna St. Vincent Millay's felicitous translations from *Les fleurs du mal* it is hardly necessary to point out how much she resembles Baudelaire in her mood of sad jesting.

Troilus and Criseyde. It is evident in Dunbar and Henryson; the Scotch, with their bawdy funeral wakes, have always been peculiarly aware of the close juxtaposition of laughter and tears.

But it was not till the Elizabethan period that the mood of tragic laughter reached its maturity, and not till the end of the period, at that. Earlier Elizabethan literature was likely to be merely a checkerboard of tragedy and comedy in the style described by Drayton as

the English strain
That cannot long one fashion entertain.

To be sure, even near the beginning of the period one finds farce and tragedy fused in Marlowe. The fusion is evident in *Tamborlaine* and *The Jew of Malta*, where one feels in the author a humorous relish of the tragedy. Here and there in *Dr. Faustus* is the same treatment of suffering as a bitter joke, as when, for instance, upon Faustus' remarking, "Come, I think hell's a fable," Mephistopheles replies, "Aye, think so still, till experience change thy mind." Marlowe's savage humor, however, is an exception. Generally speaking, the humorist and the tragic hero of Elizabethan drama began by alternating scenes with each other in the earlier plays, and only gradually approached closer and closer till they became a single person in contradictory moods, such as Hamlet, and then moved still closer until they became a single person in a single complex mood, such as Webster's Flaminio or his Vittoria. To make this fusion possible, not only was the broad clowning of early days gradually refined into high comedy, but—what was more important—the hero was transformed, by the admiration which Elizabethans began to feel for aristocratic melancholy, from a self-reliant being who was troubled about nothing except the outcome of a single crisis in his life, into a being who felt a melancholy anxiety about human life in general. Then in later drama the hero passed from chronic, melancholy anxiety to melancholy resignation, and from melancholy resignation to melancholy amusement with a hopelessly insane universe.

It was Shakespeare's successors, rather than Shakespeare himself, who anticipated our century in evolving this last type of humor, unless, indeed, we account Shakespeare the creator of Palamon in *Two Noble Kinsmen*, of whom it is said,

> Palamon's sadness is a kind of mirth.

Two Noble Kinsmen is soaked with tragic humor, and its ironical close is the very essence of the mood. Theseus, with a melancholy smile, comments on the outcome:

> The conquered triumphs:
> The victor has the loss.—Oh, you heavenly charmers,
> What things you make of us! For what we lack
> We laugh, for what we have are sorry!

The Two Noble Kinsmen has had an evident influence on Edna St. Vincent Millay ever since she first read it as a child of nine or ten; and it is to Fletcher, Webster, and the other Elizabethans that we must look, I think, to find the principal literary source of her sad jesting over the universe.

It is true that the mood had not been entirely forgotten between 1630 and 1920. Swift, Fielding, and Thackeray had kept something of it alive for two centuries. And Thomas Hardy possibly felt it more deeply than any other modern writer, though in his novels his expression of it is marred by his ingenuity in contriving tragic plots. On second reading of Hardy's novels one is tempted to feel that the tragic faults of his heroes and the remorseless onward grind of a mechanical universe would have been powerless to achieve catastrophe had not the author (not fate or doom or Satan but Thomas Hardy himself) stood by frantically jerking the strings and violating all the mathematical laws of chance in order to make his stories turn out wrong. In his poetry, however, Hardy was a true tragic humorist, at his best in those scenes in *The Dynasts* that show the battle of Waterloo from the point of view of worms in the earth and of spirits at an astronomical distance from the earth.

Before *Aria da Capo* was written Edwin Arlington Robinson also had felt this sad and humorous mood; I often think he felt it more warmly than Hardy. Obviously the mood cannot be genuine, in any poetic sense, without warmth. In order to be transmuted into poetry the tragedy must pierce to the very core of the poet's heart, and the humor must tickle his very heart root also. The terrible and uncontrollable sense of humor that attacks one a few days after one's appendix has been removed throws one into what, I imagine, is the physical counterpart of the tragic humorist's spiritual state. At least that seems to have been Robinson's spiritual state throughout his life. Like the hero of his *Ponce de Leon*, he looked at life, always, "with a twist of pain that might have been a smile."

Still, when all is said, no one except the seventeenth-century Webster and Tourneur and their associates has been precisely in key with the mood which evolved in America after the war and first reached significant

literary expression in *Aria da Capo*. The early seventeenth century and the post-war years of the twentieth
century had a great deal in common. The grim and
shuddering jokes in Webster's and Tourneur's plays
would all have been to the fancy of the average man
on the street, in 1920. After the wholesale slaughter
of the World War, everyone understood "interne's
humor" like that in Webster's *Devil's Law Case*,
wherein a surgeon, seeing a supposedly dead man
open his lips to groan, exclaimed, "What, is the wind
in that door still?" In 1920 everyone understood un-
dertakers' jokes also—a type of humor which had
reached its perfection in Dekker's *Old Fortunatus*,
wherein a son, as he was about to show his father's
corpse to a mourner, discovered that it had suddenly
disappeared, but disguised his astonishment with the
nonchalant explanation, "Oh, our father has stepped
to agree with Charon about his boat-hire to Elysium."
And as early as 1920, though the gangster era had
scarcely begun then, most people understood murderers' jokes also—the kind of humor that led killers in
Webster's plays to refer to throat-cutting and stran-
gling as making gifts, to the victims, of "winter
plums" or "choke pears" or "true love knots." Nowadays, of course, the gifts are "a ride" or "a necktie
party." And the World War taught men to jest even
in the act of taking their own lives, in the spirit of
Webster's character who explained, in the act of suicide,

> To kill oneself is meat that we must take
> Like pills, not chew't but quickly swallow it.

As for jests in the moment of violent death, there were
many in the World War, as there had been many in
Webster's plays. Thus Vittoria, in Webster's *The*

White Devil, challenged her murderers, "Sever head from body, we'll part good friends," and Flaminio, of the same play, on being advised to recommend himself to heaven before he was murdered, replied, "No, I will carry my own commendations thither." And a moment later, feeling his voice going, he whispered, "Oh, I have caught an everlasting cold."

Furthermore, during the World War even mourning for a beloved one was sometimes mingled with jesting, for grief was so general that a mourner lost his sense of distinction, and, if he could not season his grief with irony, felt as apologetic as Beaumont and Fletcher's old Lord Calinax, who excused himself for sobbing over the body of his dead daughter: "You all have fine new tricks to grieve, but I ne'er knew any but direct crying."

This resemblance in temper of twentieth-century society and seventeenth-century literature was soon to lead not merely Edna St. Vincent Millay but T. S. Eliot and Herbert Read and other poets and critics to feel that perhaps the poet's one road to freedom in a disillusioned and scoffing age was to emulate Webster and Middleton and Ford and Tourneur, or rather to go farther than they had done, by writing, not tragedies with a pretense of farce in the conversation, but farces with an undercurrent of tragedy. This form, they felt, might make it possible for the poet to survive even in an age hostile to deep feeling.

It is undeniable that a hard surface of bitter humor is a protection to the poet in many ways. For one thing, it protects him from ridicule, for a reader who is inclined to accuse the poet of morbidity or sentimentality is disconcerted by the half-smile playing about the poet's lips as he makes his most tragic utterance.

Second, it assures the poet that every reader will observe only as much tragic earnestness as his nature is capable of responding to sympathetically. Third, it protects the poet from the moistly clinging sentimentalist who flourishes even in the least sympathetic age. Emily Dickinson well understood the need for such defense:

> Mirth is the mail of anguish,
> With which it caution arm,
> Lest anybody spy the blood
> And "You're hurt!" exclaim.

Edna St. Vincent Millay commented to the same effect:

> So far, indeed the world may mock at me,
> But if I suffer, it is my own affair.

And, fourth, since the spirit of an age necessarily penetrates the poet's own nature, perhaps a hard surface of humor seems to him most valuable as a protection, not against the public, but against himself. Herbert Read says that a poet cannot feel assured of his own dignity unless he is armed with the sense of proportion which humor gives, preventing him from exaggerating his woes to gratify his sense of self-importance. And also, in an age that accounts it unmanly to grovel and weep, the mood protects a poet against his own temptation to break down in self-pity, for when one is screwed up in agony that demands an outcry, laughter affords almost as much emotional release as a groan. But a far deeper poetic justification for the mood lies in a sense that one is getting even with an omnipotent and hostile universe by jeering at it while it annihilates one. There is something profoundly moving about a puny human being daring to confront doom as a dandy, a fop, making himself, as Wallace

Stevens has expressed it, "a connoisseur of elemental fate."

And, finally, deeper than all this lies the profoundest justification of all for the mood, though only the greatest poet would be capable of feeling it to its depths and expressing it. Tragic humor in its deepest poetic sense would mean the achievement of such freedom from egotism that one could honestly see a joke on one's self and laugh with one's whole heart at one's incongruity in the universe, even while one was suffering. (Perhaps Santayana alone, in our century, has fully achieved that ultimate tragic humor, in his prose-poetry.)

As a consequence of some such convictions as these, soon after *Aria da Capo* appeared there were many recommendations that a form of drama somewhat resembling it be adopted as the distinctive expression of our age. In France Jean Cocteau began to experiment with adaptations of Shakespeare's tragedies to be played by chalk-faced Pantaloons. In America Charles Chaplin was urged by the intelligentsia to play *Hamlet* on the screen. In London T. S. Eliot advised poets to use the style of the music-hall comedian as a medium for tragic utterance. "Jazz as a medium for tragedy" became a watchword among poets for a time. But most of these projects were still-born. As late as 1934 W. H. Auden published two plays in the manner. His *Dance of Death* and *Paid on Both Sides* are tragic burlesques of the politics and social convictions of our time. But, in spite of them, it seems to me that *Aria da Capo* still stands almost alone as a poetic achievement in this field.

One reason for the success of *Aria da Capo* is that Edna St. Vincent Millay is so steeped in the seven-

teenth-century imagery comparing life to a stage play
that she can make stage puppets of her characters
without losing a jot of their appeal to our human
sympathies. The overtones of seventeenth-century utterances about man as a player

> Who struts and frets his hour upon the stage,

as a being who feels in the hour of catastrophe that

> When thunder sounds, heaven likes the tragedy,

and who can think of death itself as another stage rôle,
saying with his last breath,

> I am in the way to study a long silence—

the overtones of many such utterances as these by
Shakespeare and Webster seem to be ringing above the
talk of the stage puppets who represent the human
race in *Aria da Capo*, and they give them richer significance. A poet less steeped in the spirit of the seventeenth century than Edna St. Vincent Millay is would
have been bound to write out of key with this imagery
and to lose all the heightening of effect that comes
from its echoing in the background of the reader's consciousness.

The other reason for her success, as I see it, is her
sensitiveness to musical effects. The musical title of
the play was much more of a novelty in 1920 than it
has become since then. Musical titles came into vogue
almost immediately after *Aria da Capo* was performed.
Aldous Huxley's *A Melody by Scarlotti* and Amy
Lowell's *Gavotte in D Minor* were published soon after
it. Next came a gush of musical titles from the three
Sitwells and after that a flood of them for poems and
novels, both in America and in England. A glance at

current issues of *Poetry*, the *Criterion*, etc., shows that the mode is not yet wholly past.

But the influence of music on *Aria da Capo* goes much farther than the title and the tripartite division that the title imposes upon the play, with the third part repeating the first. The resemblance to music comes out most strongly in the interweaving of themes, so that, in much the same way as in *The Lamp and the Bell*, one hears echoes of the past and anticipations of the future while a certain action is going on. In *Aria da Capo* this is managed by having the voices of Pierrot and Columbine, off stage, interrupt the shepherd's story. Thus, as the shepherds take their first step toward modern civilization by making their wall, we hear the inane voices of the harlequins quarreling, reminding us that their futility is a sample of the civilization toward which the happy and serious shepherds are moving. Again, just as the shepherds begin their first dispute over property, Columbine incongruously appears, demanding *her* hat, informing them that it is *her* scene, making the whole notion of property seem ridiculous, since she in her pink skirts is so tiny and faded as to seem utterly insignificant in comparison to the heroic size of the shepherds in their brilliant blue and red cloaks. And once again, when the shepherds have reached the climax of their hate, the thin and flippant voices, off stage, of Pierrot and Columbine, depleted by a decadent civilization till nothing is of moment to them, accentuate the weight and seriousness of the shepherds' problems. And if these interruptions of the harlequins are like pizzicato phrases in a high treble interpolated in the grave music of the shepherds' talk, they are balanced by the interruptions of the stage manager, Cothurnus, the spirit of tragedy, in a voice deep and measured as the voice of fate itself. The play is very like a string quintette of eighteenth-century music, and the harmony with which the parts answer one another lends a sense of heightened significance to the simple or flippant speeches, giving them in combination a meaning far beyond their surface meaning. This formal symmetry, like that of classical music, is indispensable to a play in which the subject matter is so lawlessly ugly, and in which the author's mood is so blackly pessimistic. It was necessary that this play, depicting the endless nightmare of history, be written in a form of beautiful symmetry; just as it was necessary, later, that Millay's *Epitaph for the Race of Man* be written in a strict form such as a sonnet sequence, rather than in free verse. For a chaotic report of chaos is nothing at all. As Professor Elmer Stoll has suggested in one of his studies of Shakespearean tragedy, a work of art must report even ultimate ugliness and meaninglessness in terms of formal beauty; otherwise the deep and grave irony that makes us aware of ugliness and meaninglessness as a tragedy is absent. This is the lesson that none of Edna St. Vincent Millay's successors in the making of farce tragedy was able to learn.

VI

SECOND APRIL
In a Time of Self-Doubt

IN 1923 two significant prizes were awarded to
poets: the Pulitzer prize to Edna St. Vincent
Millay[1] and the *Dial* prize to T. S. Eliot for his
Waste Land. The extreme difference in the two prize
books marks dramatically the parting of the ways for
two poets who in 1920, when *Aria da Capo* was written,
had seemed to hold the same vision of the world. At
that time both of them, sharing a strong love of the
seventeenth century, were looking with the ironical
eyes of John Donne, the ironical smile of John Webster, at a shimmying, joy-riding, baby-aping, bootlegging, fortune-making, fortune-wasting, sex-crazed
world, and finding in its whirling insanity a philosophy of despair. In 1922, however, when their prize
poems were made, they were far apart. T. S. Eliot was
leading a flock of followers straight on into the desert
of nihilism, among the cacti and Joshua trees of
symbolism, marquetry, obscurantism, and caricature,
whereas Millay was walking the Maine seacoast of
her childhood, finding in her unshaken love of earth
and ocean and the noble aspirations of past ages an
impregnable defense against the disintegrating forces
of her time; and she was meeting all the devastating

---

[1] The prize was awarded for a group of poems published in the *American Miscellany* in 1922, and for the ballad *The Harp-Weaver*.

logic of nihilism with the proud cry, rather like that of Descartes, "I care, therefore I am!"

The logic that she had to defend herself against was that of David Hume, belatedly making itself felt in poetry. Every advance in human logic has eventually affected society as a whole. But it takes a long time for an abstract philosophy to enter into the casual thought of men, to blend with their daily life, to become assimilated with their longings and aversions, to merge with their sensations, and finally to express itself in the unstudied and inevitable attitudes of poetry. It is not surprising that one hundred and eighty years went by before a skepticism like Hume's was "felt in the blood and felt along the heart" by the poets. Of course poets, like other persons of a philosophical temperament, had been aware of Hume ever since the eighteenth century, but only with the intellect. They had read him in the same spirit as Hume himself occasionally had regarded his own conclusions, with a chuckle at the incongruity between his logical inferences and his daily life, with its comfortable backgammon-playing and church-going and consistent study. But when poets with their whole nature as poets finally felt Hume's conclusions, it was with no impersonal interest but with a gnawing physical distress that was literally driving some of them to suicide and leading others to wish that they had never been born. For it had become impossible for them to behave any longer as if the world made sense when to their minds it patently did not.

In 1921 events had prepared the way for a whole-souled attention to a nihilistic philosophy. That year, for American art, marked the end of a drunken jag and the beginning of a vile headache. In other words, it

marked the end of reckless and exultant tasting of
sensual experience and the beginning of a horrible distrust of everything—of the outer world, of the past,
of the future, even of one's self; particularly, indeed,
of one's self. At the end of the war poets had been
avid of experience, any kind of experience. Their
mood might have expressed itself in the cry of Faustus:

> Ah, might I see hell and return again,
> How happy were I then!

They saw hell, but in 1921 they discovered that the
return was not easy. They had renounced past and
future and gambled everything on the instant. Reality, for them, had lain in the immediate sensation
alone. Rationality was merely a barrier to sensation,
leading to such awkwardness as E. E. Cummings ridi-
culed on observing his friend's "acute sentience whose
white-hot lips however suddenly approached can
never quite taste the wine which their nearness
evaporates." This failure to taste the present moment
was in the view of the jazz poets the only tragedy of
existence. Tzara, the high priest of Dadaism, was giving logical expression not only to Dadaism but to the
philosophy underlying practically all poetry of the
war years—the poetry of imagism, of naturalism, and
of vorticism—when he preached: "Dada, abolition
of the memory; dada, abolition of the future; dada, to
respect all individualities in the madness of the moment."

But now poets discovered that by excluding past
and future they had destroyed all individualities. And
not only that, but they had lost the moment itself.
For they found that the past shuts tight against the
future and that they had squeezed away their very self-

hood by shutting themselves within the present instant. Conrad Aiken, first of the new school of poets, described the nothingness of the immediate present, as he saw it:

> It is a stage of ether, without space,—
> a space of limbo without time,—
> a faceless clock that never strikes.
> Here the dark synapse between nerve and nerve;
> the void, between two atoms in the brain;
> darkness, without term or form, that sinks
> between two thoughts.

Malcolm Cowley was another of the first seers of the nothingness of immediacy. He saw time like a serpent squeezing the meaning out of each instant, squeezing the personality out of each human body:

> Time is a boa about the neck of these people,
> Constricting slowly.
> See, they are choking; their skin
> Goes dead white under their rouge.

Poets, along with all the rest of the human race, became, to their own vision, nothing—a mere geometric point in a cyclonic wind of nothingness. Their only sensation became a tortured, raw awareness of a raging tempest of time. Desperately they struggled to find some bracing standard of judgment within themselves, some lasting desire, some stability in grief or disappointment, some respect for their lost illusions, even, that would give them at least a sense of direction in the storm. They could grasp nothing at all. The stupid public, of course, was erecting the flimsy barricades of "efficiency" and "success" and "standardization" against the cyclone of senseless change. Poets saw those contemptible shifts for what they were, and to their despair added weariness with a human race so cipherlike that it could not even call forth the saving emotion of pity.

From that day until this, poetry has been obsessed by the nightmare of time. Nothing to match this obsession is to be found in the poetry of any previous period. It is true that in the Elizabethan period a sad awareness of time permeates the poetry of Shakespeare and the others. But through Elizabethan poetry time moves with a grave, measured footfall. The poet sees a shape of beauty approaching from afar; he clasps it to his heart; he feels it torn away by the stern, inexorable hands of fate; and he sees it retreating into the far mists of memory, still beautiful, still meaningful, still worthy of desire and worship. In Webster's *White Devil* a lover could cry with his whole heart:

> I could wish time would stand still
> And never end this interview, this hour!

The lover's bliss might be fleeting; he might enjoy only the poor benefit of a bewildering minute, but in the age of Elizabeth he had no doubt of the eternal worth of the object of his desire. In the twentieth century, however, a lover who finds his mistress divine at one instant, might find it hell if he were bound to her in the following moment. The lover T. S. Eliot describes in his *Prufrock* sees time working within his own desires, sifting his passion into dust and its object into the ashes of limbo. Eliot's Prufrock, on his way to make or not to make a proposal of marriage, reflects that there is

> Time yet for a hundred indecisions
> Before the taking of a toast and tea.

The difference between Webster's and Eliot's lovers shows, not so much a difference between Webster and

Eliot, for they have a strong affinity for each other, but a difference in the philosophy of selfhood in the seventeenth century and in the twentieth. Elizabethan poets had not dreamed of conceiving of the self in Hume's fashion, as a chance succession of fleeting sensations. Consequently, to them time was an enemy, but not an annihilator.

In the nineteenth century, on the other hand, there began to be some faint premonition of our terrible devil-worship of time as sole reality. Tennyson, seeing the groundlessness of an optimism based on nothing but the mere facts of evolution, sometimes felt all human values slipping away from him in incessant universal change. He mused upon

> The sound of streams that swift or slow
> Draw down Aeonian hills, and sow
> The dust of continents to be.

And listening to this noise that time makes he felt in his heart a foreboding of finding no abiding values, nothing worth loving, because

> Love would answer with a sigh,
> "The sound of that forgetful shore
> Will change my sweetness more and more,
> Half dead to know that I shall die."

But Tennyson, in such moods, had only one intelligent reader, his friend Thomas Henry Huxley. The fear of time as a power drawing the iron out of the universe, sucking reality out of everything but itself, washing away the foundation from every standard of value— all this Tennyson expressed in such vast terms of geological ages that it seemed not to matter, in the nineteenth century. Anti-sentimentalists read rot into his words and rejected them. Sentimentalists read rot into his words and embraced them with tender tears. It was not until 1920 that Tennyson's philosophical poetry could be read intelligently by anyone but a scientist, and by that time he was so out of fashion that scarcely anyone bothered to read him, with the noteworthy exceptions of Edna St. Vincent Millay and George Dillon.

At the end of the nineteenth century, in France, Mallarmé came closer than Tennyson to expressing the bottomless instability of the so-called "solid" universe. In his poetry he tried to reflect flowing change within the instant, by alluding to objects of sensation as if each object were merely the fleeting gesture of a dancer. If he had possessed Santayana's ironical humor, he might have anticipated Santayana's remark, in 1921: "The world is a perpetual caricature of itself; at every moment it is the mockery and the contradiction of what it is pretending to be." James Stephens expressed the same vision as Mallarmé's and Santayana's when he wrote, in 1923:

> Naught can be stayed; for as the eye
> Rests upon an object nigh,
> It is not there to look upon;
> It is mysteriously gone;
> And in its place, another thing
> Apes its shape and fashioning.

This fact, which is of course no truer in the twentieth century than in the age of Heraclitus or of Aristotle, did not matter to poets so long as they felt within themselves a mysterious power of selecting momentary sensations and weaving them together into a coherent Platonic pattern, discarding irrelevancies with a sure instinct, and forming, out of emotion re-

collected in tranquillity, an abiding world of ideal
standards, by which they might judge the imperfec-
tions of the natural world, with its ceaseless change.
In 1914 Rupert Brooke was still able to boast of this
power:

> Proud in their careless transience moved
> The changing faces that I loved;
> Till suddenly and otherwhence
> I looked upon their innocence.

He was convinced that he possessed within himself a
recognition of significance that would carry away
from the fleeting and fluid moment an element of
beauty to store in the memory.

Exercise of this power to judge the moment was,
however, precisely what the jazz age gave up. It had
no standards of selection; in fact, it despised standards
of selection as a narrowing of experience. Every degree of fastidiousness, it was assumed, was also a degree of stagnation. Standards of beauty were either
an affectation or a cowardly escape from reality.
Aldous Huxley expressed the current contempt for
the man of aesthetic standards:

> Beauty for some affords escape,
> And they find happiness in eying
> The gorgeous buttocks of the ape,
> Or autumn sunsets exquisitely dying.

But with the passing of standards went poets'
awareness of themselves as abiding personalities. By
1921, when poets wished desperately to regain their
sense of dignity, of a power to judge life, of abiding
selfhood, it seemed to them that it was truly non-
existent, that the so-called "self" was no more than
"time dripping through the veins," to use the fine

phrase of Malcolm Cowley. In *The Lamp and the Bell* Millay had let one of her characters exclaim playfully,

> An hour is like an ocean
> The way it separates one from oneself!

There was nothing playful in Conrad Aiken's expression of the same conviction, a few years later:

> The moment falls between us
> Wide as the spangled nothingness that hangs
> Between Canopus and Aldebaran.

This horror of what he may become in the next minute, not merely reversing his present tastes in the style of Dr. Jekyll and Mr. Hyde, but losing all interest in the preoccupations of that personality, colors all Aiken's poetry. There is no more bleakly despairing poetry in all the past world than his *Preludes*, in which for the last ten years he has recorded his obsession with incessant change outside and inside the shell of his body:

> This is the world: there is no more than this.
> The unseen and disastrous prelude, shaking
> The trivial act from the terrific action.
> Speak: and the ghosts of change, past and to come,
> Throng the brief word. The maelstrom has us all.

And younger poets, growing up in the 1920's amid this sort of despairing utterance, caught the contagion of horror. Stephen Spender has written,

> Without that once clear aim, the path of flight
> To follow for a life-time through white air,
> This century chokes me under roots of night.
> I suffer like history in Dark Ages, where
> Truth lies in dungeons.

It seemed to most poets inconceivable that great poetry should ever be written again, since the great

101

poetry of the past was obviously written with the
conviction that there was something in the universe
that mattered, something of such profound and abiding significance that trying to express it was an act
of religious gravity, a sacrifice at the altar of the cosmos. Yet on rereading this poetry it seemed to poets
in the 1920's that it was written under a hallucination
as absurd as Titania's infatuation for Bottom—a hallucination that stupid and ugly notions were of abiding beauty and dignity. Richard Aldington, in 1922,
expressed what most poets were feeling when he said
that the *Divine Comedy* could never have been written
had Dante not been sustained by lies. Aldington said:

> One might contrast the conception of poetry held by a writer
> in the age of Dante (when the "noble" topics for a poet were
> held to be War, Love, and God) with the conception that a
> modern might have, seeing that we consider war disgusting and
> barbarous, that our theories of love are largely physiological,
> and that most of us hold that the gods are made by men, not
> men by gods.

Poets did not give up to futility without a struggle.
Almost *en masse* they left distracted America in the
early 1920's. They emigrated from New York to London, from London to Paris, from Paris to Rome, to
Russia, to Egypt, to the Orient, seeking a place where
thinkers were still finding stability in their environment and self-respect and aspiration in themselves.
The quest was fruitless. In London they found Yeats,
far from the happy isle of Innisfree, able to think of
nothing but the horrors of the present state of the
world, and bewailing the passing with the times of
ideals that he had supposed were "above the murderous treachery of the moon." He was groaning, in
1921:

We who seven years ago
Talked of honour and of truth
Shriek with pleasure if we show
The weasel's twist, the weasel's tooth.

They found the traditional themes and forms of poetry dried up into the sterile and simpering verses of the "Georgians." And they found the rebels against tradition infected by the despair of their American visitors, and already echoing the dolors of Aiken and Eliot.

They found the most significant prose writers of Europe busy revealing the mind of man, not as a rational machine, but as a wind-blown rubbish heap of accidentally associated ideas. In London they found Dorothy Richardson showing the mind hurried along by the passing minutes faster than it could lay hold on meaning, scrambling along in a squatting, pouncing run, like a man after his hat. They found James Joyce revealing thought in the act of taking shape, showing it as an amoeba-like writhing and splitting of unformed impressions, ugly and senseless. In Paris they found Remy de Gourmont and Gide and Proust making the same exposure of human consciousness, showing man to be not a creature of reason, but a victim of chance associations of ideas in his early childhood. They found the poet Paul Valéry, the literary idol of Paris, anticipating a time when we shall cease to claim even a Proustian tangle of accidentally associated impressions as our own knot of selfhood, for as Valéry said, the physics of the future will undoubtedly find means of wishing our wishes upon us, so that we shall be unable to determine whether we are desiring a thing or whether an outside power is desiring it through us. (It is hard to see why this should have startled Americans who had already been wished into a World War by a persuasive press, but it did, in fact, add to their depression.)

In Germany they found Einstein speaking the language of universal relativity, which they could only translate into further corroboration of their despair—to the quizzical astonishment of the happy and energetic Herr Einstein, who, on hearing their story of how he had knocked the last prop out from under the faith of modern civilization, shook his gray mane ruefully as he marveled, "Lieber Gott, habe ich wirklich das alles getan?" In Russia they might have found help, I think, by seeing how sturdily our basic human aspirations shoot up again after a civilization has been cut back to the very roots, but the visitors stayed only long enough to learn that in Russia all an artist's energies had to go to provide food and shelter for the next day. In the Orient they found a beautiful pattern of art and life being ruthlessly sacrificed in a scramble to enter the wild hurly-burly of the very civilization from which the American visitors were trying to escape. There was no help for them anywhere.

One might think that, under the circumstances, the rational thing would have been for poets to stop making poetry. But there was no compulsion on them to be rational in the demonstrably irrational world of 1921. And, anyway, a poet incubates poetic impressions as a hen sits on potatoes or round stones, if there are no eggs for her to hatch. There is no way to turn the literary temperament into one that does not brood.

As poets settled down to work again after their restless and unhappy wandering over the earth, after the war, they were convinced of two things. The first was that poetry today can have only one mood—that

of cynical irony. The other was that its method must
be deliberately incoherent, honestly reflecting the in-
coherence of life. And it should be, they felt, a hit-or-
miss mingling of scraps of older literatures with comments on the twentieth-century world. The incongruity of the scraps of old literature in the new setting
would express the cynicism of the poet, it was felt;
because the nobility of the old would effectively set off
the vulgarity of the new; and, on the other hand, the
patent truth of the vulgar new would show the underlying falsehood on which the nobility of the old
rested.

Both of the elements in the new method owed a
good deal to the example of James Joyce in his novel
Ulysses. Inasmuch as his intention in *Ulysses* had been
to exhibit half-formed thoughts in the act of being
displaced by other half-formed thoughts, in a con-
tinuous stream of consciousness, Joyce felt that the
conventional grammatical sentence, with a subject
and a predicate and a period, was a deceitfully complete form of expression. He devised a literary "impressionism" very much like the impressionism that
the French painters initiated at the end of the nineteenth century. It was a kind of dot painting with
words. A noun phrase, or an adverb, or a pronoun
might stand alone as a sentence. On the other hand
half-a-dozen sentences might be run together as if
they were a single clause, or a dozen words might be
printed solidly as one. Or a word might be changed
into another before it was half spelled out, because of
some sudden new association suggested by its initial
sound. It was an outgrowth of the old method used in
Tristram Shandy, of course; but it was elaborated to
express occult vagaries of chaotic complexities in con-

sciousness such as dear simple-minded Uncle Toby could never have dreamed of.

The method influenced poetry greatly during the 1920's, not so much in the direction of grammatical license as in the direction of removing all marks of coherence between simple statements. Since poets wished to show the mind as a storm of ideas no more connected than snowflakes, they abjured conjunctions, relative pronouns, participial phrases, and all other suggestions of causal relationship, and relied upon mere contiguity to express the relationship of one idea to another. I am afraid this description of the method suggests a greater simplicity than it has. The poets were aware that thoughts succeeding one another are not really separate in the same fashion as snowflakes. The new one comes and fills the mind before the old one has quite faded out. The image that Hilda Doolittle ("H. D.") used to describe the flight of ideas is better than mine. In her *Palimpsest* the dim and blurred succession of our human thinking is compared to old photograph negatives, laid one on top of another, endlessly. This method of laying one impression on top of another is the method that T. S. Eliot used in his *Waste Land* and later in his *Ash Wednesday*. It is the method that his many admirers and the admirers of James Joyce are still using, a method which is becoming more and more acceptable to the reading public and which will undoubtedly have some permanent influence on the course of English style—that fascinating river which, as constantly and as subtly as the stream of consciousness itself, has been transforming itself from century to century since the time of *Beowulf*.

As for the poets' new method of literary parallelism,

or what one may call marquetry—their habit of inserting phrases from earlier literatures into the welter of present thought—that, too, owed something to Joyce's *Ulysses*. As its title suggests, Joyce's novel is written with Homer's *Odyssey* hovering continually over the author's consciousness, making him ironically aware of the ugly difference between Homer's happy, objective story and his own tortured, subjective one. He has made his story a faithful parody of Homer's, following in minute detail every episode of the *Odyssey*. This seemed to Joyce the most effective way of giving artistic order to something which he must reveal as intrinsically disorderly and anarchic, namely, the insane welter of daily life in the twentieth century. The device is brilliantly effective, in theory. How effective it is in practice is something that each reader of *Ulysses* must determine for himself.

Poets' widespread use of this method of intertwining older literature with their own writing owes much more to T. S. Eliot than to Joyce, I think, and I think Eliot is partly indebted for it to Mallarmé; but he gives full credit for his very original and effective use of the method to Joyce, to whom Eliot says future writers will be indebted in the same way as future mathematicians will be indebted to Einstein. And Eliot's use of the method is, by the way, a sort of literary Einsteinian relativity. In a world where all thought is a meaningless illusion, a relative meaning can be given to it by setting the sharply contrasted thoughts of different centuries against one another, thus revealing a distinctive quality in each. Therefore, Eliot drops single phrases from the classics into his observations of the life about him whenever an ironical appreciation of their incongruity brings them to his mind. If he changes the phrases at all, it is only to syncopate their rhythm a bit in fitting them to their jazz surroundings. Thus the opening phrase of Olivia's song in *The Vicar of Wakefield* bobs up with a jazzed accent in Eliot's account, in *The Waste Land*, of a joyless copulation between a grimy London stenographer and a pimply youth:

> When lovely woman stoops to folly *and*
> Paces once more about her room alone,
> She smooths her hair with automatic hand
> And puts a record on the gramophone.

Undoubtedly the sudden and surprising vision, in this sordid room, of the sentimental and unfortunate Olivia, with her eighteenth-century decorum, accentuates the squalor and ugly commonness of the twentieth-century atmosphere. It is an effectively ironical method, provided that the reader is familiar with the quotation.[2]

But not one in a hundred of Eliot's hidden quotations is so easy to identify as this one. His *Waste Land* holds hidden quotations from the Bible, from Buddha, from the Upanishad, from Vergil, Ovid, Augustine, and so on and on down to recent writers. And the quotations are seldom from anthology excerpts of the classics. If the reader's study has not corresponded with the author's, he is lost. One might expect some hint from quotation marks or an introductory phrase that Eliot is quoting. But this would have been contrary to the obscurantist cult of the day.

The cult of intentional obscurity owes most to Gerard Manley Hopkins, that nineteenth-century

---

[2] Most bewildered readers of *The Waste Land* have discovered a few explanatory notes in the back of the book. But they know how few of the disguised quotations are indicated there.

Catholic mystic, whose poetry was published for the first time at the end of the World War, being at once extravagantly admired by those readers patient enough and sensitive enough to become aware of its hidden beauty. Hopkins believed in poetry being dark at first reading, or even at sixth reading, in order that when the meaning finally appeared, it might, as he said, "explode." To Hopkins' admirers among twentieth-century poet cynics it seemed that, in the heyday of the crossword puzzle, this device of tantalizing obscurity was poetry's only hope of appealing to the gnawing restlessness of the modern mind. The same excitement which attended the discovery that "supralapsarianism" was the word fitting the longest line of a newspaper puzzle might, it was felt, attend the discovery that the meaning of an obscure line in a new poem depended on one's recognition of its context in Dante's *Inferno*, and the excitement of finding it might carry the phrase alive with passion into the soul.

Perhaps a single rather trivial example will illustrate how this works, at least in an inept mind. Eliot's poem *Cousin Nancy* describes the serenity with which the Bostonian aunts of a "flapper" are able to watch her shocking behavior because they are sustained by the knowledge that on their shelves are

> Matthew and Waldo, guardians of the faith,
> The army of unalterable law.

On reading these lines the first very feeble explosion in the reader's mind is likely to be the discovery that Waldo is Emerson—naturally enough a guardian of inviolable truth for these old-fashioned Bostonians. The next explosion reveals that he is associated, not with the biblical Matthew, but with the poet Arnold.

But now the mind is likely to backfire. I, for one, was convinced that the next line belonged in *Paradise Lost*, and I sought it there long and earnestly, moment by moment disliking Nancy and her aunts more intensely. Suddenly, with a tremendous explosion, I realized that the line came from George Meredith. In profound mental easement I sighed, "Well, that's that," and dismissed the poem from my mind. Not till a year later did I happen to reread *Cousin Nancy*, and only then, with a mind free from the nervous strain of delayed explosions, did I calmly observe that the point in the last line lies in the identification of Nancy with Satan, who in Meredith's sonnet is shown unable to go farther in his marauding desecration than the divine will permits. Balked and abashed, he gazes at the serene wheeling of the starry heavens overhead,

The army of unalterable law.

The explosive appreciation of obscurantist poetry is, as is obvious, a very different experience, psychologically, from the old-fashioned appreciation of older poetry, in which the meaning grew like a widening flower, revealing more and more of its heart to a reader who was released from the tension of search altogether, living momentarily in a trance of wonder, a spellbound attentiveness that made him wiser and more observing than his usual distracted self. But that attitude was not modern.

The question of plagiarism cannot be raised by any intelligent reader of Eliot, Aiken, Ezra Pound, Elinor Wylie, the Sitwells, Archibald MacLeish, Wallace Stevens, and many of the other poets who use this method of marquetry or mosaic work. The effectiveness of plagiarism depends on its not being recognized.

The effectiveness of this method, on the other hand, depends upon recognition that many lines are not the poet's own. The object is usually caricature, and caricature is meaningless without a recognition of its likeness to something. It is this which differentiates marquetry from the borrowings indulged in by·great and original poets of earlier periods. It is true, obviously, as Eliot points out, that Vergil and Dante and the Elizabethans borrowed a phrase or a figure of speech whenever they wished, and regarded it as their own if they improved it or at least changed it by adapting it to a new environment. But it was not necessary that Vergil's contemporaries should realize that one of his images was an adaptation of Homer. Its beauty and significance would be almost as great if Vergil had been the first to use it, and Vergil would probably have been proud to be the first. This is very different from the twentieth-century frame of mind. Eliot would be ashamed, I think, if he had made up one of the serenely beautiful phrases that appear in his poetry. It would seem an anachronism, almost an indecency, to him to indulge in a primitive poetic sensation, even if it were possible for him to experience such a one with a sense of newness. He would feel like a middle-aged man suddenly thrown back into the mental state of a boy of three.

It was generally felt in 1921 that everything beautiful and memorable had already been said and stored away in the vast libraries of the world. Our age was intellectually bankrupt. There were no fresh metaphors to be used (except ugly ones); there were no birdlike liltings or organ pealings of new rhythms to be discovered; there was no petaled curve of a fresh phrase to startle the discoverer with its simplicity and grace; there were no exultant new aspirations to struggle up into great speech as if a sea gull were struggling upward through the crevasses of the wind. The literature of the future could no longer be a direct reflection of life; life was grown too monotonously arid for that. It must reflect the worked-out soil of older literature, using the old figures of speech, the old combinations of words. But it must make something new of them by setting them sharply against new moods, against disillusionments and despairs that directly contradict them. A rose petal becomes something new when a boutonnière is unfastened and ground under the heel into the gravel. It becomes an ironical commentary on the weakness of roses and the harshness of gravel. One must expect nothing more than this revelation from poetry in an age when, to use the words of Eliot's *Waste Land*,

> The dead tree gives no shelter, the cricket no relief,
> And the dry stone no sound of water.

This was the world in which Millay's *Second April* appeared. Can anyone who read it in 1922 ever forget the bewilderment with which one met the simplicity of its old right ways of saying things? This poetry was pre-symbolist, pre-vorticist, pre-Dada, pre-jazz, pre-imagist, pre-vers-librist. One stammered, "But poetry can't be like this any more!" And then one stammered again, "But it is!" For *Second April* was no bouquet of strawflowers, dusty with disintegrated metaphors and sentiments. It was no imitation of an imitation of Swinburne, himself that "damnedest simulacrum," as Walt Whitman once called him. These poems were the irrepressible emotions of a human being drinking in the world of 1921. In *Second*

112

April there was revealed recognizably the same world that Aiken and Eliot and Pound and the Sitwells and Wallace Stevens were living in—the same world of disillusionments, of world-weariness, of enmity with dizzily speeding time. But these sentiments were the soil from which the sturdy selfhood of an artist was sucking the mysterious chemicals that make the flower of poetry, poetry as the ancient world understood it, poetry with metaphors and phrases that were at the same time lovely and new—metaphors and phrases as like and yet as unlike those of earlier poetry as a new-springing tree is like and unlike an older one.

Poetry made no "progress" in this book, as it had done in *Aria da Capo*. But there are circumstances under which standing still is the greatest of achievements. In the world-wide dust storm of dissolution and frenzied change Millay set the stubborn roots of her being against life and held fast. In a period when the soil of poetry seemed too thin and shifting for any faith at all to endure, she gave us a book of poems standing like the blue flag in her allegory:

> On its roots like iron claws
> Rearing up so blue and tall,
> It was all the gallant Earth
> With its back against a wall.

Second April does not stand absolutely alone as evidence that pure poetry had survived the World War. In Greece Hilda Doolittle was finding and expressing a few fitful gleams of beauty. In Ireland George Russell was still singing out his Platonic mysticism. In America Sara Teasdale had recently published her *Flame and Shadow*, and Robert Frost was meditating a fresh and unsophisticated utterance of beauty. But these were a very few short and isolated poems. No other poetry of the day stood up so straight and tall as *Second April*.

Of sheer, unadulterated poetry, perhaps the purest example in the book is the *Ode to Silence;* yet, if I am not mistaken, it is the least known of Millay's poems. It has been a bit too pure even for her warmest admirers in our journalistic age, for it holds no scrap of interest for anyone indifferent to beautiful cadences and fresh and lovely imagery. It is as unhuman in its beauty as Shelley's *Queen Mab*. Yet it is a revulsion from the same noise-racked and dizzy world that called forth Eliot's *Waste Land*, and its mood is, if possible, more depressed than Eliot's, for it is a cry after utter annihilation, a longing for a final and dreamless death, wherein the noises of the world shall at last cease to jangle in the brain. And there is irony here as truly as in *The Waste Land*. Only here the irony is that which pervades so much great and sad poetry, in that the expression of despair is for the poet wings away from all sorrow into the realms of divine order and refreshment.

How effortlessly new and genuine the imagery of this poem is may perhaps be best illustrated by the use of imagery drawn from archeology and geology, in the lines commenting on the departure from the populous world of the muse named Silence,

> Of whom there now remains
> For sages to decipher and priests to garble
> Only and for a little while her letters wedged in marble,
> Which even now, behold, the friendly mumbling rain erases,
> And the inarticulate snow.

But throughout the poem one image drifts into another in modulations as serene as the modulations one finds everywhere in Shelley or Milton, however

114

troubled their subject may be. And the more literal pictures are as clear to the visual imagination as is the imagery. Flowers Millay has the skill of picturing in words that differentiate them from all other flowers—a skill that seemed to have died with Drayton after he described the marigold as "meridianus sitting in a maze." As unmistakably right as that is her line,

Stiffens the white narcissus *numb with sleep*,[3]

or her reference to "the heavily sweet blue hyacinth that *blossoms underground*."[3] As for the music of the poem, the lines run from monometer to octameter in a fluid metrical pattern, and the rhymes ring and repeat themselves and are lost and then echo once again in a continually varied succession. And the succession of vowels and consonants makes, as always in her poetry, a violin timbre of which one used to suppose that Yeats alone, of living poets, possessed the secret. The sound of all the poem is almost as lovely in quality as the throbbing vibrancy of the lines near the close:

Out of the urgent heat
In some clear glimmering vaulted twilight under the odorous vine.

I suppose that the *Ode to Silence* is the most daringly unfashionable poem written by any member of the twentieth-century intelligentsia. In the first place, it is an ode, and the ode was, supposedly, as definitely out of 1920 fashion as pantalettes. And in the second place, its mythology is that of classical Greece—which was definitely forbidden to poets by the despots of the poetry magazines and anthologies. And worse than that, it deals with the muses, who above all other classic figures were taboo. And as if bringing in

[3] In both quotations the italics are mine.

115

the Nine Sisters were not the supreme iniquity, Millay writes of a tenth, the Muse of Silence, "sown of Zeus upon a dream of death." This *Ode to Silence* might so easily have been a defiant *tour de force*. Instead, it is as gravely moving as a Beethoven sonata.

Part of the secret of the fresh life in *Second April* is that Millay dares to bring the past into the present in this way. The nervous forcing of themselves to be contemporary was one cause of sophisticated poets' conviction that they had lost their selfhood. Seeing the follies and faults of taste in their earlier selves, they were continually trying to bring themselves up to date by cutting off everything that those earlier selves had admired. This severance shortened the singing robes of poetry till they resembled women's skirts of the day. Millay alone is not shorn and exposed to the raw wind of cynicism by her dislikes.

Obsessive dislike for a tradition may be as crippling to a poet as an obsessive liking for it. For instance, Millay alone was saved from the crippling effects of sentimental Tennysonianism because, in a day when Tennyson's name was above all other names anathema, she alone felt no compulsion to be as unlike him as possible. One need only contrast her poetry with that of Ezra Pound to see the difference. Whenever I read the grave and lovely music of Pound's early poem, *Virginal*, I am convinced that he was intended by an all-wise but impotent creator to be the Tennyson of the twentieth century, the melodious evangelist of Freud as Tennyson was of Darwin. But in his horror of such a destiny Pound has kicked against the pricks of his natural instincts until his style resembles nothing so much as machine-gun staccato, and his ideas resemble the resultant wreckage. A little honest indulgence of an admiration for Alfred Tennyson, and all might have been well. Millay, on the other hand, with defiant courage dares to include in *Second April* a poem about her love for the early poems of Tennyson, and she includes another poem based on Tennyson's *Lancelot and Elaine*. As a reward for her courage, she is thereafter uninhibited in using everything that she is able to learn from Tennyson's harmonious and pellucid utterance.

Millay's poem *Elaine*, by the way, reveals another enrichment of her style by devotion to past poetry. The delicate turn of thought and phrase that is characteristic of Ovid gives most of its charm to Millay's lyric. Ovid, for instance, commented on Narcissus' reflection: *Tecum venitque manetque; tecum discedit, si tu discedere possis.* Every stanza of *Elaine* holds this sort of repetition with a half-turn of the thought, as when, for instance, in the fourth stanza Elaine stammeringly retracts her perhaps conceited assumption that Lancelot will not have forgotten her by the summer after her death:

> You needs must think—if you should think—
> The lily maid had died.

And in the last stanza Elaine's wistfulness again changes a repeated thought, but this time she returns to the belief that Lancelot will perhaps think of her and mourn for her. She says that her ghost will watch

> To see you speak, the way you speak,
> And smile—if you should smile.

With love of the capricious Ovid flourishing beside a love for the overearnest Alfred, there was no occasion for Millay to worry for fear either poet should warp her originality out of shape. And *Second April*

117

reveals Sappho, Catullus, Chaucer, Donne, Herrick, Webster, Milton, Coleridge, and Keats also sustaining her style, not by plagiarism and not by marquetry, but by subterranean nourishment and enrichment of a style that is indisputably her own.

Her love for the great thinkers and singers of the long and varied past is part of the reason why Millay, as well as the school of Pound and Eliot, cries out against the ugliness of our times and yearns for a better and earlier period of the world's history. She carries on the traditions of the past, she says,

> For the sake of dim things
> That were once so plain.

Yet I venture to believe that it is not real nostalgia for the days of yore that Millay feels. I think she would not have been so fine a poet in any day but ours; at least she assuredly would not have been the poet-that-she-is in any other day. Her longing is the poet's longing to carry all the great and noble past into the living present, and at times she groans that the burden is too great for her. But she alone of the poets who are deeply acquainted with the past refuses to shirk the burden. She will not compromise by setting up in her poetry broken marble torsos of ancient poetry and then setting up opposite them obscene mud statues which she calls by the name of the present day. The other poets of the early 1920's were rather like cooks making jam. They forced their fruitful imagination through a colander, squeezing away every drop of their inspiration derived from the past, and then triumphantly exhibited the remaining mass of seeds and skins as the essence of our day. But Millay is too egoistic for that. "I am today," she feels, and she refuses to squeeze herself through a sieve and deplete herself. Instead, she eats the past as if it were a eucharistic wafer and makes it bone of her living bone.

I wish that I did not seem to be disparaging the poetry of Eliot and of Aiken. It is their philosophy— their cramping theory of poetry and existence that I am quarreling with, and not the greatness which they sometimes achieve in spite of their theories. In *The Waste Land* there is Eliot's description of the hopeless crowds on the streets of London, reminding him of the damned in one of the circles of Dante's hell; that passage is so great and so moving that it belittles praise—at least it is far above any praise that I can give. And there is fineness in Aiken, too. His loveliest poetry is as authentically beautiful as the paintings of Whistler, which to me at least his *Preludes* resemble in their hypersensitiveness. They strain the limits of my perceptions of subtle philosophical ideas just as Whistler strains my perceptions of twilit colors. But the pessimistic theory of the school of marquetry and obscurantism was, on the whole, paralyzing to simple grace. It frightened many a young poet into silence because, as one of them complained,

> At my back I always hear
> Eliot's intellectual sneer.

After all, the so-called logical poetry of nihilism was just as illogical as any other. It was only great when it forgot that nothing can be held fast and known clearly. Aiken could not have expressed his horror of time had he not temporarily ignored his conviction of his dissolution by time and proceeded to hold fast and clarify his understanding of it. A poet may bind himself with a thousand cords of logic, but he always

119

leaves one foot free to kick at fate. Millay is more logical in her illogicality. She refuses to cripple herself at all.

Millay's assumption of her own sturdy and compelling selfhood is utterly unreasonable. By all the unanswerable logic of physics and sensationalist philosophy and behaviorism she isn't really a self at all. And yet there she stands. And believing in herself as if she were God, she has something that answers to an absolute foothold in the universe and she can look at the whirl of the Democritean snowstorm and find shapes and patterns in it—patterns determined by her likes and dislikes.

Once assuming that she is herself, her other permanences are easy to establish. Time is constantly destroying what she loves? Yes. That is the theme of her *Journey, Passer mortuus est, Song of a Second April, Rosemary, Alms, To a Poet That Died Young, Ebb, Mariposa, The Death of Autumn, And You as Well Must Die.* Time in itself is nothingness? Yes. That is the conclusion of *Spring:*

> Life in itself
> Is nothing,
> An empty cup, a flight of uncarpeted stairs.

But she is nothing? Poetry is nothing? Grief is nothing? A thousand times no. Her own "fierce and trivial brow" is more real to her than all the stormy atoms of the universe as science sees it. Her belief in art holds poetry to be a permanent reality which may bind her to the men of a thousand years from now, whom she salutes in *The Poet and His Book.* And her awareness of grief for her dead friend makes the unconsciousness of an automaton inconceivable. Much in her nature was changeful as time itself. Yes, she knew that. Her heart, she said, was "a house where people come and go." But this pain caused by the first incursion of death into her life did not change, except with the change of a tree striking its roots deeper and deeper and growing in complexity and significance. Perhaps it was the piercing insistence of grief that was her salvation in this critical and destructive time. Whatever else was an insane illusion in a world of nothingness, that, she knew, was real. Pain is the one unarguable reality. Acedia may be confused with nullity, but agony may not. And so pain became a solid rock on which to base her conviction of her own selfhood and on which to build her poetry.

VII

THE HARP-WEAVER
In the Heyday of Behaviorism

A SENSE of personal identity as strong as ever was revealed in the next book of Edna St. Vincent Millay. If she felt her nature changing, it was not as a sand dune changes in the wind, but as a plant changes during its summer growth.

I tell you I am what I was and more,

she said in one of her new sonnets. But her assurance of her own selfhood no longer came from the sharp twist of agony in her mind. Back in 1921, the year *Second April* was written, pain had saved her from the listlessness of self-doubt which was afflicting other poets. But in 1923, the year *The Harp-Weaver* appeared, few lives were more steeped in sunlight than hers. This was the year of her marriage to Eugen Jan Boissevain. This year her poems were published in England, as well as in America, and some of the most brilliant minds in Europe were becoming aware of her for the first time. With her marriage she suddenly became very wealthy, and she was free to indulge her lightest whim. The wide world lay all before her, in which to travel and explore. And she was strangely beautiful, and was still young enough to feel a girl's zest for her new life as a fairy tale come true. Under the circumstances it would have been strange if *The Harp-Weaver*, like *Second April*, had been an outcry against intoler-

122

able suffering. It is true that sorrow for her dead friend lives on; it is expressed in the poem *To One Who Might Have Borne a Message*. Under all her life, ever since her young friend died, there has sounded the dark note of inexorable mortality. And there is a quiet comprehension of all suffering in all the poems of *The Harp-Weaver*. This book is not an exultant asseveration that all life is cakes and ale merely because she has herself been well served. But sharp grief no longer stands as her bulwark against the doubt of her own existence suggested by an utterly skeptical age.

The black nightmare of nihilism, however, was by 1923 perhaps troubling poets a little less, although this was the year when poetry was taking most serious account of psychological behaviorism. All the diffuse skepticism of the age seemed to be precipitated in this new mechanistic psychology, which denied validity not merely to one's independent selfhood but even to one's passing consciousness. However, as soon as people see their ghastly convictions neatly ticketed and subjected to scientific investigation, their convictions are likely to lose much of their horror. Thus in an earlier century the idea of the earth being uprooted as fixed center of the universe had lost much of its power to make people unhappy as soon as they had ceased to envisage the devil spurning their world off into space and had become familiar with astronomical charts showing the earth's circuit around the sun. And similarly the despair of poets at losing assurance of their selfhood seemed less surely founded on unarguable reality as soon as they saw their fears corroborated not by philosophical speculation but by psychological experiments, with the definite limitations inherent in any piece of scientific research. A pessimistic metaphysical mood covers all the world with darkness, but pessimism based on laboratory experiments casts only broken cloud shadows, like those that sweep over wide miles of Kansas wheatland. The wheat still shows gold, even through black shadow; and there are great billowing tracts of it in brilliant sun, untouched by shade. Life always shines through as just life, to the authentic poet, no matter what science may say of it.

It is not science itself, but belief in the ghost stories of science that weakens poetry. We are likely to forget that Elizabethan poets saw life under somewhat the same conditions of scientific skepticism as poets meet nowadays. If in the sixteenth century the self was not doubted in quite the same way as today, it had not been conceived in the same way, and with the loss of assurance of an immortal soul, all seemed to Elizabethans to be in doubt. Elizabethan dramatists were convinced that it was best not to speak much of the very uncertain soul, but to deal with people in purely physical terms. In expressing human emotions almost exclusively in terms of the muscular manifestations that accompany them Elizabethan literature agreed, in fact, with the precepts of twentieth-century behaviorism. And, also, in its emphasis upon worldly accomplishment Elizabethan literature was in agreement with John Broadus Watson's teaching that a normal life is an affair of socialized muscularity. If Elizabethans did not have a cocksure psychologist to inveigh against the morbidity of a poet's too inactive and introverted life, they had Queen Elizabeth (whose brisk political theory supplied a sort of behaviorism) to pronounce that a man is no more than what he does. Elizabethan poets accepted extreme introversion as a disease. Middleton described it as such, and cried,

> O wake from drowsy and enchanted shame
> Wherein thy soul sits, with a golden dream
> Flattered and poisoned!

But this did not hinder a poet from sitting with abstracted brow until he had dreamed his plays through. It was hard to bluff an Elizabethan. And three centuries later Millay showed herself similarly unbluffed in her poem *The Dragonfly*, in which she defended her own introversion against the charge of morbidity.

Nor was Elizabethan science more reassuring than ours about the reality reported by one's sensations. Even in the infancy of physical science the body was already denied authority as a reporter of a reliable world. During the lifetime of Shakespeare Sir John Davies wrote, "I know my sense is mocked with everything." And Donne wrote, "The stars, the sun, the sky which thou admirest, alas, have no color, but are fair because they seem to be colored." Elizabethans, however, with their physical robustness, did not allow the colorful world to grow pallid to their senses merely because it appeared colorless to their reason. When twentieth-century poets are advised by a scientist to enjoy a sensation exactly as if it had not been proved to represent an illusion, they are apt to feel as self-conscious as an inexperienced actress under the Kleig lights of Hollywood, who is directed to behave as if she were drenched in the freshness of dawn. On the other hand, Elizabethan poets experienced sensations belittled by science as unquestioningly as painters, until very recently, have still been able to do. So recent a painter as George Inness was probably physicist enough to be thoroughly convinced that there is no color in the objective world, but the conviction seems not to have detracted from his enjoyment of a vermilion chimney against a patch of sapphire sky. A painter knows that a sensation, no less than Popeye the Sailorman, is what it is, regardless of any interpretations that the science of any age can make of it. But a sophisticated poet must have a deep thirst for sensation in order to realize that.

This is not to say that poets, when they come to interpret the meaning of their sensations, can arbitrarily contradict the science of their day. Poets have been known to write verse carping at science, but it has never been good poetry, not even when a Wordsworth or a Poe has lapsed into it. Poets and philosophers are equally helpless in this regard. Unless they can go into a laboratory and disprove scientific pronouncements, they have no right to contradict them. The science of one's day may be inadequate and mistaken, but it is, to the non-scientist, simply the air he breathes, and he is as helpless to breathe a different air as a mountaineer is helpless to draw a breath of the salt sea rather than the breeze off a glacier. Dante had to breathe the air of medieval logic, Milton of astronomical science, Tennyson of Darwinism, and poets in 1923 of behavioristic psychology. Poetry must come from the whole personality. If a poet refuses to accept something that his reason tells him is true, he is dead, poetically speaking, because his entire nature is not aiding in the struggle toward significant expression, and anything less than that will not create poetry. If all the tremendous urge toward articulation that makes up the poetic impulse is lacking, verse becomes a mere wicker-work of dead and dry phrases.

But, fortunately, it is only actual experimental science that poets need accept. They need not accept the philosophical speculations of any scientist, whether he be a Robert Andrews Millikan, averring that he has seen Jehovah in a white and wind-blown beard ride in the tempest and direct the storm of starry nebulae, or whether he be a Watson, setting psychological standardization up as arbiter of all aesthetic and moral values. In his exchange of opinions with Bertrand Russell, within the pages of the *Dial* magazine during 1922, Watson seemed quite honestly pitiful of Russell's old-fashioned notion that philosophy still would have something to say in an era of behaviorism. Rereading Watson's remarks, in which he was, all unknowingly, speaking not as a psychologist but as a very callow philosopher, one is apt to forget that he was, after all, also a scientist, that many of his statements, based on his experiments, were indubitable, and that others were not yet proved false. A poet who did not take his scientific discussions seriously in 1922 was either uninformed or stupid.

To the leading poets behaviorism had, by this time, become pretty much all of psychology; and it was a far healthier influence upon them than Freudianism had been. Poetry based on Freudianism had been a sort of twentieth-century *Castle of Otranto*, an equivalent of eighteenth-century Gothic romance. It had been shivery, spooky stuff, reflecting superstitions rather than life. But by 1923 Freudianism was exerting most of its literary influence not upon poetry but upon biography and drama. Biographers were vieing with one another in revealing the geniuses of past centuries as pitiful exhibits of sexually diseased personalities. And in the theater John Barrymore was enthralling New York by his interpretation of Hamlet as a cring-

ing tangle of Oedipus and Narcissistic complexes.
But poets, on the other hand, were becoming aware
that a more mechanistic type of psychology was turning a flashlight into the mind's dark forest and was
revealing the ominous black bear as merely the shadow
of some underbrush. And the best poets were grateful.
If a moonlit forest has just as much truth and more
poetic possibilities than a forest lighted by electricity,
yet turning the flashlight on it for a moment could do
no permanent harm to the moonlight and shadow, and
it enabled poets to observe them with a more judicial
mind.

On the whole, I should say that the study of experimental psychology has had an excellent influence on
poetry. The sharper a poet's appetite for truth, the
better poet he is, and the more kindly he feels toward
an honest investigation of facts. As for the devitaliz-
ing effects of the study, most poets, before they turned
to a definite study of psychology, had already reached
the rock bottom of despair, and for them an infant
science could not possibly debunk human life further.
It was only to the unthoughtful man, in the 1920's,
that the behaviorist's denials of a firmly integrated
selfhood were new. And it was the same with unflattering revelations about the workings of the personality. Millay, in particular, had already investi-
gated her own nature with a ruthlessness that left
nothing for any psychologist's analysis of the personality to shock her with. And she continued this
ruthless analysis in the *Harp-Weaver* volume: *Nuit
blanche* expresses the power of free association on her
moods; *Scrub* describes the power of early environment
upon her personality; *Departure* deals with the unreality of escapes from life in revery; *Curse* exhibits spite

as a motive for struggling after fame; *The Pond* and *If I Should Learn* show respect for social conventions taking precedence over supposedly unconquerable emotions; *That Love at Length* shows wounded vanity as a concomitant of despairing love; *I Being Born a Woman* shows a sexual impulse as something that may be divorced from reason and good taste. To a poet who has sat at the feet of John Donne, savage debunking of the personality is an old story.

On the whole, Millay's poetry could hardly have met a less crippling psychology than behaviorism. Did it refuse to acknowledge emotions and ideas save as a physical matter? That is what emotions and ideas have always been to her. It is no hardship to her to be asked as a poet to live within her body. She cannot live out of it. She has never been one, like Elinor Wylie or the nineteenth-century Platonists, to conceive of her body as a five-bolted prison house. Nor has she been one to dive into immediate sensation as into a relaxing element apart from ideas. At the time *The Harp-Weaver* was published, most current poetry fell into one of two classes: poetry describing a gross and inchoate wallowing in sensations with no upsurge of thought, or poetry repeating a ghostly rumor of a disembodied reality, like Gawain's voice shrilling along the wind. Some of the truest poets, blown to pieces by time, seemed to be frantically snatching at this or that rag of mist to make for themselves a corporeal presence. Such was Aiken and the speculative world he lived in. But Millay has always lived with sharp, clear sensations that can be integrated into a sharp, clear mood, and the mood is not dissipated for her by an understanding of its limitations.

Did behaviorism deny that sensations themselves

129

can exist as a conscious experience? That is simply, to Millay or to any other clear-sighted poet, none of this science's business. It has every logical right to ignore conscious sensation; it has no right to deny it. The behaviorist's mechanistic world is a real world, but a limited and closed world, with no room for consciousness in it. The poet's world is equally real, and it is steeped with consciousness. The behaviorist diagrams the living body and its universe as if they were a room with diffused lighting. Naturally he does not make a drawing of the light. The poet, with wholly different intent, comes to the room when slanting sunlight is pouring through the windows, and he paints the room solely in terms of that light—in terms of the relative brilliance and shadow that consciousness gives to the objects that it touches. The only sensuous poetry that behavioristic psychology can hurt is of the undefined sort that Millay has somewhere expressed as unflattering opinion of—poetry that sounds as if someone were playing Chopin by uncertain memory in the twilight, with the scent of honeysuckle drifting through the open window. Poets who are the dupes of literary traditions and who express synthetic saccharinities of sensation are confused and lost when a psychologist in the laboratory laughs at their pretension of being really aware of these things. But a poet who experiences sensations honestly and at first hand knows irrefutably that his consciousness is, in the beautiful phrase of George Meredith, "the sky of the senses." To be told by the behaviorist that his consciousness does not exist troubles him as little as it troubles the behaviorist to be told (by an occasional solipsistic dreamer) that none of the physical movements of the body and of the laboratory instru-

ments exist.   It is a matter solely of point of view, a
matter of seeing obverse sides of a logical dilemma.

Did the psychology of 1923 likewise strongly indicate that aesthetic standards have no absolute basis?
That could not trouble Millay's egotism.   Her own
standard of beauty is absolute for her, and she demands
no other.   In *My Heart Being Hungry* she says,

> Beauty where beauty never stood
> And sweet where no sweet lies
> I gather to my querulous need,
> Having a growing heart to feed.

And she has found by actual experience as a poet that
she can awaken in other people an appreciation of her
own standards.   What more could an absolute standard
give her?

Did behaviorism deny the existence of the will?
Not for Millay.   For to her, her will has always meant
an intense onrushing toward a definite goal, and to
the very muscular psychology of behaviorism, this is
what the will means also.

> There is no I
> Saving the need I have to go to her,

Millay's princess in *The Lamp and the Bell* said of herself when her friend was in distress.   Millay's will and
selfhood are to her what Elizabeth Barrett's personality seemed to Robert Browning, "all a wonder and a
wild desire."   And Millay's self seems to her an abiding and consistent self because her intense onrushing
toward a goal is her poet's quest of understanding and
expression of life; and thus far the intensity of this
quest has never slackened or altered.   Whether her will
exists as an absolute entity in the universe is of no
more concern to her poetic mood than the same aca-

demic question would have been to the Elizabethan hero-villain, pursuing his desire in agony, and crying,

If I have nothing else I'll have my will.

Probably to the eye of eternal omniscience Millay would be merely a clock wound up to tick off the minutes in a zestful impatience to strike twelve, but as a poet that likelihood does not especially concern her. Her progress toward her goal is what counts for her, and the eager, impetuous sound of her tick is her satisfaction.

And, last, did behaviorism reduce all human thought to the mere muscular exercise of grunting? It seemed so to certain squeamish thinkers. But it was not the most thoughtful poets who objected. For the reduction (as it seemed at the time) of all memory and all thinking to muscular movements in the throat was really somewhat like handing all the universe to poets on a silver salver, because no other thinkers are masters of the physiological elements in language to the same degree as poets. A great poet would be too modest to set himself up as a thinker superior to a great scientist, but so far as the accuracy and clarity in the vocal expression of his thoughts go, a poet is to a scientist as Heifetz is to a street-corner fiddler. No other grunting can compare in virtuosity with poetic grunting. Similarly the greatest poets have always been too modest to fancy that poetic memory and imagination are the only type of memory and thought, but they have always known that there is no other *poetic* memory or thought besides the ache in the throat for perfectly articulate expression. The colored panoramas that pass before the closed eyes of some of them (panoramas whose existence behaviorists in

1923 were superciliously denying) are, poets have always been well aware, not poetic memories at all. They become poetic only when the right words are found to express the colors. And so it is with the odors and tastes and sounds and weights and shapes and textures of their past experiences. It could be only a cause of rapture to poets (if they could believe it) to learn that successful capture of all these elusive sensations in words is practically guaranteed by the fact that their existence in the memory is in purely verbal terms and that the poet's sole problem is to grasp these verbal terms clearly enough to bring them out in vocal utterance. How heartening this would be, if it were undeniably true!

Millay has always been a bit too much of a behaviorist, perhaps, in ascribing to other people the poet's constriction in the throat that accompanies the need for verbal expression. Thus in *The King's Henchman* one of the young lovers, in the ecstasy of a first kiss, cries out in prayer that it may be granted her to "find speech for all this ache and wonder." It is doubtful that, to a lover who is not also a poet, expression in words appears so superior to other modes of expression.

But if in this regard Millay exaggerated the laryngeal muscularity of emotion and memory and imagination, her sensitiveness to sound saved her from the overemphasis upon throat movements that certain other poets were betrayed into by a too enthusiastic indorsement of behavioristic theories. In April of 1923 the poet Baker Brownell published an essay in Harriet Monroe's *Poetry* magazine which is a brilliant exposition of what many poets were deriving from current psychology. Brownell says that English poetry has been on the wrong track ever since the four-teenth century, because Langland was the last poet to be aware of words exclusively as muscular efforts. Of twentieth-century poets Brownell finds D. H. Law-rence and Sandburg closest to the right track because they pay most attention to "the gulp and grumble" of syllables. The more intensely the reader experiences an incipient movement in his throat, the more success-fully the poet's mood and ideas have been transmitted to him, Brownell thinks. And he adds, "Good poetry might well be written with no regard for sound."

From the narrowness of such a poetic standard Mil-lay's exigent ear saved her. But the large element of truth in Brownell's essay she accepts. Perhaps there is greater truth in Brownell's assumptions for English poetry than for some other—Italian, for example. English from the beginning has been a strong and bony speech, whose consonants have been far less flexible than its vowels, and no poet who has tried to ignore the strength of those consonants has ever been very successful. Every once in a while a critic arises to deprecate English poets' greater sensitiveness to con-sonants than to vowels, but no one has succeeded for long in making poets comparatively deaf to consonant-al effects and sensitive to assonance. The prominent consonants remain in the speech, whatever one may do about them, and poetry which ignores them only leaves them protruding gauntly, like the spine of an aged horse. English poetry at its best has the grace of a wild stallion. There is no use in asking it to mimic the grace of a cobra.

Though Millay's poetry from the beginning has shown an appreciation of all this, still I think that the debate about behaviorism and its application to literature deepened her appreciation of it and enriched her poetry. It may have had something to do with turning her attention to the tremendously muscular poetry of Old English times, and this resulted in her drama *The King's Henchman*, in which she imitates the vehement alliterative style of Old English. And ever since she wrote *The King's Henchman*, much of her poetry has carried more of the muscular force of Old English utterance than was noticeable in her early poetry. Edna St. Vincent Millay and Archibald Mac-Leish, I should say, are the two poets who have taken most to heart the behaviorists' discussion of thought as a laryngeal process; they are certainly the two who have profited most by it. MacLeish has given directions to his future readers for coming into emotional rapport with his poetry. He says, in his *Anonymous Signature*,

> Think,
> If you read these words in a better time,
> Of the shape of my mouth forming the difficult letters.

And elsewhere he has exulted in the way "the iron of English rings from a tongue." Millay has not discussed the theory, but she has made reading her poetry aloud an unusual physical satisfaction to the speaking voice, just as the music of Handel is an especial satisfaction to the throat of a singer. Thus Aethelwold's cry of defiance, in *The King's Henchman*,

> Now ring, ring, ring, ye hammers of wrath,
> On all the anvils of doom!

fairly pleads in the reader's throat to be shouted aloud. And his cry of tenderness to Aelfrida, "My throstle-throat, my lovely thing!" has an alliteration that is even more for the speaking voice than for the ear, as the alliterated *thr* has the very throb of a lover's tenderness in it. And in *The Harp-Weaver*, such lines as

> Love is no more
> Than the great tide that treads the shifting shore,
> Strewing fresh wreckage gathered in the gales

are a muscular combination of consonants holding the feeling for the speaker of a power that could remold the shores of a continent.

But it is not merely in its arrangements of energetic syllables giving pleasure to the throat and tongue and lips that Millay's poetry is muscular. She is fond of writing about a muscular world. One reader has complained that her poetry does not make vivid pictures in the imagination. Whenever this is true, it is due to her describing things from the inside, in muscular terms, instead of from the outside, as if she were photographing them. Thus when she describes herself running away from Paradise, we do not see her running; we feel her running:

> And my heart rose like a freshet,
> And it swept me on before
> Giddy as a whirling stick. . . . .

It is so when she describes the act of climbing:

> And I felt my foot slip,
> And I scratched the wind. . . . .

And it is so with her description of exhausted struggling onward through desert sands:

> I chase your colored phantom on the air,
>   And sob and curse and fall and weep and rise
> And stumble pitifully on to where
>   Miserable and lost, with stinging eyes,
> Once more I clasp, and there is nothing there.

And she ascribes this sense of muscular tension or relaxation even to inanimate objects, as in her reference to the "upheavèd heaven," or to the rose that "hugs the brown bough," or the bud that "sighs into the flower," or the wide-blooming flower that

> Droops for a moment and beholds, dismayed,
> The wind whereon its petals shall be laid.

Even those states that seem to most people the essence of inertia she can conceive only in energetic terms. Thus she describes the longing for death:

> Almost
> I feel my feet uprooted from the earth,
> There's such a tugging at me to be gone.

And emotional states of great intensity, which were in dubious standing among skeptical poets because they seemed so tangled with idealistic notions and sentimental exaggerations, she is able to express without fear and without reproach, because (like the Elizabethan poets) she simply translates them into inner physical sensations.

> And my quick blood went suddenly quiet in my veins,

she says, or

> Of a sudden whirred
> Her heart like a frightened partridge,

or, describing a girl feeling herself in love,

> The August night
> Was level as a lake beneath the moon,
> In which she swam a little, losing sight
> Of shore . . . .

or, describing a woman on edge with dejection:

> She inescapably must endure to feel
> Across her teeth the grinding of a backing wagon-wheel.

137

And yet all other sensations are as real to her as tactual and muscular sensations and are translated quite as effectively, it seems to me, into verbal terms.

Odors she does not perhaps describe with such precise rightness as Edwin Arlington Robinson was able to do when he told how, in an orchard, "many sweetly stinging fragile odors broke lightly as they touched him," or perhaps as Robert Frost when, in a field of haycocks, he spoke of "freshness in this air of withering sweetness." Still I am not sure that either of these phrases carries more suggestion to my nose than Millay's "sweet stench of the loam that rises sharp and chill," or her "At dusk the dumb white nicotine awakes and utters her fragrance." No other poetry of today holds so many odors as Millay's. It holds the fragrances of pinxter and privet and tansy and bayberries and hay and clover, the reek of rank thorn apples, the smell of river water and of smoking candlewicks and of closed hallways, the stenches of dead fish and of garlic and of a boar's breath, and of foul human breath as well.

Tastes she describes more clearly and far more significantly than other recent English and American poets have done, with the possible exception of Hart Crane. Crane knew how to use the sense of taste figuratively, as when he spoke of a boy's dream of Cortez riding up and

reining tauntly in
Firmly as coffee grips the taste—and away,

or when he spoke of aviators drinking "pure alcohol of space." Other American poets deal with taste sensations occasionally, but either with an effect of flippancy, as in Wallace Stevens' comparisons of various seascapes with the taste of breakfast chocolate, and

Hortense Flexner's comparison of monotonous days to "biscuits baked in a pan," or else with a rather stereotyped effect, limiting taste sensations mostly to those of bread and honey and wine. Honey still seems generally accepted as a "poetic" food; Leonie Adams, Amy Lowell, Elinor Wylie, and David McCord describe its taste. And fruits have been described often since Paul Valéry set the fashion with his famous description, in 1917, of anticipating the immediate future as if it were fruit melting in the mouth:

> Comme le fruit se fond en jouissance,
> Comme en délice il change son absence
> Dans une bouche où sa forme se meurt,
> Je hume ici ma future fumée. . . . .

But no other poet (unless possibly Wallace Stevens) distinguishes so well as Millay does between the tastes of individual fruits. She gives one the flavor of grapes "savoring faintly of the acid earth," of plums stinging the palate with the frozen sharpness of the "frosty dust" they wear, and of chokecherries—"puckered fruit that sears the mouth." Millay's poetry also takes account of the homeliest and most substantial of foods: halibut, herrings, mutton, oaten bread, cheese, baked oysters, even.

But the chief excellency in Millay's description of taste is her power to use it figuratively to describe powerful emotions. Few sources of imagery have the poetic power of imagery connected with food and drink, since the intensity of hunger and thirst makes taste more closely associated than any other sensation with the instinct to survive on the earth. This was realized by the Hebrew poets who wrote of Christ in terms of bread and of wine. But today only Millay gives a sense of great dignity to her thought by using

139

food imagery, as when one of her heroes, deceived ¹
a friend, says,

> My mind, that hath been fed so long on the sweet far⸗
>   of utter trust in thee,
> Smells at this meat,
> And turns away;

or when she says of herself,

> The anguish of the world is upon my tongue;
> My bowl is filled to the brim with it.
> There is more than I can eat.

Sounds, because of their temporal extension, are
more comforting than other sensations to the school
of poets who have the jitters over time. But Millay,
being a musician, is no less keenly sensitive to them
than the nihilists are. The living poets who seem to
me to hear sounds most distinctly are Edna St. Vincent
Millay and Conrad Aiken. I am not sure which describes sounds in a way that gives me the more pleasure.
Millay, however, has the greater capacity for giving
herself up to sound and enjoying it for its own sake.
It is interesting to set Millay's *Concert* beside Aiken's
At a Concert of Music, published two years later, because
the two poems reveal so clearly the differences in
two personalities. Both poems deal with a lover listening to music. Aiken finds himself unable to find peace
in the music, because at the first wave of the symphony washing over him, he finds that his fancy has
escaped from his present sweetheart beside him in the
concert hall and has fled to an earlier one, lingering
in the dark forest of his memory. He says,

> I run by a secret path through that dark wood
> To another time, long past, and another woman,
> And another wood.

And this infidelity of his fancy, always moved by con-
course of sweet sounds to idealize the past rather than
the present, tortures him into inattention to the music,
so that he cries,

> Alas! Can I never have peace in the shining instant,
> The hard bright crystal of being, in time and space?

It is precisely this "peace in the shining instant" that
Millay is capable of finding in her sensations, and
especially in hearing music. In her *Concert* poem she
refuses to take her lover with her to the symphony
because he might distract her from absorption in it;
and as she listens, she is not soothed into erotic reverie;
she is wakened into poignant appreciation of the
mood fusing the rhythms and volumes and tones and
timbres:

> Armies clean of love and hate,
> Marching lines of pitiless sound
> Climbing hills to the sun and hurling
> Golden spears to the ground.

Aiken, for once, I think, has written the more musical
poem, and yet Millay's rather than his is the poem of
a musician. To a musician a symphony is enough in
itself, without motion-picture effects of dream sweet-
hearts, past or present.

Color Millay uses less lavishly than several other
poets of our day. John Gould Fletcher during the
early 1920's used to make his poetry a phantasmagoria
of colors. And Wallace Stevens has sometimes used
bright colors with a barbaric lavishness. Ezra Pound's
exultation in the colors that he sees with so true an eye
is perhaps the one lovable thing about him. Melville
Cane and George O'Neill also write largely in terms
of color. But (I do not know how it is with others) I,

for one, often find poetry crowded with color as meaningless to my imagination as a smeary painter's palette. Almost everyone finds that a moving-picture which fairly reeks of the rainbow is a distraction and a weariness to the eye; and a too elaborately colorful poem affects me in the same way. Two colors are about as many as I can feel simultaneously with gratitude. I can see Marie Welch's spring orchard in rain, "silver and dark silver," and I can see E. A. Robinson's man against the sunset sky, "black-drawn against wild red," with far more pleasure than I can see the elaborate color symphonies of some of these other poets. For that reason I have always been fond of Millay's simplest color pictures, such as her memory of the girl and the man in *Cameo:*

> White against a ruddy cliff you stand, chalcedony on sard,

or of a fire kindled at twilight:

> A pack of hounds, the flame swept up the flue,
> And the blue night stood flattened against the window,
>   staring through,

or of two girls' heads:

> Side by side, the onyx and the gold,
> Two agate eyes, two eyes of malachite.

It would be a mistake to deny that Millay can make elaborate pictures in color, sharp and strong as paintings by Gauguin or Matisse. Such is her picture, in *Pueblo Pot*, of flickers, with their red and black and golden feathers and their ebony bills, wrenching indigo berries from the woodbine, their shadows

> Skimming the court and in the yellow adobe wall
> Cleaving a blue breach.

142

But in her favorite way of looking at the world, things appear to her more like etchings. Some of her pictures are like etchings printed on the ivory-yellow paper that Whistler was so fond of using. Such are her impressions of sunlight and shadow, as in her description of the view from an invalid's window:

> The sunny sky, the skimming bird beneath,
> And, fronting on your windows hopelessly,
> Black in the noon, the broad estates of Death,

or in her picture of sheep moving in a single direction up a slope:

> They crop a grass
> That's yellow where the sun is out and black
> Where the clouds drag their shadows.

And she is fond of seeing landscapes in the sharper white and black of other etchings. There is her picture of Paradise:

> White eternal lilies stand
> By a lake of ebony.

And her pictures of the Maine seacoast are likely to be etched rather than colored. She sees the coast with "sullen rocks and skies." And especially she sees it thus at night, when there is "a broken dart of moonlight splintered on the sea." Or she sees the countryside when

> Stark on the open field the moonlight fell,
> But the oak-tree's shadow was deep and black and secret
> as a well.

All those pictures seem to hold the marks of the etching plate.

I suppose that it is mostly because color is always joined with shape in these landscapes that they are so effective; and then it is partly because one is far enough away from the objects to see a clear and simple picture. Millay would seem to be farsighted, like Wordsworth; at least her pictures always have the clear and simple composition of his. She does not share the pleasure in minuteness of observation that is evident in the poetic pictures of Edith Sitwell and Margaret Emerson Bailey, or in the Lilliputian fancies of Elinor Wylie, for instance—something that goes only with nearsight, I fancy. Millay praises other poets' attention to tiny pictures; she has called attention to the accuracy of Abbie Evans' miniatures, as in her lines,

> Through the blazing mica grains by a road well-known
> Watch the small red spider.

And Millay herself knows how to paint a small object clearly; she makes one see the hummingbird:

> that small bird with iridescent wings
> And long incredible sudden silver tongue.

But she describes tiny objects as mere flecks in a larger picture. Her eye always seems to find it a relief to look at a landscape as a whole.

It is not merely color and shape that she welds together into pictures of extreme simplicity. In the phrase "the dahlias bleed," she has in three words expressed the color, the shape, and also the movement of petals loosened from a flower in late autumn. And again she welds three separate sensations into a single impression in the lines,

> Whippoorwills wake and cry,
> Drawing the twilight close about their throats,

wherein the second line not only suggests the plaintive quality of the call, but expresses one's narrowing vision in decreasing light and also one's increasing chill as darkness comes on. Again in the lines describing fire,

> The white bark writhed and sputtered like a fish
> Upon the coals, exuding odorous smoke,

one becomes aware simultaneously of color, shape, movement, sound, and odor. The single clear impression comes so inevitably that the thing looks easy. But such a mess as most poets make of complexities of sensation!

Sometimes, though not often, Millay carries this mingling of sensation into synaesthesia, or the description of one sense in terms of another—that favorite device of Carl Sandburg and Amy Lowell and the Sitwells. This she does in her description of brilliantly colored flickers against an adobe wall:

> Powerful was the beauty of these birds;
> It boomed like a struck bell in the silence deep and hot.

This, however, is not so characteristic of her as her welding of two literal sensations together in a condensed phrase such as Milton, and scarcely anyone after him, knew how to use. Thus Millay speaks of the road of human life as traveled by "the desperate foot, blind and torn." Or she speaks of the startled forest deer standing "with listening hoof." In such phrases she not only welds sensations into a phrase of extreme simplicity, but she makes the phrase express an emotion as well, as again in her "wondering candles" that lit the Carian day.

Reading poetry written since the World War, I wonder if in our complex and bewildered day the gift of achieving simplicity is not the richest and the

145

rarest of all poetic gifts. Most poetry of our time, whatever other beauties it may possess, lacks complete integration into wholeness. Often a poet's various senses seem to be canceling the effect of one another, as if he were listening to a Brahms symphony with a draught down his spine and a bad breath at his shoulder and a red exit light troubling his vision. And often a poet's sensations seem to be called up for reprimand by his reason, which tells them they are exaggerating or distorting their reports of the world. And often a poet seems to be hysterically arguing with his reader, who may, he fears, be taken in by the twentieth-century scientist's denials of things that the poet holds precious. Most harmful of all is the poet's constant wonder as to how he is appearing to the scientists, with a resultant jumping in and out of his own personality, as if he were a photographer running behind the camera to supervise an alteration in his own pose. Poetry, of course, can write about science and still remain beautifully integrated poetry. Millay's Euclid sonnet has proved this, and so have MacLeish's poems about Einstein. But it is disastrous to be constantly interrupting a poem on another subject with the question, "I wonder what Einstein (or Watson or Terman) would think of me now." All that must have been disposed of for good and all before the poetic mood comes on.

None of these things troubles Millay in her *Harp-Weaver* volume. The line of every poem is as miraculously single and clear as the line of a Beardsley drawing. And let no one suppose that this is because she elects to treat life with an obtuse and obvious simplicity that comes from unawareness of its subtleties and confusion. Probably Millay's love sonnets reveal a greater knowledge of the complexities of love than any others that have ever been written. Certain moods of lessening love have never been treated by any poet in the world except her, so far as I know. And certainly there is nothing in Ovid or Freud or Plato or Jung that she seems to have disregarded, in writing her love poems. And yet she can reduce all the welter of her experience to such simplicity as that of the sonnet concluding,

> I only know that summer sang in me
> A little while, that in me sings no more.

I suppose that it was the intensity of her emotions that enabled her to keep her head at a time when many poets were doubting themselves because psychology doubted them, and others were screaming themselves hoarse with rage because some of their claims for poetry were proved nonsense when they were tested in the laboratory. Millay has said somewhere, "I know what I know," and that simple fact has always saved her from being disconcerted by scientific experimentation. If a psychologist, looking at her from the outside, says he sees no evidence of consciousness in her, that troubles her as little as it troubles a girl to have her suspicious father walk past a summer-house convinced that there is no boy there, holding her hand in a dark shadow. Millay's own intense appreciation of her consciousness is enough for her. Of course the psychologist, as a matter of fact, is right. But then Millay is right also. A poet's consciousness does not show from the outside, any more than anyone else's does. It seems absurd, really, that any poets should have worried for fear they were walking about the world in a somnambulistic coma merely because they

147

could not prove to others that they were not. But I think the reason they worried was that the nervous shocks of our age actually had reduced many of them to a state in which they were little more than somnambulists. They kept wishing they could feel, but they did not know what to feel or how. This debility of their own was the real cause, probably, of the poetic paralysis which some of them ascribed to knowing too much of an unsympathetic science. Millay may be happy or unhappy or angry or loving or perplexed; she may be in any one of a hundred different moods; but when she is writing a poem she is never debilitated or unconscious. Whatever her mood, she is intensely alive in every one of her five senses, and all her senses are fused in a single controlling mood and purpose. Her poems represent only those moments in her life when she has succeeded in becoming utterly at one with herself and intensely aware of the world.

VIII

THE KING'S HENCHMAN
Our Problems a Thousand Years Ago

BY 1926, when *The King's Henchman* was being written, the general public of America had reached the height of the gay wastrel mood to which poets had abandoned themselves at the close of the war. With the Florida land boom at its height, and with instalment payments enabling every man to spend his income a year before he earned it, American frenzied finance was a spring being coiled tighter and tighter until it had almost reached the tension at which it was to snap—in the stock-market crash of 1929. With a fast automobile at his disposal, with bootlegging arrangements conveniently made, and with family ties comfortably loosened, the average efficient American had dropped all ethical and pseudo-ethical obligations except the one of "getting by," and was spending his days and nights breaking his earlier speed records in search of new thrills. When he dreamed of the future, it was of faster automobiles, stronger bathtub gin, and wilder dances than the house-shaking Charleston. Still shouting the sentiments of the jazz poets of 1918, he had not as yet felt the contagion of the poet's ensuing mood of disgust and foreboding.

It is fascinating to watch a mood spread through a complex society. A black cloud no bigger than a man's hand appears in a single poem or philosophical essay, and, long after the original author's mood has cleared, the blackness of his disgust and foreboding may go on spreading and spreading among multitudes of people. A mood of a single philosopher or poet spreads among poets first, then among serious readers and writers of prose, then among popular novelists and journalists, until by and by it is being expressed by the men on the street corners, by the barbers and the politicians. The mood of *Aria da Capo*, of *Punch, the Immortal Liar*, and of *The Waste Land*, which in 1920 and 1921 had expressed the conviction of three poets that our life is a tragic farce, best dismissed with a twisted grin of pain, was not to reach the average American until 1934, when five-year-old Shirley Temple was to teach millions of disgusted Americans to sing,

> Life's just a buggy-ride,
> So laugh, you son-of-a-gun!

But some years before 1934 the leading poets had decided that this attitude was, after all, not the last word in cosmic criticism, and they were beginning to search the rock bottom of despair for a little soil in which some positive belief might grow.

By the irony that pervades human life, every step of the popularization of a conviction is, to the man who first expressed it, a partial condemnation of it, and he invariably changes his conviction as others adopt it. For every truth is complex beyond the possibility that any apprehension of it, by whatever genius, will express its proportions perfectly; and, of course, as a shrewd and subtle expression of a conviction is accepted by other men and amplified and reiterated and reformulated again and again, the disproportions become greater and greater, so that the flaw in the original conception becomes clear to its author. Perhaps unintelligent disciples are the most valuable corrective that an earnest poet or philosopher can have.

By 1926 the nihilistic attitude toward life, though it had not yet reached the general public, was widespread among poets, and it was beginning to reach the readers of prose as well. In that year Theodore Dreiser's *An American Tragedy* was published, and much to the author's surprise reached a large circle of readers. Most of them, to be sure, dismissed Dreiser's gloomy indictment of civilization with an incredulous shrug and a smile of superior knowingness, but hundreds of readers were deeply impressed by his hopeless picture of the bewildered, uprooted populations of our cities, and a few other serious novelists began to adopt and re-express Dreiser's philosophy of despair. In the same year Oswald Spengler's *The Decline of Western Civilization* was published in English translation. This revealed to a wider public the same grounds for pessimism that had been troubling the poets for years, for it expressed the impotence of the human race to defy inexorable and all-destroying time. Like the poets, Spengler hypostatized time; he made it a satanic deity with a will of its own which there is no use in defying. Spengler convinced many people that our civilization is in its death throes, not because of any avoidable stupidity of ours, but because no civilization can postpone the foreordained day when it will be crushed under the wheels of that Juggernaut which is the time cycle.

Such prose studies of their moods set a number of poets to a more thoughtful appraisal of human traditions, searching for principles of soundness which they had been ignoring. Of one thing they became certain, that a society with every belief uprooted is the ugliest and most meaningless of all possible societies. It has, they became convinced, not even the virtue of superior honesty; for if no belief is true in an absolute sense, neither can there be absolute truth in the dogmatic assertion about the cosmos which utter cynicism makes. And a belief that has grown in a race for a thousand, two thousand, three thousand years, that has resisted the inertia and self-indulgence of men and given them a power of working together and making a fair form in the midst of chaos, has a certain mythical truth, even though it partly contradicts another belief as deeply rooted in some other race. Such reasoning as this was, in 1926 and 1927, moving several French poets to give up their former cynicism and return to the Catholic church, in the belief that the Catholic myth is the noblest one that men have ever conceived. The same reasoning was leading T. S. Eliot to espouse Anglo-Catholicism, as a dignified conception of man holding a mysterious and sustaining mythical truth that would enable him, Eliot felt, to face the chaos of modern society with fortitude and Christian resignation. His prayer in *Ash Wednesday*, published in 1930, was to be

> Teach me to care and not to care;
> Teach me to sit still. . . . .

Other poets were searching farther back in human development than Christianity for beliefs with a sturdy and tenacious life in them. As an aged man, tottering out for his last walk in the spring sunlight, looks with a sense of miracle at toddling tiny children, with such varied and complex life before them, so poets who felt that our civilization was sinking into the last sickness of old age looked with a sense of miracle at primitive societies, with all the long, long road still to travel of eager, flourishing life and growing ambition and careless pride and cruel insolence and cynical disillusionment and decay. By studying a primitive society poets felt that they could perhaps distinguish between the seeds which bring forth the wheat and those which bring forth the tares of civilization, and perhaps find some answer for life's seemingly inevitable tragedy.

A number of poets were studying the undeveloped races of today, no longer through envy of their supposed sensual license and freedom from rationality (which had appealed to poets at the close of the World War) but because it now seemed that one might, by observing and comparing these races, find out which beliefs of the entire race of man are rooted most firmly in an earthy life. Hartley Alexander and Lew Sarett and Mary Austin were studying American Indians; D. H. Lawrence and Osbert Sitwell and Hart Crane were studying the civilization of Old Mexico; Hervey Allen was studying Negroes and South Sea islanders.

But many other poets thought it more profitable to study the ancient beliefs revealed in *The Golden Bough*, in which ever since 1907 Sir James Frazer had been publishing his studies of the primitive practices and beliefs that had gradually taken shape as the principles underlying great and complex civilizations, notably the Greek and the Roman and our own. Ever since T. S. Eliot had woven allusions to *The Golden Bough* into his *Waste Land*, it had become the fashion among poets to study it, and some of them were deeply moved by the tenacious racial memory which came to light when they compared the beliefs of early societies with our own only half-acknowledged beliefs. Archibald MacLeish's *A Pot of Earth*, published in 1925, was one of the first of many poems, after *The Waste Land*, which aimed to express a confused awareness, in our modern life, of things that our ancestors knew more plainly and instinctively. In MacLeish's *A Pot of Earth*, a thirteen-year-old girl, watching her doll float away on a stream (like Adonis in primitive myths) has a confused sense that she is seeing something which has been seen often before and that many, many women before her have shared this feeling of sadness. She thinks,

> We have known this thing
> A long time. . . . . There is a thing we know.

In 1926 MacLeish wrote of such a mood again, asking,

> Why do we stand so long
> To watch the fall of moonlight on the sand?
> What is it we cannot recall?

This troubled wonder about a hidden racial memory that colors our moods is the *leitmotif* in most of MacLeish's later poetry. He says of himself,

> I was born of the race of Gaels in the outland.
> It is a troubling thing
> To remember the singing of rivers you have not heard.

Our modern life, he says, is a stair built by our ancestors, which each of us mounts without understanding why our impulses move us in that direction. The tragedy of our present civilization is that we no longer recognize our impulse to climb. In his *Hamlet* MacLeish says,

> We know what our fathers were but not who we are,
> For the names change and the thorns grow over the houses.

If we could only know ourselves to the depths as our fathers knew themselves, he feels that we would find the human stability and dignity that our generation so sadly misses.

The French symbolist poets and Irish mystics, especially, felt the need of studying our strange racial memory. Guillaume Apollinaire, one of the leaders of the French symbolist group, was one of the first to recommend a study of ethnology to poets as a source of poetic truth. The Irish mystics have been (especially in recent years) less inclined to anthropological study, more inclined to believe that understanding of our remote ancestors will come to us intuitively, if we will allow ourselves to be quiet enough for the deeps in our nature to be revealed. George Russell, in 1928, wrote a poem warning parents to give their children freedom and solitude, in order that they may absorb the strange symbolism of common objects, which have acquired life-molding power in the racial memory. He says,

> Let thy young wanderer dream on.
>   Call him not home.
> A door opens. A breath, a voice
>   From the ancient room
> Speaks to him now. Be it dark or bright,
>   He is knit with his doom.

Yeats also came to believe that our dim racial memories are a source of power to us and that we should struggle to make them clearer. Yeats has gone so far as to assert that the thought of a poet is actually a kind of magic when it works with ancient symbols. The human brain, Yeats and other poets in the late 1920's were beginning to believe, has no power of expressing or apprehending abstract truth, which is an utterly inhuman thing; but in the course of ages it has gained the power of communicating deep and significant convictions by mentioning, with the right emotional nuance, concrete objects about which our ancestors' emotions have been wrapped for thousands of years. Our so-called thoughts, in other words, are really half-memories of our ancestors' sensations and emotions, and the best we can do toward apprehending and communicating fundamental realities is to describe something before which we have stood in a bewilderment of terror or reverence or delight and ask our neighbor whether in him, too, the thing awakens a troubled sense that it has been of significance for a long time, that it means more to him than he has any words to express. Everything that moves us deeply, poets feel, is a part of that racial memory which constitutes the most significant part of each of us.

That is the reason the more radical symbolist poets have abjured coherent statements in their poetry. The logical interpretations that we make of our occasional shudders of half-knowledge are likely to be all wrong, and they send our thoughts off on a wrong track, so that we lose our feeling that a certain object has a deep significance for our nature. But the poet who lightly weaves together only the essential qualities in the moods that overwhelm him may actually reach communication with the hidden natures of other men, revealing to them unsuspected depths in their own natures, unsuspected relations to the universe, and so making them more alive. In this way the poet may become, as Yeats put it, a "magician," freeing us from the dizzy whirl of shifting superficial fashions and from all the hopelessness, the acedia, of a rootless modern life. The poet may, with his subtle appeal to a race-old longing within us, reveal to us a self beneath our superficial discontented moods—a self which has been at home in the world for a long time and which feels a piety for the aged earth and heavens. Thus the poet may give us back a faith that life is very old and greatly enduring and strangely worth while.

I think that the psychologist Jung was partly responsible for the poets' widespread interest in racial memories in the late 1920's. Jung seemed to be expressing a theory that a racial memory is something more than absorption of the books and music and proverbs and legends and rules for conduct which all of us meet from early childhood, and which of course fuse in our minds into a great, formless notion of the way the human race in general thinks and feels. To the symbolist poets, at least, Jung seemed to be saying that our very brain structure holds memories of the earlier life of our race, so that on first meeting a complex sensation for which nothing in our nurture and experience has prepared us, we may be startled profoundly by a sense of its overwhelming significance, merely because our remote ancestors were moved by it. Jung's psychology has become almost a Bible to some of the symbolists.

In 1926 Millay was among the first of American poets to be touched by the new mood, the feeling that the early history of our race is intensely significant to us, and that by studying it we may steady ourselves by learning to thrust our roots deeper toward the bedrock of fundamental human nature. The difference between Millay's *The King's Henchman* and some of the symbolists' studies of primitivism is chiefly one of method. Millay will never consent to believe in half-expression, however convincing an argument for the need of it may be. A need for clarity is something bred in her bone, and a conviction of its supreme worth is to her an intuitive revelation as unarguable as any revelation in moonlight or drifting water or withered leaves that comes to a symbolist. Whatever intuitive certainties other men's ancestors have given them, her ancestors have given her the certainty that words ought to fit together to make statements. Clear speech comes to her as instinctively as a neat completeness of melody comes to a thrush.

It seems strange, considering the importance that primitive racial memories have assumed in poets' minds, that Millay's *The King's Henchman* remains, with the possible exception of MacLeish's *Hamlet*, the only long modern poem that interprets our Anglo-Saxon ancestors.[1] I suppose that is partly because the period is a hard one to study. It is much easier to read, in the modern English of *The Golden Bough*, about the sources of classic legends than it is to study the *Anglo-Saxon Chronicle* and *Beowulf* in their original form. And yet during the 1920's there was an impulse among poets to study Old English. Hilda Doolittle has said that she was deeply interested in the sound of *Beowulf*, when she was a student at Bryn Mawr, but that she failed the course. Hart Crane and Ezra Pound and (after Millay wrote *The King's Henchman*) Archibald MacLeish and Stephen Spender and W. H. Auden have shown the influence of Old English rhythms on their verse. As early as 1921 there was enough interest in Old English to warrant three new translations of its

[1] Its closest kin in recent poetry is T. S. Eliot's *Murder in the Cathedral*, but that poetic drama makes no pretensions to the sort of historical realism that Millay is concerned with. This is true also of Robinson Jeffers' *At the Birth of An Age*. Both men are content with wild anachronisms.

poetry. Of these translations by Professor Spaeth, by Scott-Moncrieff, and by Ezra Pound, the rendering of the *Sea-farer*, by Pound, was probably the most poetic and certainly the most influential in poetic circles. It led to Pound's preaching force and freedom of accent to the many young poets in his circle, and so had something to do with the loosening up of English metrics which is characteristic of our day.[2]

But no translation of Old English can give what Millay and other poets were chiefly seeking, namely, a revelation of what it felt like to be a member of a more primitive society. Poets wanted the sense of being inside their ancestors of long ago. As a man may be startled by noting an unconscious gesture of his own hands, such as his dead father used to make, and may realize, by the brief gesture, how he is growing into likeness with his father, how—as it seems to him—his father is actually still living within his son's body, even so poets have been moved by filial piety when they discover how naturally they may repeat ancient words and how deeply their moods may answer to them. But this feeling comes to a poet only when he knows the ancient language. Millay gives far stronger evidence than Pound or any other poet of our time does of having actually learned the oldest form of English, of knowing the feel on her tongue of *Beowulf* and the *Chronicle* and the *Riddles* and *Charms* and the *Husband's Message* and the *Sea-farer* and the *Wanderer*.

The sense of physical force that comes from repeating the unpolished old words is in itself a revelation

[2] It had, I think, much to do with preparing the way for the printing of Gerard Manley Hopkins' roughly rhythmical poetry, which has had a further influence of its own upon twentieth-century rhythms.

about our ancestors. This language is not a mere language of the head, a mere matter of the tongue and the scheming brain, as so much of our smooth modern speech seems to be. Old English seems to be spoken from the waist up. One gains from it a certain comprehension of Old English reticence. No one, surely, would go to the trouble of expressing himself in this language unless he felt a strong conviction, an inner need of speech. One clumsy, heavy word after another is heaved from the lungs and with awkward deliberation is set upon another to build an unwieldy, rudimentary sentence. It seems no wonder, as they used this language of strong initial accents and heavy consonants which seemed to come with such force from the lungs, that thought itself seemed to our ancestors a matter of the body rather than of the head. It was to them a *breost-hord*, a hoard within the breast, an actual physical weight that oppressed them. It was hard work to think in those days, and the thinking was done with the whole man. Millay catches that feeling when she makes her Aethelwold speak of his thought being "on his heart," and makes him long for "emptiness" of mind again. He longs, as for supreme felicity,

> To ride into Wales, with a spear in the hand again!
> And a shout in the blood again!
> And an empty mind.

Thought and emotion were frankly one in those days, and emotion was frankly a physical thing. "Longing burns against the blood," we are told in *Beowulf*. Millay, who described her own longing in such terms —as filling up her lungs with brine and fire with every breath she drew—was naturally drawn to this single-heartedness and bodily consciousness of her ancestors.

160

Of course, such thought was often stupid and, according to our ideas, tragically mistaken. It is with no idea that in early English society she would find and reveal a perfectly thought-out code of conduct, applicable to modern society, that Millay has made her poetic study of early England. Nor has she made it to gratify an instinct to escape to a golden age of innocence, before problems began. In her earlier drama, *Aria da Capo*, the two shepherds, at the beginning of their scene, represent such a mythical age, full of sunlight and flowers and peace and singing. That conception serves very well for the purposes of allegory, but it will not serve for a realistic historical study like *The King's Henchman*. Human life, Millay believes, has always been beset by tragic problems, and so she makes *The King's Henchman* a tragedy. And yet, beneath the tragedy, she shows us something marvelously and magnificently solid, something on which one may rest as on the foundations of the world.

This solid foundation is not a code of morals. The code of *The King's Henchman* is not ours, could not be ours. Eadgar, king of England, sends his best friend Aethelwold to judge whether a beautiful girl is worthy to be his bride. Aethelwold finds her so incredibly beautiful that he sends a false report to the king and marries her himself. When the king, on coming to visit Aethelwold, learns of the deception, he stands with arms locked across his breast, sternly waiting for Aethelwold to make the atonement of suicide. Translated into twentieth-century terms and acted with modern settings, the code would become ridiculous and ugly. A man expects his dearest friend to sacrifice the greatest need of his life in order to give him a girl to whom he is bound by no betrothal, whom

he has never even seen, for whom he can have no affection at all. Common sense would tell us that the
thing for two friends to do under such circumstances
is to have a little talk, at the close of which one of
them would relinquish what means so little to him
and so much to the other. Failing that way out of the
initial difficulty, if a man has told a lie to his friend
in order to encompass his desire, who and what is a
king that he should think a paltry lie to him is un-
deserving of forgiveness and only to be made right by
the sacrifice of a life? It all seems very arbitrary and
silly.

But underneath the code is something else—a willing-
ness to accept the noblest code that one can conceive
of and try to live up to it. Aethelwold has accepted
the code. He is no modern democrat or communist,
nor is he a reader of essays on the right to be happy.
He believes from the depths of his soul that his highest
duty is to obey literally and implicitly his king and
his blood brother. He believes that only blood re-
venge can blot out a dishonor. And believing these
things while they do not hurt him, he must believe
them also when his tragic desire has made him wish
to believe otherwise. By killing himself rather than
to compromise with his beliefs, he becomes in our
eyes a man—a man who is something more than the
cleverest of all the beasts. Watching Aethelwold die
by his own hand, we know, with something deeper
than reason, that the strongest compulsion upon
human nature is to find a code of behavior that satis-
fies the most lively intelligence and then to live up to
it, however much it hurts. And if our keenest modern
intelligence is really no less stupid than Old English
intelligence, if the highest code of conduct that we

can conceive of will become, from the point of view of another generation, ridiculous—what of that? We shall have proved our nobility by struggling after something that we have conceived to be noble.

This compulsion to try to be noble seems to be the racial memory that works most deeply within us, and from farthest back in the human race. It is something like this which the symbolist poets are trying to bring to our deepest awareness when they remind us of objects and sensations which to our earliest ancestors were closely associated with their struggles after nobility. And if one asks why the symbolists or indeed Edna St. Vincent Millay herself cannot come out and say in plain words that this is what the racial memory is all about and let it go at that, of course the answer is that dogmatic words have nothing to do with the matter at all. No one ever set out to be noble because of a statement in an essay or a copy-book that nobility is very noble indeed. Ideas that play across the surfaces of our minds have nothing to do with the deep current of conviction that really moves our lives.

Before Millay can reach our almost forgotten faith in aspirations after nobility, she must convince us that her story is true, must win us to what Coleridge calls "a willing suspension of disbelief." So long as *The King's Henchman* is just a play or a libretto, setting effective phrases against a musical accompaniment, it is nothing. Writing a historical tragedy in these days when we know so many ways of being skeptical is a tremendous task. In Shakespeare's day it was not so hard. Shakespeare put his hero into one period or another of the world's history just as he would have dressed him in a crimson cloak or a blue one or a purple, with no idea that the time was more than his garment. Shakespeare made Cymbeline king of an early England that is nothing at all like the early England over which Eadgar rules in *The King's Henchman* and it does not matter, because we know that Cymbeline's kingdom is really a combination of fairyland and seventeenth-century London. Elizabethans did not watch the play to find out how their ancestors felt about the world. They took it for granted that they felt and acted as Elizabethans did. But in the twentieth century we, with our ever gnawing sense of time, come to history and to historical dramas in a very different spirit. We want very much to know whether our ancestors had something that we have lost, whether they had something that we can regain, whether they were free from something that is plaguing us. But in order for a drama to tell us anything about this, it must first convince us that it is showing us our ancestors. And Millay has taken pains to show us an England that is in accord with all that we know of it from history and literature.

She has chosen her period wisely. She has refrained from going back so far into the mists of time that human figures appear shadowy and ill-defined to us. She gives us a time when, we know, life sounded and smelled and tasted and looked more or less recognizably like the world today. And she chooses a century when she has the completed literature of a period to guide her. And she has chosen a century in which the language was changing sufficiently so that she can suggest its vigor without abandoning a natural modern English speech, though she has, with strictest fidelity, used not a single word of which the root, at least, had not entered the language before the Norman

164

Conquest. During the rule of King Eadgar, from 944 to 975, the language and the poetry were taking on a few modern characteristics. Though it is a hundred years before the Norman Conquest, already the poetry is showing traces of rhyme and regular meter. Therefore Millay, without too much incongruity, can represent the forceful everyday speech of her characters by an irregular blank verse, heavily alliterated, and can show them singing rhymed ballads. But she convinces us from the beginning that these are old English times, indeed, by opening the play with a song by the gleeman which is in the four-stressed alliterative and unmetrical (though heavily rhythmical) Old English verse. Just as *Beowulf* contains the gleeman's song of the *Battle of Finnsburgh*, which is in the style of an earlier day, so Millay, in this opening song, carries us back to the time of King Cynewulf, two hundred years before King Eadgar's reign. The gleeman is chanting the story of Cynewulf's death, on his mistress' doorstep, where he is set upon and assassinated by his enemies:

> Stroke upon stroke, Sledging and slaying
> Swashes the sword, Shivers the shield. . . . .

The energy of Old English poetry is in her imitation of it, yet she did not find this material in poetry. The story of the gleeman's chant she found in the prose of the *Anglo-Saxon Chronicle*.

At the conclusion of the song the noisy shouts of the drinkers begin. It is the *bencsweg*, the "bench-noise" which in *Beowulf* we are told always arose as the drinking recommenced at the conclusion of a song. Then these people who seem to us to be in such an early world begin to lament that they could not have lived in the earlier, more heroic world of the song. That is true to the feeling of the Anglo-Saxons. Even in the time of *Beowulf* there was romance attached to an earlier time. Thus the dragon's treasures belonged to a splendid day a thousand years before. And in the Old English poem *The Wanderer* the poet felt, no less than a twentieth-century poet, that times were growing very bad, that the earth day by day was sinking into decay. It is ironical of Millay to remind us of that. Perhaps, after all, our earth and our civilization are still in the first throes of adolescence.

The men and women sing a kind of "charm" to the gleeman and his harp—that instrument that was the mirthwood to the Old English. And then one of the feasters tells of the friendship of Eadgar and Aethelwold, and how Aethelwold saved the king's life. In spirit it is like the story of Wiglaf's comradeship with Beowulf in slaying the dragon, for as Wiglaf, out of courtly deference, left the actual slaying of the dragon to Beowulf, his king, so Aethelwold, in saving Eadgar's life from a wild boar, instead of slaying the boar, "hugged the great head backward" so that the king might have the dignity of killing his enemy himself.

There are many reminiscences of *Beowulf* in this court scene in the first act of *The King's Henchman*. The scene is laid in a drinking-hall much like the Old English *meodo-heal*, and the men on their rough benches are drinking mead, as the Old English did on their *meodo-setl*. But King Eadgar, to pledge Aethelwold, calls not for mead but for wine in a handsome cup, as in *Beowulf* King Hrothgar gave Beowulf wine in *wunder fatum* (in cups to marvel at). The dress of the women is faithful to Old English fashion. King

Eadgar yearns for a bride whom he may adorn with heavy ornaments. He vows to

> Weigh her down with them, that she might not walk
> But leaning on my arm.

That is in the fashion of Queen Wealtheow in *Beowulf*, who is *goldbroden* and *beaghroden* (adorned with gold and with bracelets). King Eadgar's taste for weight in ornaments reminds one of the taste of King Hrothgar, who gave Beowulf "the heaviest neck-ring that was ever heard of upon the earth." It is natural, with such taste, that Eadgar should dream of the noise his bride's garments will make, when she wears "bright silk that clashes like a sword."

The feeling for the out-of-doors in *The King's Henchman* carries still more of the spirit of *Beowulf* and the other Old English poems. Aethelwold makes a horseback journey with the gleeman, who sings to him on the road. Thus in *Beowulf* "many a young man went on a joyous journey, riding on a white horse." And the swamp in which Aethelwold meets his love, Aelfrida (who has come there to recite a charm on Halloween) has the eerie look of Grendel's fen. In the wan moonlight (as in the *wanre niht* of *Beowulf*) Aethelwold gropes on misty paths (like the *misthleotum*). His challenge of a "slinking shadow" there recalls the *sceadugenga* (the shadow-goer). The forest is a wilderness filled with snuffling wolves, like the *wulfhlith*. And there are boars and ravens in the forests, as one is reminded in *Beowulf* and in the Old English gnomic verses. In Aelfrida's home by the sea cliffs the wind blows always, as on the *windige weallas* of *Beowulf*, and the sea gulls trouble Aelfrida as they troubled the poet in the *Sea-farer* and the *Wanderer* and the exile in

The Husband's Message. The intense joy at the breaking and scattering of winter recalls the *wuldortorhtan weder* (the glory-bright weather), in which winter was scattered in *Beowulf.* And the sense of the spaciousness of the earth outspread beneath the skies is suggested as strongly as in *Beowulf.*

But more meaningful than the literal descriptions of the Old English world are the symbols and imagery which Millay makes her characters use, showing natural objects already possessed of spiritual significances for them, through the associations which their ancestors have built up around them. Thus wolves have become a symbol for sensuality and savagery. Dunstan, the archbishop of Canterbury, hearing the jesting about the lusts of the flesh, sighs

> Ah me,
> In what a wilderness,
> And snuffled at by wolves,
> Build I the house of God!

Millay has not ignored the importance that wolves must have assumed in the minds of these people, since King Eadgar, as a matter of history, imposed a tribute which led to the extirpation of wolves in England. Of course, in actual Old English literature, the world "wolf" is used repeatedly as a symbol in compound words, now admiringly, to express ruthless strength, and again contemptuously, to show bestial savagery in a man's thoughts.

The wind and the tides are favorite symbols both to the Old English poets and to Millay. The wind is usually the wind of fate, as in *Beowulf,* wherein fate *forsweoth* (swept on in a mighty wind) and brought the warriors to the terror of Grendel. Likewise the mourners in *The King's Henchman* seem to hear the wind of

168

fate in the trees outside, as Aethelwold is swept on by
fate to his death. This is one of the ancient images
that symbolist poets have found most moving to us
still. Thus Archibald MacLeish makes us feel the
power of fate upon our civilization when he says,
"America is west and the wind blowing." Millay's
Dunstan finds the wind of fate too strong for his warn-
ings to Aethelwold, and he sighs,

> I shout into the wind, that beareth my words nowhither,
> > but only back
> To mine own ears.

The tides stand, usually, in Old English poetry, and
again in Millay, for the restless rise and fall of human
passions; and the turn of the tides stands for human
perplexity. The ocean in storm stands for the noise and
zest of battle. Sunny daylight stands for life, of course.
And the horse also is a symbol of life. Thus in *The
King's Henchman* the mystery of life and death are contrasted:

> The horse standeth in the smithy door with lifted hoof,
> > and shivers against the flies.
> And thou liest there.

That, surely, is a reminiscence of the image used for
death in *Beowulf:*

> Nor doth the swift horse paw in the courtyard.

And the men in *The King's Henchman* refer to made
objects symbolically, also, with the feeling about
them that the Old English would have had. As bright
tapestries signified beauty in *Beowulf*, wherein the
tapestries, shot with gold, gleamed on the wall, so
Aethelwold naturally uses a reference to them to express his love for Aelfrida and his loss:

> Here sharply endeth and is seen no more
> The golden thread in the woof.

And in the days when a house was not something taken for granted, it became easily a symbol of security and civilization. Thus in *Beowulf* the deserted Heorot, with the winds blowing through it, appeared to the Old English a symbol of a civilization being destroyed by fate. It seems natural, therefore, that in *The King's Henchman* Eadgar should speak of his attempt to establish a strong civilization in England as the building of a house. His task has been, he says,

> Hewing and heaving,
> Setting stone upon stone,
> Building England.

Literally and figuratively, then, Millay has given a very strong illusion of showing us actual early England. Why was it worth doing? Why, if she is merely giving us the spirit of the Old English poems and chronicles, would it not be better for us to read the old poems themselves, in our search for reassurance of ancient stability and nobility in human nature? Well, nothing else takes the place of reading old literatures at first hand, of course, but *The King's Henchman* is, obviously, not presented as a substitute for that. It is not a mere imitation of Old English poetry, but an interpretation of it in terms of twentieth-century needs. And as each of us is not a deeply imaginative poet, it is valuable, in every age, that a poet should do this thing for us. The more of the past our poets can interpret in terms of our own age, the richer our age becomes. The past is meaningless to us until we interpret it in terms that pierce sharply into our everyday concerns. Our interpretation may be all wrong, ridiculously inadequate, but we cannot help that. It is, at least, an effort to see the truth; whereas, if we simply look at old poems as museum pieces, we are doing nothing but tiring our eyes and our spirits.

Thus Millay turns to the Old English period and reads it with all the light she can bring to it from the entire history of English literature and twentieth-century psychology. She tries to express the simple as it looks to the complex. In other words, she makes an intensely subjective study of a period which its own literature pictures only in simple, objective terms.

The Old English did not understand their own motives as we do (or think we do), and they would have despised an attempt to understand them. Their villains were wild beasts or devils. Grendel and Grendel's mother are the villains in *Beowulf*. The villains in *The King's Henchman* are, to the characters of the action, no less absolute and objective. The villain of the action, to the minds of Dunstan, of Maccus, and of Aethelwold, is Satan himself, and his evil agent is womankind—not a woman, but Woman. Dunstan is trying to force celibacy upon his clergy, and he is urging it upon the king. "*Solutus es ab uxore?—ne quaere uxorem*," he earnestly warns Eadgar, and he refuses to bless Aethelwold's errand of seeking a new wife for the king. Maccus accepts the same belief. "All women," he assures Aethelwold, "are daughters of the Evil One." Aethelwold and Aelfrida believe that they have met through evil witchcraft on Halloween, and Aethelwold believes that an evil supernatural power is contributing to his punishment. He tells Aelfrida,

Ywis, in the month of the wolves I wedded thee,
And thou shalt rend me yet.

171

This is as much as any of the characters understand
about Aethelwold's temptation and fall, and these
broad outlines are all that any Old English poem
would have given us. But Millay interprets the whole
action as a matter not of supernatural powers but of
subtle complexities of character.

She shows Aethelwold betrayed to temptation by
the exceptional fineness of his nature. He is essentially
a poet. During the springtimes when other men have
been making love, he has been thinking "on the
Lenten-tide and the white thorn." His standards of
enjoyment are higher than those of his friends, and
his sense of beauty is finer than that of the men who
enjoy women easily. All the girls of average good
looks about the court appear and sound much alike to
him. He says,

> So many dry leaves in a ditch they are to me,
> These whispering girls,
> A little fairish and a little foulish,
> And all alike, and mightily underfoot.

It is inevitable that when he sees a woman of remarkable grace he shall love her with an intensity that his
easily satisfied comrades, and even King Eadgar, can
have no comprehension of.

And Aelfrida's villainy is analyzed quite as sympathetically. We see her, not as a member of a naturally
infernal sex, wantonly enticing men to hell, but as a
girl prevented from developing much independent
judgment, except about household matters. She is not
allowed to express any judgment about a man's af-
fairs. A woman was at that time, even to the man who
loved her, merely a body, or a Maypole to hang rings
and bright ribbons upon. One could not expect too

172

great exercise of fortitude from a young girl of sixteen or so under the circumstances.

And Aelfrida's downfall is subtly devised. When she betrays her husband's lie to the king by appearing in her full beauty before him, she has been under the most irresistible temptation that could befall a girl of her nature. She could have resisted considerable temptation. Aethelwold has cheated her of a chance to be queen of England, but she can forgive that. She is regretful when she thinks of what she has lost—the incredible marvel of waking in the morning to find, as she says,

Great Eadgar, the Dove of Albion, and the Hawk of the Dane,
Asleep like a child in my bed.

Still, since she loves Aethelwold, it does not seem unforgivable that he has cheated her. She could give up a kingdom for him. But that should he have sent back a message to the king that she is ugly, that is too much. And when, on top of that, she is asked actually to make herself ugly while the king, the king of fairyland itself to her simple mind, looks at her, it is more than her young girl's vanity can bear. In a flash of rebellion she makes herself lovely as possible. What young girl would have shown more self-control?

And yet, understanding all, we cannot forgive all. After the betrayal, when Maccus, kneeling by the bleeding corpse of Aethelwold, warns Aelfrida to draw back her skirts, and she instinctively obeys, we glory in his contemptuous comment,

So,
I would not have thee foul this blood.

And when the king dismisses her as a being with "a narrow heart," we dismiss her, too, as unworthy of pity.

173

And it is likewise with Aethelwold. Sympathizing with his agony of contrition which is yet not strong enough to override his great passion, understanding that his temptation has been, humanly speaking, insuperable, we yet wait as sternly as Eadgar himself for him to make atonement, and we should have despised him if he had not wrung our hearts with pity for him by killing himself. Aethelwold perhaps could not help his fall, but he would not be Aethelwold to us if he had not tried to be more than human, had not judged himself by a standard higher than he could live by.

Thus the twentieth-century comments upon the ethics of the tenth. The code of the time we see as not overintelligent. The judgment of the time we see as narrow and severe. Men then judged one another according to a black and white of absolute good and evil. We, watching them, judge them by the complex shadings that make up the subtle natures of human beings as we understand them. And yet, such is the power of the drama upon us, our judgment corresponds with theirs in the end. Men cannot be utterly noble, we believe, but we still believe they should judge themselves as if they could be. Thus we feel about Shakespeare's heroes, and thus, with the full light of twentieth-century psychology beating upon them, we judge the people of Old English times as they are interpreted in *The King's Henchman*. So long as tragedy can move us in this way, the racial memory of some strange impulsion to seek good and to abhor evil is not dead within us.

IX

THE BUCK IN THE SNOW

In Quest of Earth Virtue

A NEW and lovely mood, a little like a revival of religion, swept over America in 1927, a sudden conviction that after all, even in our century, it is possible for a man to be more than an automaton in behavior and a sensualist in instinct. It was a transient mood, and in many people it soon altered into something ugly, and yet its finer traces have not even now passed utterly away. It marked the end of the jazz age.

In May of 1927 the public turned to the worship of a face, which for a year it insisted upon seeing daily in the newspapers and in the cinema newsreels—a young Scandinavian face on which was written plainly a virile innocence and eagerness. It looked as if life were a matter of high purposes and high joys, and as if the world were young. For a few days people imagined that they were paying tribute to supreme sportsmanship, to a daring crossing of the Atlantic by air; but when in the course of the next few weeks a half-dozen men flew across the Atlantic without creating much excitement, while the worship of Lindbergh grew more and more ardent, it became clear that the Atlantic flight was to the public a mere symbol, and that this adoration was for a young man who looked as if he were capable of soaring in spirit. The incredible flood of speeches and editorials and poems and essays that were poured out in Lindbergh's honor all expressed a single mood—a mood of marvel that there was reality in those qualities which Americans had long imagined to be the "phoney" virtues of motion-picture heroes, that a man was actually walking the earth who possessed independence and sincerity and modesty and self-control. Nothing shows more clearly how low belief in the human race had fallen than the unfeigned tears with which men spoke of these simple and, it had once been supposed, fundamental human qualities.

This was the main manifestation of people's sudden imperious longing for a belief in humanity. But during the same year another human being began to be widely discussed as genuinely worthy of honor. Mahatma Ghandi was the subject of many essays which expressed a tentative belief that in another and far country a member of an alien race, uncrippled by the conventions of a "Christian" civilization, might today, no less than in bygone days, be an unselfish man, a lover of humanity, even a saint.

To Edna St. Vincent Millay it seemed that this newly humble and eager mood of the public might be enlisted to rectify a gross injustice. If the public wished subjects for hero-worship, there were Sacco and Vanzetti, showing the steadfastness and loving-kindness under adversity that are the attributes of hero and saint. For these obscure Italians had been arrested years before and, after a mock trial, thrown into prison, ostensibly on a charge of murder, but really, many people were convinced, for holding an anarchistic political philosophy. And the behavior of Vanzetti, in particular, during his long stay in prison had given some of his watchers a new revelation of the

gentleness and forgiveness that may flower in the human heart. For months Edna St. Vincent Millay de-
voted all her energies to the task of rousing Americans
to demand a fair trial for these men.

But lethargy and injustice triumphed, and on the
twenty-third of August, in 1927, the two were finally
executed. And Millay's mood curdled into bitterness
against a human race that was capable of killing men
for being gentle and filled with high faith. The execution was, of course, a salient injustice; but I think it
was the poetic irony of Sacco's and Vanzetti's deaths
that touched her so deeply, and made these two
humble and ignorant Italians seem so much more
piteous than the victims of other injustices which are,
without stinging through our callous human com-
placency, committed on our earth every day. For here
were two sweet-tempered men who believed, with a
deep sincerity beyond all question, that human nature
was essentially good; they believed that men need
only be freed from restraints in order to behave
generously and nobly; and they were put to death by
the men in whom they expressed such naïve faith—
were put to death, in fact, for no other reason than
that they did express this faith. Millay concluded
that their faith had been absurd and preposterous.
Man, she said, was to her mind quite obviously the
worm that the Moody and Sankey hymnbooks had
described him as being. And she cried out that our
human civilization was degenerating, that our American political structure was like a farmland that has
become depleted:

> What from the splendid dead
> We have inherited—
> Furrows sweet to the grain, and the weed subdued,
> See now the slug and the mildew plunder.

This outburst against the legalized murder of Sacco and Vanzetti, *Justice Denied in Massachusetts*, was among the first of many controversial poems to be published in England and America. In the same year as it appeared, the first extensive translation of Russian Soviet poetry was made, and this helped to turn poets' attention to the possibilities of poetry as a propagandist instrument, which had been largely forgotten since the beginning of the nineteenth century. Robinson Jeffers, Archibald MacLeish, Stephen Spender, W. H. Auden, Cecil Day Lewis, Julian Bell, and others soon caught up the new mood of partisan hero-worship and denunciation. The Sacco-Vanzetti trial, the Reichstag trial, and various phases of the communistic experiment have set a new school of poets to writing furiously about political systems and events; and the new school has repudiated as anemic the introverted poetry of hair-spun distinctions that had been obsessing so many writers. Edna St. Vincent Millay set a fashion for "taking sides" in poetry, for spurning away those readers who do not agree with one's political judgments. She commanded:

> Cruel of heart, lay down my song.
> Your reading eyes have done me wrong.
> Not for you was the pen bitten,
> And the mind wrung, and the song written.

But this controversial mood, though it has given us much verse, has not given us much poetry. It is not that the arguments by which the propagandist school of critics have been trying to foster it are untrue. Poetry that squeamishly skirts away from a subject that deeply moves its author is finicking and sickly.

178

Yes. A poet who is not deeply moved by political
questions in a day like ours is deformed and insensi-
tive. Yes. And insensitiveness is antithetical to
poetry. Yes. Still the fact remains that poetry is not
achieved every time an eager and talented writer
takes up his pen to convert the world. Shelley
himself, in such brashly determined moods, occasionally wrote very weak verse. To reach poetry one has
to climb up above a controversial mood as truly as one
must climb above any other, and it is harder to sur-
mount a controversial mood than some others. So far
as poetry is concerned, much of this interesting
journalistic verse is no more than a shriek of ill-temper
that seems about to break into a whimper. I must admit that even such a mood—every mood—can make
poetry. Macbeth's

> The devil damn thee black, thou cream-faced loon!

is in that mood exactly. But it has reached the height
where poetry dwells by being seen for precisely what
it is—an explosion of jangled nerves, whereas most
controversial poetry presents jangled nerves as something quite different and nobler.

I suppose that one trouble with controversial poetry
is that it stirs up the reader's egotism by making him
aware of himself instead of making him think simply
and self-forgetfully about the poet's theme. A fist
shaken in one's face cannot help making one feel self-
conscious and prejudiced in one's own favor. And a
poet shaking his fist at the reader is as much out of
character as a mathematician shaking his fist at his
students. Both are far from a world of ideal convictions. It is impossible to watch one's effect on the pub-

lic and make poetry at the same time; and this is no less true when one's object is to irritate the public than when it is to make money by soothing it. I feel sure that there is no subject of such immediate and violent controversial interest that it cannot become the theme of poetry; but the poet must approach it as simply as a tiny child, that may run to its father through a rain of machine-gun bullets. It usually takes time for a poet to transcend his ugly ill-temper and reach this purity and simplicity of intention. It took time for Millay to do it.

The encouragers of controversial poetry have made much of Dante's inclusion of Guelf and Ghibelline political squabbles in his *Inferno*. Perhaps Dante invariably transmuted these squabbles into pure poetry. I cannot tell, for I am deaf to a great deal in poetry of a foreign language. But I know this: The Farinata passage in the *Inferno* is marvelous poetry. It is supreme poetry. No one can watch Farinata in the flames, as under the gaze of his unscathed enemy he "straightened up with breast and front as though he had Hell in great scorn," without crying bravo for our magnificent and ridiculous human pride and stubbornness, that doesn't know when it is beaten, even in eternal hell-fire. But Dante here is not arguing with his bitterest enemy; he is drawing his portrait and giving him his due. Dante has climbed as high as Mount Everest above the plane of their political bickering. This is not the plane of *Justice Denied in Massachusetts* or of *To Those without Pity*. But give Millay time. Who knows what she might be able to do with the theme of Governor Fuller in hell?

Fortunately Millay included very little about the Sacco and Vanzetti trial in *The Buck in the Snow*, which was published only a few months after the execution. However much her political conscience may nag her, her poetic conscience generally controls it and holds her back from merely journalistic expression. This is the reason, I think, that passionately political critics writing for some of the weeklies have been inclined to disparage Millay of late years, and that the reading public itself has shown a disposition to nag and fuss at her, pleading for more "current events," whether political or personal, in her writing. Most of us would rather have a newspaper than a volume of Shakespeare with our morning bacon and coffee; and it is such a breakfast-table mood that often overtakes us when we pick up a crisp new book with its fresh-smelling paper. It stimulates an appetite for pungent novelty rather than for poetic worth. But Millay, keeping step with the times and feeling its emotional tension to the degree that only a poet can feel it, has yet learned to control herself (with a few lapses) and exercise the patience by which current problems may be distilled into a single limpid drop of poetry.

There is poetry, but not limpid poetry, it seems to me, in *Hangman's Oak*, *Wine from These Grapes*, *Sonnet to Gath*, *To Jesus on His Birthday*, and *The Anguish*— poems which express something of her tribulation of spirit over the Sacco-Vanzetti trial. Not until two years after these poems appeared did she publish a poem holding a crystalline distillation of the meaning of her long turmoil. Then, in the *New Republic* for August 27, 1930, appeared a poem of such silvery Vergilian phrasing as only Edna St. Vincent Millay, in our century, is occasionally able to attain. From the first line one feels, in descant against the hopeless cry of pain, the celestial, singing rhythm that dis-

181

tinguishes great poetry and that can never be aped by
poetry on a lower level:

> Where can the heart be hidden in the ground
> And be at peace, and be at peace forever,
> Under the world, untroubled by the sound
> Of mortal tears, that cease from pouring never?

It is interesting to see that this ultimate essence of her
mood is not direct pity for the persecuted, but rebellion against the pain of not being able to express
righteous indignation adequately, when one is on fire
to sear out the very eyes of a tyrant. The pain of such
repression moves her to hope for oblivion after death,
as a thing preferable to an impotent immortal awareness of human woes:

> Anguish enough while yet the indignant breather
> Have blood to spurt upon the oppressor's hand;
> Who would eternal be, and hang in ether
> A stuffless ghost above his struggling land,
> Retching in vain to render up the groan
> That is not there, being aching dust's alone?

It is not so nobly unselfish a mood as the one she had
imagined she was expressing in the earlier unrealized
poetry. It is, in fact, like most of her poetry, intensely egoistic—but the mood has at last been accepted as exactly what it is. It has become inevitably
and perfectly realized. It has become poetry.

Strangely extravagant, monstrously wasteful would
seem to be the transmutation of human experience
into poetry. So far as the world of pure poetry is concerned, two men were put to death unjustly and thousands of men were driven into a frenzy of rage over the
injustice, millions of angry words were spoken and
tears were shed; and it all had, as almost sole result,
that a single one of the people so deeply moved should,

after years of unhappy pondering and abortive efforts
at expression, speak of man as "the indignant breather." But in the high, ruthless, and inhuman world of
pure poetry the single pellucid phrase seems to be a
not negligible result. For an utterly simple poetic
phrase seems never to have been achieved at less expense. In all the poetry of all the races of men there
is not an uncountable number of single phrases with
that innocent Homeric rightness. It is queer how inimitable they are. The violent thirteenth line of this
sonnet in memory of Sacco and Vanzetti set quite a
fashion among poets of metaphorically retching and
vomiting in controversial verse. But the phrase "the
indignant breather" set no fashion among poets for
referring to a mood of all mankind, revealing its
physical manifestation, and suggesting the brief mortal existence of the mood and of the puny human race,
which has a sense of its deserts so high above its
powers to exact them from fate—all this set down
with utter literalness and a diamond concentration, in
three words. And yet the phrase looks, as pure poetry
always looks, as if it were the unpremeditated and
effortless utterance of a child.

Even though, in her first rage against the unjust
execution of Sacco and Vanzetti, Millay screamed out
her belief in Calvin's doctrine of total depravity, her
dream of the ideal man has never been a dream of a
being with his natural instincts trodden out. Rather,
he is the man in whom the innocence of his natural
instincts has never been perverted. Millay has herself
taken a vow (in a rather unsaintly mood, to be sure)
that she will never again defraud her "innocent
senses" of their own. And this vow is in key with

the whole range of her poetic philosophy. Naturalness and tolerance are, to her, the basis of human
goodness. The saint and hero is he in whom

> Pity shall be governor
> With Wisdom for his guest.

Is this ideal man the "philosopher king" of Plato?
Not quite, for Plato would reverse the hierarchy of
these virtues, making wisdom the governor of pity.
Millay is not so fully a Platonist as many poets have
been. She cannot share Plato's worship of pure wisdom, apart from its human embodiments. In fact, it
is disembodied wisdom that horrifies her in the Sacco-
Vanzetti sonnet that we have quoted, in which she
shrinks from an immortality of knowing without
being able to act upon her knowledge. And elsewhere
she confesses,

> Wisdom, heretic flower, I was ever afraid
> Of your large, cool petals without scent.

Ideas move her only after they have entered a human
brain and are committed to the accidents of our human
life. For her it is the sad, sweet fragrance of earth
that gives ideas their loveliness.

Few poets have been farther than Edna St. Vincent
Millay from Plato's view that our human bodies and
senses are a dark prison, shutting the light of pure
wisdom away from our souls. To be sure, she admires
Plato's metaphor by which he described the philosopher's bewilderment in his daily life within his body.
Twice she has used this Platonic figure of the black
cave. In an early sonnet she says,

> Then is my daily life a narrow room
> In which a little while, uncertainly,
> Surrounded by impenetrable gloom,

> Among familiar things grown strange to me
> Making my way, I pause, and feel, and hark,
> Till I become accustomed to the dark.

And in *To the Wife of a Sick Friend* she speaks of a man's intelligence that illumines, for her, the Platonic cave of the world. She pleads:

> Shelter this candle from the wind,
> Hold it steady. In its light
> The cave wherein we wander lost
> Glitters with frosty stalactite,
> Blossoms with mineral rose and lotus,
> Sparkles with crystal moon and star,
> Till a man would rather be lost than found.
> We have forgotten where we are.

But obviously neither passage expresses unadulterated Platonism. In the second one, from *To the Wife of a Sick Friend*, it is the seventeenth-century English variant of Platonism with which she is in accord, just as she is in accord with so much else in the seventeenth century. Here is the very sensuous Platonism of Henry Vaughan, who in his *Silence and Stealth of Days* used Plato's cave metaphor as movingly as Millay has done. Not pure reason, but a personality, intelligence in a beloved human embodiment, lights the world for both Vaughan and Millay.

Moreover, in *To the Wife of a Sick Friend*, Millay is very much the twentieth-century introvert, rather than the ascetic idealist of Plato's *Republic*, for her cave is not so much Plato's cave of general human ignorance as it is the cave of her own solipsistic isolation. She says that we stand

> Each in a sudden, *separate* dark.

Here is the same feeling of loneliness that haunts so much of Aiken's poetry, the terrible loneliness of realizing that, for all we know, each of us is dreaming alone in an utterly empty world, and that all the peopled globe, all the astronomical distances of the universe, as each one of us knows them, belong to each one singly, unshared and unseen by anyone else.

But for all that Millay is no solipsistic pessimist. She has full faith in poetic intuition as a miracle breaking through this isolation. A richly endowed and sympathetic human intelligence can bring about the magic of communication and bring isolated members of the human race into a single lighted universe, she feels. And she is interested only in this warm and humanized universe, not in the cold serenities of Plato's metaphysical realm of pure ideality. After the philosophers and poets of the earth have died, leaving their impersonal utterance of wisdom to the world, then, she says, in her *Dirge without Music*,

> A formula, a phrase remains—but the best is lost.
> The answers quick and keen, the honest look, the
>   laughter, the love,
> They are gone.

Plato's ideal wisdom is to her merely a formula, a phrase. The candlelight in the cave of sense is enough for her. She does not crave the featureless sunlit air outside our bodily existence. Having said that, one must remember her poem *On Thought in Harness*, in which she does indeed urge the falcon of her thought to escape all bondage to the sensuous world, to leave the "air filled with earthy dregs" (as Ovid put it), which underlies the weightless ether of ideality. She cries to her falcon,

> Forsake this wrist, forsake this rhyme;
> Soar, eat ether, see what has never been
>   seen, depart, be lost,
> But climb.

186

Still, this is only one poem, and a passing mood, it seems to me. Usually her falcon is happiest in the atmosphere of our planet earth, pursuing another high-flying bird, as a falcon is supposed to do.

In fact, the existence of the good, the beautiful, and the true in the Platonic realms of essence holds little comfort for anyone nowadays, apparently, unless possibly for Santayana. To our modern temperament goodness, truth, and beauty seem nothing at all unless they are a human possession; and, as a consequence, the meaning of the entire universe seems to most of us to have a very precarious existence in the human mind alone. We leave the miracle of abstract and communicable logic unaccounted for, and we think of truth as being the slow accumulation of merely human and animal knowledge and wisdom. If all eyes and brains were annihilated, then, it seems to us, as we look out at the blinding flame and blinding darkness of a mechanistic universe, truth itself would be lost. Truth, as we know it, appears to be something that has slowly evolved out of the warm and fertile earth, even as our bodies have done.

Before Edna St. Vincent Millay and the symbolists there had been little poetry about this earthly truth. But very recently many other poets have begun writing of it. In the early 1930's, especially, George Dillon, Raymond Holden, Marie Welch, Joseph Auslander, and George Russell have expressed a warm and eager affection for this earth truth. George Russell called it *The Virgin Mother*, and he asked,

> Who is the goddess to whom men should pray
> But her from whom their hearts have turned away,
> Out of whose virgin being they were born,
> Whose mother nature they have named with scorn,
> Calling its holy substance common clay?

187

One of the greatest and most influential poems in *The Buck in the Snow* is Edna St. Vincent Millay's apostrophe to this earth-grown truth, which she conceives under the metaphor of the Tree of Knowledge, described in Genesis. And conceiving of truth as a tree, she manifests toward it that protective tenderness which stirs in her for any green and growing thing; and with the same inimitable solicitude which she felt for the blue flag in the bog, she calls to human wisdom to be careful in its climb:

> Grow not too high, grow not too far from home,
> Green tree, whose roots are in the granite's face!

For she is afraid that our knowledge may grow top-heavy with abstract speculation and lose its earthy virtue. She calls out the warning:

> Taller than silver spire or golden dome
> A tree may grow above its earthy place,
> And taller than a cloud, but not so tall
> The root may not be mother to the stem,
> Lifting rich plenty, though the rivers fall,
> To the cold sunny leaves to nourish them.

She is sure that such a complex growth as is all the science and the speculation of modern man, leading him to interpret even the incredible spaces of astronomy, cannot be healthy and sound unless it becomes rooted in deeper understanding of the earthy nature of our human intelligence:

> Earth's fiery core alone can feed the bough
> That blooms between Orion and the Plough.

The consequence of such a philosophy is that she, and other poets following her, are feeling a new piety for the earth. Poets have become worshipers of earth, in a way, and are convinced that the life which is

188

lived in closest relation to the earth is the holiest. Many poets have gone so far, in certain moods, as to feel that in our human emergence from the other animal life on our globe we made some fundamental early mistake, which accounts for our human woes. Robinson Jeffers, especially, has maintained this. He has said,

> Humanity is the mold to break away from,
> The crust to break through,
> The coal to break into fire,
> The atom to be split.

And he has avowed his belief in a "wild God of this world" who has nothing in common with human religion. He declares,

> You do not know him, you communal people, or you have
>   forgotten him.
> Intemperate and savage, the hawk remembers him.

And he adds,

> I'd sooner, except for the penalties, kill a man than
>   a hawk.

What is this mistake of the human race that other animals are free from? It is the mistake of sentimentality, said D. H. Lawrence—"faked love has rotted our marrow." It is fatigue and weakness, said Elinor Wylie and George Dillon and Merrill Moore. It is the degeneration of animal lust and hate, said William Faulkner. It is greed and intolerance, said Edna St. Vincent Millay. It is the artificiality of a rational consciousness, said Robinson Jeffers and Harold Cook and James Rorty. It is our bondage to language, said Conrad Aiken and Rolfe Humphries and Virginia Moore and Hart Crane. The mass of poetry containing all these views yet has fundamental unity, for it is all marked by the conviction that the human race, in developing the power to think and reflect, has lost its straightforwardness and developed a false complexity that makes it uncertain of its desires and grotesque in its behavior. "We recognize ourselves by a wrong laugh," as Archibald MacLeish puts it. Or, in Leonie Adams' phrase, man is "the natureless creature that has confusion to his part." It is self-concern that ails us.

The first twentieth-century poem to express a revulsion against our human self-concern, as compared with an animal's lack of egoism, was a sonnet by Santayana, in which before the World War he expressed an abhorrence of human self-sickness:

> I would I might forget that I am I!
>
> . . . .
>
> Happy the dumb beast, hungering for food,
> But calling not his hungering his own. . . . .

Later, in a prose essay, he set down his belief that an animal may "keenly enjoy the momentary scene, never conceiving of himself as a separate body or as anything but the unity of that scene, nor his enjoyment as anything but its beauty." This attitude has, in the last fifteen years, resulted in a flood of poetry expressing envy of the animal's closeness to the world about it. All the intensity of the poet's longing goes out to this magical, free awareness, this dream consciousness, free of the past, free of the future, free of self-sickness. After Santayana, Edna St. Vincent Millay was the first to utter the mood in a lyric cry. In 1921 the flight of wild swans caught her up out of sickly subjectivity:

> I looked in my heart while the wild swans went over.
> And what did I see I had not seen before?

Only a question less or a question more:
Nothing to match the flight of wild birds flying.
Tiresome heart, forever living and dying,
House without air, I leave you and lock your door.
Wild swans, come over the town, come over
The town again, trailing your legs and crying!

No other mood has so united poets of divergent temperaments and poetic theories as this one. Robert Tristram Coffin and Marie Welch are the two who have lately made this mood the center of their poetic lives and who have written most fully, and sometimes, perhaps, most beautifully, of animal innocence and joy; but literally hundreds of writers have followed Millay out of doors and caught the contagion of her delight in the ecstasy of animal movement and the beauty of animal forms.

There is pleasure for Edna St. Vincent Millay in feeling the touch of the world as she imagines an animal may feel it. She muses:

Black bird scudding
Under the rainy sky,
How wet your wings must be!
And your small head how sleek and cold with water.

Or she imagines the coolness of dew on the bat's wing:

Wan ghost between
Two lights, the shadowy flitter-mouse,
Half seeing and half-seen,
Swoops in the glimmering even;
The early star he knows,
And her cool wave upon his ribby fin.

The live colors of feather and fin excite her more than the colors of flowers. The "jeweled fish" is a symbol of summer's beauty to her; and year after year she exults anew at the colors of the returning flicker.

EDNA ST. VINCENT MILLAY

"The golden flicker with his wing to the sun," she calls it in *Moriturus;* and in *Pueblo Pot* she sees the birds "flashing the wonder of their under-wings."

And her poetry shows delighted awareness of the quality of bird voices—of "the wood-cock's watery call," the "nicker" of the woodpecker, the ceaselessness of the pigeon's droning (which she imitates in the rhythm of her line,

> How they conversed throughout the afternoon in their
> monotonous voices never for a moment quiet),

the almost articulate syllables of the nightingale, the "chuckling" of the bobolink, and the "serene and pitiless note" of the skylark "like a crystal dart."

This sensuous delight in birds and beasts is not a new thing. No, it has always existed—in Theocritus, in Anacreon, in the young Vergil, in Petrarch, in Chaucer. . . . . But it has always been rare in its enchantment, and today's poetry is richer than that of earlier periods in this one aspect, I think, for I know of no time in the past when animals were, as today, the most popular theme in poetry; and out of today's great mass of loving comment will surely be saved a surprisingly large remnant of beauty.

But another side of such poetry about animals is like nothing in the past and could not have existed sooner. I mean it could not have arisen until the theory of biological evolution had not merely been formulated and generally accepted, but also had become part of the unconscious background of our thinking. It took some notion of the vast stretches of evolutionary periods and the abandonment of a man-centered theology to enable us to look at men and beasts as almost indistinguishable comrades, making their ignorant journey

192

through time. Thus Edna St. Vincent Millay, in *Epitaph for the Race of Man*, sees the dinosaur and the "cretaceous bird" as beings close to us in nature and even close to us in time, for she sees man also as a creature

out of ooze
But lately crawled, and climbing up the shore.

And in the gross ugliness of the dinosaur she sees not the grotesquerie of a museum fantasy, but a creature embodying something closely akin to the "stench of man" in our cities whose sewers pollute the streams, and to our overgrown materialistic civilization wherein we trust to the physical powers at our disposal to save us from extinction.

And therefore Edna St. Vincent Millay can write of animals, even of the tiny ant, with no condescension, but with wonder at the gulf in understanding that separates two earth-dwellers so alike in their customs:

Now forth to meadow as the farmer goes
With shining buckets to the milking-ground,
He meets the black ant hurrying from his mound
To milk the aphis pastured on the rose.
. . . .
In chilly autumn on the hardening road
They meet again, driving their flocks to stall,
Two herdsmen, each with winter for a goad;
They meet and pass, and never a word at all
Gives one to t'other. On the quaint abode
Of each, the evening and the first snow fall.

In her musing upon this gulf in sympathy and understanding between man and the animals that are such close blood kin to him, Millay comes nearest to genuine agreement with Calvinism. To be sure, she sees man in a world not made for him, a world which existed without him for countless aeons, wherein the older animals are far more at home than he, and this evolutionary concept is radically different from the old Calvinistic view of the making of the universe and of man's place in it. And yet the counterpart of the old notion of "original sin," setting man apart from the other animals, persists.

> If lustful goats and serpents envious
> Cannot be damned, alas, why should I be?

asked Donne rebelliously in the seventeenth century, and a similar note of injury appears in the twentieth century, not merely in Edna St. Vincent Millay, but in most poets who write about animals—a feeling that the human race has been discriminated against. The animals shrink from us, and become contaminated and unnatural if they are forced to associate with us, poets feel. And yet poets feel that the deepest source of human joy and virtue is a life lived as close as possible to the wild and innocent beings that inhabit our globe. This complex mood is Millay's when she observes a baby fawn,

> Asleep on the moss, his head on his polished cleft
> small ebony hooves.

The theme of the poem is the fawn's refusal to accept her presence when it awoke:

> I would have given more than I care to say
> To thrifty ears, might I have had him for my friend
> One moment only of that forest day:
> Might I have had the acceptance, not the love
> Of those clear eyes.

But the fawn seems to feel immediately an instinctive hostility, and it leaves her to muse:

> Was it alarm, or was it the wind of my fear lest he depart
> That jerked him to his jointy knees,

194

> And sent him crashing off, leaping and stumbling
>   On his new legs, between the stems of the white trees?

Before the World War this new humility of men before animal innocence and wisdom would have seemed a mere sentimentality. But after the "war to end war" had, they feared, sown the seed of even more deadly conflicts, poets began to look with new eyes at the creatures that would probably have the wit to survive the slaughtered human race upon this globe.

> High on his naked rock the mountain sheep
>   Will stand alone against the final sky,

Millay said, musing of the ultimate destruction of our planet. For she was sure that long before that day there would be nothing but the ruins of our steel towers to indicate that on this earth there had once existed

> Most various man, cut down to spring no more.
> Before his prime, even in his infancy
> Cut down, and all the clamor that was he
> Silenced, and all the riveted pride he wore,
> A rusty iron column whose tall core
> The rains have tunneled like an aspen tree.

This sonnet sequence, *Epitaph for the Race of Man,* is the incomparably beautiful expression of the tragic conviction, but other poets have brooded on the same idea—Archibald MacLeish, Carl Sandburg, Robert McBlair, Daniel Hickey, Djuna Barnes, Robinson Jeffers. All have felt that in this human interval animals are not merely after, but before their time.

Can men comfort themselves by reflecting that during our little interval we may hold in serene possession a beauty greater than that of animals, which the best of the human race have achieved? No, for men cannot reproduce themselves exactly, as animals do. Shakespeare in his sonnets might beg a beautiful boy to beget sons, that the future might marvel at his grace, but we think that no replica of the idol of Shakespeare's heart is walking the earth today. And Edna St. Vincent Millay's certainty that, when a human being dies, its beauty will never be exactly recovered makes the pathos of her most beautiful elegy to her young friend:

> But your voice, never the rushing
> Of a river underground,
> Not the note the white-throat utters,
> Not the feet of children pushing
> Yellow leaves along the gutters
> In the blue and bitter fall,
>
> Shall content my musing mind
> For the beauty of that sound
> That in no new way at all
> Ever shall be heard again.
> . . . .
> All your lovely words are spoken.
> Once the ivory box is broken,
> Beats the golden bird no more.

And so it is even of the things which men create. Millay, piecing together some beautiful shards of a past civilization, appealed to the beauty of the birds, the flickers, above her, for consolation. But their beauty seemed to answer, "I cannot console the broken thing; I can only make it whole." The shards of the ancient pot crumble into dust, but the underwings of the flickers remain as bewilderingly burnished as when flickers flew above those early men at the time the pot was in the making.

Edna St. Vincent Millay's volume, *The Buck in the Snow*, holding her poetry of human ideals and con-

troversy and her poetry about animals, expresses two
sharply contrasted moods—love of life and rebellion
that human life is not nobler. But love of life is the
stronger. Death is more conceivable to her now than
it was when she wrote *Second April* and expressed a
yearning for oblivion. She is beginning to believe, as
a very young person cannot believe (except with the
surface of the mind) that death will overtake her in
the end; and she recoils in horror at the anticipation
of that utter extinction. Like Donne or Mallarmé, like
Pascal or Amiel, she is fascinated by her own horror
of nothingness. It is relatively easy for her to say that
any suffering is preferable to nothingness, for, being
an Elizabethan in spirit, she has a zestful curiosity that
makes sharp suffering the next best thing after sharp
joy in this world. And so she writes,

> Life, were thy pains even as the pains of hell
> . . . .
> Yet must I cry, So be it; it is well.

This choice, for her temperament, is not hard. But in
Moriturus she has made a merciless analysis of life at
its lowest and most worthless ebb, ugly and senseless
as the wash of an old boot or an orange peel against
the sea sand, and even that seems to her to be worth
fighting for, so that she says in anticipation of her last
struggle with death:

> With all my might
>   My door shall be barred.
> I shall put up a fight,
>   I shall take it hard.
> With his hand on my mouth
>   He shall drag me forth,
> Shrieking to the south,
>   And clutching at the north.

197

It is principally this sense of the incredible and price-
less miracle of consciousness and physical sensation,
in a monstrously insensible universe, that makes her so
interested in wild animal life; for in the animal of the
forest, and especially in her favorite, the deer, life
seems to her to be experienced in its essence, without
the ugly conflicting desires, the ignoble twisting and
deforming of nature that make much of human life so
unheroic. And therefore with a feeling of finding the
first pure spring of a river which afterward has become defiled she looks at the wild deer. In the title
poem of her book, *The Buck in the Snow*, she sees in the
simplicity of such existence and in its extinction all
that she loves and dreads most in the world:

> How strange a thing is death, bringing to his knees,
>   bringing to his antlers
> The buck in the snow.
> How strange a thing—a mile away by now, it may be,
> Under the heavy hemlocks that as the moments pass
> Shift their loads a little, letting fall a feather of snow—
> Life, looking out attentive from the eyes of the doe.

In this volume Millay is searching much farther
back than the Old English times of *The King's Henchman*, trying to find the sources of what is good in our
human natures. She has gone as far back as the innocent animal life on the earth; and there, it seems to her,
we may make a fresh beginning of studying those bewildering and fascinating problems which make the
good and evil of human life.

X

FATAL INTERVIEW
Conversation with the Immortals

THE volume *Fatal Interview* is undated poetry. Save for the turns of twentieth-century speech it might have been written in the time of Shakespeare. Save for its sonnet conventions it might have been written in the time of Sappho. For it deals with the subjective states of a lover. Sappho, according to legend, for love and grief leaped from the Leucadian cliff. A modern girl, according to newspaper headlines, for love and grief leaps from an airplane. Is there much difference in their despair? Alcaeus might write of Sappho's love in a very different way from that in which Robinson Jeffers might write of a twentieth-century girl's passion, but to Sappho and to her inarticulate sister of today their plights probably looked much the same. However much objective poetry about love may differ from age to age, subjective love poetry, close to the heart of human impulse, throbs with the same systole and diastole always.

This timelessness of *Fatal Interview* worried reviewers, though it did not worry all of them for the same reason. One of them discovered an apparent divorce from the current events of the author's life. Literary insincerity glared from every line in the sequence, he averred, after his investigations had shown him that this poetry of reckless and troubled love and final

199

separation was written while the author was living quietly with a husband of eight years standing. . . . .

(At this point, Gentle Reader, Mr. Eugen Boissevain scratched a deeply bitten marginal comment on my manuscript to the effect that the assumption in the foregoing sentence was a lie. With a last gasp of deference to the opinions of Moses, I assumed that it was merely my adverb which was at fault—life with Miss Millay being notoriously disquieting. But I was not long allowed that casuistical refuge; and now, as it seems, the word of the Lord has come upon me, and I, all unwilling and unworthy, must be the first post-Victorian critic on record to state in cold print, in a book designed to stand on a family booksfelf, that a still breathing married woman, name and dates given, has written a poem of extra-marital passion, not as a literary exercise in purple penmanship, but as an honest record of immediate experience. But—who knows?—perhaps a Diogenes of the next century, waving his lantern in the dustbin of twentieth-century journalistic criticism, may impute it to me for righteousness.)

And now, after this bow to the facts of life, I should like to ask the carper against *Fatal Interview*'s sincerity what earthly difference it can make to a work of art whether it celebrates an event of the preceding hour or of twenty years ago? Too many reviewers of poetry, it seems to me, have started as newspaper reporters. News twenty-four hours old is dead; a sonnet celebrating an event that did not take place on the same day is to them, by analogy, insincere. By such logic surely the only sincere form of romantic art would be that recorded by the photographers whom Hollywood lovers bribe to follow them about the beaches, from embrace to impassioned embrace. A diary would hardly constitute sincere art, for a kiss would be ended before it was recorded. Long before *Fatal Interview* was published, however, Millay had made known her conviction that an emotion which does not sink deep enough in the heart to reach the timelessness of art is not worth recording. Moreover, within a sonnet sequence the "sincerity" of one violent emotion depends upon its relation to another violent emotion, just as in a portrait the sincerity of one line depends upon its relation to another. The extreme crest and trough of a passionate feeling come close to contradiction, and only an artist above and beyond them, able to see them together, to see the beginning and end, can make a unified and truthful whole of the two feelings. Ordinarily this requires time. But to say that rising above one's feelings in this way means that the feelings have become false is nonsense. The only way to rise above a feeling as a poet is to climb up through it. There is no possibility of cheating, not even by a Verlaine living in debauchery while he writes a delicate and perfect love lyric.

Other reviewers were worried about the divorce of *Fatal Interview* from the political problems of 1931. Having watched Millay march in the Sacco-Vanzetti parades, they had assumed that she would never again break lock step with current political and economic progress. Yet here, in the second year of the depression, appeared a book which revealed no awareness that stock markets had crashed, that banks were closing, that Republicans were looking apprehensive, that Democrats were looking anticipatory, that communists were looking smug. There was no mention of

technocracy in this book. Reviewers reminded Millay
that this was no time in which to behave as if romantic
feelings or personal feelings of any sort were worth
recording. In fact, a new literary school was beginning to deny that we have personal feelings any
more. All feelings in a modern society, whether we
realize it or not, are communal ones, they averred, and
literature henceforth must recognize this truth by
dealing with humanity in large blocks, as class units
rather than as individuals. A million sex-thwarted
women might make a respectable unit in a poem of
the future, but the distress of a single lovelorn one
would be silly and meaningless. Just why a million
ciphers should add up to more than nil is something
that the extremists of the new school have not made
altogether clear.

And still another reviewer, who had been anticipating something "snappy," in the style of *Figs from
Thistles*, leafed through this new book with a shrug,
and, becoming aware of a note of high seriousness,
instead of reading it, he yawned out his conviction that of all old joy, a twentieth-century love-
sonnet sequence is most boring. After all, one is
tempted to agree that, in the course of three millenna,
everything that can be said about love has been said.
And, yet, so long as the human mind, as well as the
human heart, is still awake, there is bound to be more
love poetry, as freshly thoughtful and as moving as
any written in the past. For passion, to the major
poet, is the heart of his restless and luminous searching of all the universe. As Middleton said in the
seventeenth century:

> Love has an intellect that runs through all
> The scrutinous sciences, and like a cunning poet

Catches a quantity of every knowledge,
Yet brings all home into one mystery.

In that sentence will remain a justification for a new sequence of love sonnets so long as men exist, surely, or at least so long as the most sensitive of them continue to think with passion and to feel with their intellect.

More than any sonnet sequence since Elizabethan times *Fatal Interview* is filled with subtle acknowledgment of what has been said about love by earlier poets. In a sense it may almost be called a daydream of conversation with the immortals. For to a greater degree than any of Millay's other books this is poetry of overtones. The phrases are not flute music, but violin singing, rich with the vibration of a thousand far-off memories of earlier utterances. And though it is not necessary to analyze a violin note in order to appreciate its timbre, yet I suppose that the artist who hears the overtones most distinctly loves the timbre of a Stradivarius the best. Likewise *Fatal Interview*, though it is far from being poetry exclusively for scholars, is, I think, enjoyed most by those scholars who know most intimately the poetry of the past and who hear, ringing high and clear above Millay's phrases, like horns out of fairyland, the phrases of Sappho and Ovid and Catullus. An illustrious throng seems to be gathered here: Sappho, Aeschylus, Euripides, Theocritus, Vergil, Ovid, Catullus, Chaucer, Sidney, Spenser, Greene, Peele, Shakespeare, Middleton, Dekker, Daniel, Ford, Drayton, Fletcher, Herrick. And a very few poets of more modern times appear here as well: Goethe, George Meredith, Hopkins, Emily Dickinson, Baudelaire, and Rimbaud.

If Millay were a mere borrower, this company would cheapen her, as it cheapens Longfellow to place his borrowed phrases beside their originals in Dante. Imitators usually reveal themselves by a finicking refinement in their use of a borrowed sentiment or by a stiffness in the rhythm of a borrowed phrase, like the jiggling rigidity of line in copies of great drawings. But Millay is not imitating earlier poets; she is merely holding her own in conversation with them. She might have said of this company, as she said of the mates of Zeus in her dream:

> Freely I moved among them and at ease,
> Addressing them, by them again addressed.

Not that there are any of the paraphernalia of imaginary conversations in this sonnet sequence. It is a subjective drama of passion, and nothing extraneous to the passion is allowed to obstruct the sonnets' onward sweep from mood to mood. One is in the central current of pure feeling from the first sonnet to the fifty-second. But in Millay's mind, impregnated by the poetry of past ages, great utterances of earlier poetry rise as if a voice were speaking, and she passionately replies—not with the "Indeed!" or "How true!" to which most of us are limited in our conversations with the mighty dead, but sometimes with half-assent, sweeping imperiously on to a new aspect of the idea, and quite as often with flat dissent, contradicting vehemently and eloquently. Often, speaking as a woman, she shows the obverse side of something that a male lover has said.

The title, *Fatal Interview*, taken from Donne's sixteenth elegy, might suggest that Millay's conversation is chiefly with Donne; and she does, in fact,

contradict him more often than she does any other
poet. It would be difficult for any poet of our day to
keep Donne out of his poetry altogether. One sees his
shadow in the writing of Rupert Brooke, T. S. Eliot,
Elinor Wylie, John Crowe Ransome, Herbert Read,
Aldous Huxley, Leonie Adams, and Sacheverell Sitwell, and his shadow's shadow in the imitators of
these people. T. S. Eliot traces Donne's influence on
the twentieth century to Dean Briggs's reading of him
to Harvard Freshmen from 1905 onward. But Dean
Briggs did not introduce Donne to Rupert Brooke in
Cambridge University, or to Gamaliel Bradford some
years before 1906. It was just time for appreciation of
him to revive. Our century loves thorny, tangled
poetry like that of Donne and Hopkins.

It seems to me that Millay admires Donne no more
than some of these other twentieth-century writers
do—perhaps less. She has an affinity with Donne's
honesty; like him, she exposes the noble and the
despicable elements in her nature with equal lack of
hesitation. She shares his obsession with sexual love.
She has something of his puzzlement over the relation
between the mind and the body. She has his occasional sardonic passion, fusing thought and sensation at white heat. But his grossness and his Gargan-
tuan exaggeration are not hers, nor his deliberate obscurity and distortion, nor his habit of speaking with
his tongue in his cheek and lifting an eyebrow if one
invariably takes his grand passions seriously. One
may find deep feelings beneath a jest in Millay; one
does not find in her, as so often in Donne, only a
sullen jest beneath a pretense of deep feeling. In fact,
I suspect that she is so continually aware of him
chiefly because he arouses an antagonism in her.

But let us look at the sonnets of *Fatal Interview* in order. It is impossible to indicate here more than a few of the myriad literary memories that ring through almost every line of the fifty-two sonnets, but perhaps an analysis of the first sonnet may give a hint of their nature.

The first sonnet reveals that sharp duality of the poet's nature which made Millay once describe herself as "a harlot and a nun." In other words she is, by spiritual inheritance, of Renaissance temperament— both a pagan and a puritan. From the fourteenth century onward poets in love have been troubled by two natures within themselves. The glory of the flesh and the austerity of otherworldliness have possessed them alternately. The more ardent their passion has been, the more apt they have been to end their expression of it with a recantation. One finds the mood in Chaucer, who, after writing one of the most sympathetic love stories in all literature, closes his *Troilus and Criseyde* with the appeal to "yonge fresshe folkes" in love:

> Repaireth hom from wordly vanyte,
> And of your herte up casteth the visage
> To thilke God, that after his ymage
> You made, and thynketh al nys but a faire,
> This world that passeth soon as floures faire.

Two centuries later Sidney was making the same sort of recantation of his *Astrophel and Stella* in his sonnet, "Leave me, O Love, that reachest but to dust," and Greene and Spenser and Donne and even Shakespeare were sometimes breaking off their celebration of love with an assertion of its vanity and its danger to the intellect or the soul.

Millay's first sonnet is, in a sense, an answer to such

retractions. She admits the reasonableness of them, but knowing the superiority of the life of pure ideality does not prevent her from choosing the other life. For, accentuating the reckless mood of the sequence, her praise of a better life comes not at the end but at the beginning of this experience of love. She has been living in the untroubled world of abiding glories, the world of Platonic ideas, of intellectual beauty. But now she is in danger of being dragged down by an earthly experience that will hold no abiding happiness. And though she cries, "Up, up, my feathers!" as Donne had cried, "Up, up, my drowsy soul!" she knows well enough what the end will be. She will not deceive herself with the hope that this new love will be more than a physical thing. Like Donne, she realizes how much mere chemistry has to do with love.

> I am a little world made cunningly
> Of elements,

Donne had said in accounting for his amorous feelings, and Millay, realizing that her lover is no more than such a combination of elements, ponders:

> What thing is this, that built of salt and lime
> And such dry motes as in the sunbeam show
> Has power upon me?

Like Donne, she knows how the body clogs the soul's flight upward. Donne had cried to God,

> No soul (whiles with the luggage of this clay
> It clogged is) can follow Thee half way.

Millay admits that bodily love "clogs" her flight. Also Spenser, as well as Donne, had seen the aspiring soul's danger in love:

> Drawn with sweet pleasure's bait, it back doth fly,
> And unto heaven forgets her former flight.

207

And Greene had reminded his Margaret of the superior glories of a spiritual life, concluding with the warning,

And shall thy plumes be pulled by Venus down?

But Millay, though still struggling, is already eager to make the sacrifice of her wings and "to journey barefoot with a mortal joy."

Obviously this opening sonnet, so vibrant with overtones of past poetry, is not a plagiarism. And obviously it is not a piece of marquetry, like Eliot's *Waste Land* and parts of Aiken's *John Deth* and of MacLeish's *Hamlet*. For Millay is not calling past poetry to mind in order to disparage herself or her age. She is conversing with past poets naïvely, not satirically, and with that rarest sort of naïveté that has survived learning and exposure to sophistication. Absorbing poetry of pure feeling, she has made another poem of pure feeling. And yet its originality is incontrovertible. Originality is proved by the way that a poem, like an arrow, flies straight to its goal. It is impossible to imitate that intense onward flight of a freshly inspired utterance. And the form of a Shakespearean sonnet puts original feeling to an especially severe test. Most modern sonnets on the Shakespearean model begin with a swift and promising phrase, but settle into a jog trot long before they reach the emphatic rhyme at the close. Even Shakespeare himself, in one or two sonnets, snapped off his concluding couplet with an air of "Oh, what the hell!" But this sonnet sweeps straight on to the close. The most poetic lines are not the opening ones; they are the question in the third quatrain:

What thing is this
That hastening headlong to a dusty end
Dare turn upon me those proud eyes of bliss?

"Dare" is the supremely poetic word there; and no thumbing of dictionaries or of poetry anthologies, nothing but a need in the heart could have found it. Read this sonnet beside the poems of Donne and Sidney and Spenser that enter into it, and it becomes not less, but more beautiful, as well as more peculiarly Millay's own. She seems to be within the sonnet in person; one sees the flushing of her "fierce and trivial brow" as she confronts these poets on their own ground, telling them that there is much to be said for the course they advocate, but that she, God help her, must take the other road.

In the second sonnet comes the revulsion from her choice, like that of Faustus as soon as his bargain with the devil is irrevocable. She has submitted, has thrown away intellectual freedom for the obsession of love, and even before there is a beginning she foresees the dreary end:

> This love, this longing, this oblivious thing
> That has me under as the last leaves fall
> Will glut, will sicken, will be gone by spring.

The imagery is that of Donne and Daniel and Shakespeare, but once more with a difference. Donne had said, rather vulgarly,

> But love us draws:
> He swallows us but never chaws.

Millay, in her revulsion, is ready to acknowledge love as such a gross and merely physical thing, but as a woman she denies that the experience can be so casual or so painless as Donne suggests. She says, on the contrary, that the wild beast, love, will not let her escape without deep and angry wounds. Nor will she practice that insincere Elizabethan flattery that mars so many sonnets, that pretense that the pain of a lover's desire is changeless. Daniel had said,

> When men shall find thy flower, thy glory pass . . . .
>
> . . . .
>
> Fresh shalt thou see in me the wounds thou madest.

Millay knows better; she strongly suspects that she will recover; but she also knows her life will be affected by the experience of ephemeral passion long after the wound has healed. After the lover has been forgotten, still

> The scar of this encounter like a sword
> Will lie between me and my troubled lord.

She is there, however, for once in complete agreement with Shakespeare, who spoke of the after-effect of love as

> The scar that will despite of cure remain.

In the third sonnet she quarrels outright with the "shrewd and wise" seventeenth-century poets who had laid down the rules for woman's behavior in love. They liked a woman to be sly and coy, even the best of them. Donne had told his mistress:

> Though love is got by chance, 'tis kept by art.

Milton had loved his Eve's

> Sweet, reluctant, amorous delay.

Shakespeare had shown all his heroines, even the inexperienced Juliet, aware of this preference of men. Each Shakespearean heroine is aware, as Cressida puts it, that

> If I confess much you will play the truant.

Millay proudly proclaims that these are not the rules by which she intends to play. She holds her honesty, her self-respect, dearer even than the attainment of

her desire. She will not stoop to lead her lover to believe that her "compass to another quarter veers."
She scorns such advice as Shakespeare's Cleopatra
might have given her:

> Little surrender, lavishly receive.

She proclaims her woman's nature as generous and
liberal, though Elizabethans did not like either adjec-
tive applied to women in their possession; and she proclaims her liberality in a metaphor that seemed gross
to Elizabethan poets, by identifying her nature with
that of the earth. Elizabethans had felt that even a
man was coarsened by comparison to the earth. Marlowe's hero-villain Tamburlaine, for instance, was
"gross and like the massy earth." And to make such
a comparison of a woman was felt to be an insult. The
Earl of Rochester cynically flaunted his mistress'
likeness to the "kind, seed-receiving earth." Donne
in his third elegy called a promiscuous woman a
"plough-land." And Dekker in *Northward Ho* char-
acterized a citizen's wife as entertaining her lovers "as
meadows do April." But Millay proudly acknowl-
edges her earth likeness, and she lifts the comparison
to blameless beauty:

> But being like my mother, the brown earth,
> Fervent and full of gifts and free from guile,
> Liefer I would you loved me for my worth,
> Though you should love me but a little while,
> Than for a philtre any doll can brew,
> Though thus I bound you as I long to do.

The next sonnet is far less fine. Few comparisons are
so hackneyed as the comparison of the beloved to a
physician; Chaucer and Spenser used it, and then it
passed into proverbial common speech. It is only Mil-

211

lay's peculiar honesty of accent and force of utterance that make the fourth sonnet, despite its commonplace imagery and its deliberate archaisms, her own. She is indisputably herself, even on the bed of lovesickness, for she is an exasperated invalid, not a listless one. The fifth sonnet likewise uses a stock comparison of the lover to a wretch pining in a dungeon. But no other poet uses the image with so much muscular energy, as if Samson himself were pent up and at any moment might

> Up with a terrible arm and out of here.

I do not know many lines with such a tiger spring in them as that one has.

A decidedly unpretty feminine mood is in the sixth sonnet, a mood that not one poetess in a million would acknowledge—the wish to scratch the self-esteem of the one who is ignoring her. But then throughout all the first nine sonnets, describing a love as yet unrequited, there runs a turbid current of noble and ignoble feelings such as no previous woman poet had been willing to acknowledge—a mingling of exasperation and impatience and even scorn for the object of her love, along with the worthier emotions of worship and despair. Thus in the third sonnet she bolsters up her vanity with the perennial boast of the disappointed woman, "I could have him if I would stoop to take him." And in the seventh sonnet she taunts the unresponsive man with his prudence, with basking in the orderliness of a life that will not admit the wild irregularity of passion:

> Small chance, however, in a storm so black
> A man will leave his friendly fire and snug
> For a drowned woman's sake, and bring her back
> To drip and scatter shells upon the rug.

212

And in the tenth sonnet she exhibits that terrible
feminine relentlessness in pursuit that has urged many
a man to the ignominious flight of a scared jackrabbit.
She will never give up the chase, she intimates, not
even when they are both dust upon the wind. Donne
had analyzed the ugly aspects of masculine moods in
this pitiless fashion, but only Millay (until she set a
fashion for other poets) made such a ruthless analysis
of feminine moods.

In the sixth sonnet she is making a charge peculiarly
wounding to masculine vanity. She is taunting the indifferent and scholarly loved one with finding it safer
to be in love with the women of past literature than
with her. This preference of his amounts to what
Byron would have called "a mild old-gentlemanly
vice"—this "pale preoccupation with the dead," as
Millay calls it. It indicates, she insinuates, a lack of
virility, a nature unequal to the ardors of a living
woman. She taunts him with the solicitation:

> Call Cressid, call Elaine, call Iseult in!
> More bland the ichor of a ghost should run
> Along your dubious veins than the rude sea
> Of passion pounding all day long in me!

How can such a mood make fine poetry? It is spite-
ful, it is petty, it is coarse. And yet it is none of these
things, because the ugly mood is crossed with tenderness and humor. The unwilling, exasperated outburst
of tenderness in the epithet "egregious boy" cancels
all the gloating bitterness from her prophecy of a time
when he will be wasted with age, amorous but impotent. The surface of the feeling is flippant and spite-
ful, but its depth is earnestly passionate, even com-
passionate. Here is the same irony of mood as that
revealed in Donne's *The Dream*, a poem in which

Donne, like Millay's egregious boy, chooses a phantom mistress instead of a real one. It seems that Donne makes his choice of a mere dream cynically, callously, grossly (or, if you will, with a priggish idealism), until there comes the (as if were) involuntary revelation of his agony of thwarted love for a real woman. For he suddenly breaks out with the cry,

> And so I scape the pain, *for pain is true*.[1]

Irony is one of the greatest of poetic qualities and one of the least imitable. Poetasters may insist and insist upon their feeling until, perhaps, the reader consents to believe in it "for their much speaking." But only a genuine and fine poet can insist and insist upon a mood until the reader suddenly sees that it is no more than a surface covering a deeper mood which the poet is unwilling to speak out. So here, in Millay's sixth sonnet, the surface mood of spite struggling with humor and an almost tearful tenderness suddenly, in the last line, seems to be torn apart like fog upon the wind, revealing a stormy depth of elemental feeling like something in Webster or Shakespeare:

> the rude sea
> Of passion pounding all day long in me.

The eighth sonnet, likewise, expresses a surface mood of hostility. It transposes the Elizabethan prophecy of virginity yielding to deflowering death (familiar in Shakespeare, Middleton, and Marvell and many poets since their day). The earth that resembles her own nature will one day take possession of the man she loves, Millay says. With a sort of triumph she anticipates the day when the earth will break

---

[1] The italics are mine.

through the coffin lid covering the beloved's face, and he will endure

> That shameful kiss by more than night obscured
> Wherewith at length the scornfullest mouth is met.

But the despair and horror of the undermood are plain enough throughout.

The greatest virtue of this sonnet is, it seems to me, the contrast expressed in the lines,

> While the blood roars, or when the blood is rust
> About a broken engine. . . . .

It would be hard to match that metaphor with another modern one as magnificent. Poetry holds no more than a half-dozen fine metaphors based on the inventions of our machine age. Writers today have been urged and reurged to such modernity of expression, and heaven knows they have struggled and experimented. Many a writer has stared at a roaring automobile engine and has stared at a junked automobile and has racked his brain for imagery based on either of them. But he has not seen this image of life and death. Such a vision as this one—the vision of a human heart stopped forever and the blood dried in the veins—is something that is not accomplished merely by struggling for modernity.

Only a poet capable of such powerful originality of imagery would have dared to write the next sonnet, taking up the most tiresomely reiterated, the most hackneyed, the most hopelessly depleted of all figures of speech—the comparison of eyes to stars. Millay loves to show defiant loyalty to the rags of outworn literary expression, whenever they incur the critic's scorn. She often snatches up a metaphor that has become a cliché and is passionately tender toward it, as

215

toward a doll with its nose worn off. Such childlike eager affection would give morning freshness to the use of any metaphor. And indeed it is an impertinence for a critic to say of any metaphor that it has become too jaded for further employment. To a strong imagination a metaphor is not an ingenious device to express a feeling. It *is* the feeling. One feels, in Dickens, how utterly impossible it would have been for him to change his metaphors. If he saw a man like an afternoon shadow of someone else, then an afternoon shadow of someone else he was; and Dickens was helpless as a four-year-old to make his imagination picture the man in other terms. So it is with Millay in this ninth sonnet. She sees her lover's eyes as stars, and the mere fact that several million eyes since Laura's and Juliet's have been compared to stars does not make her lover's any less starlike. And so, by some miracle, this sonnet is as if no other had ever been written, and those disturbing eyes with their stormy lashes become unlike any others in the world. I know of only one finer pair of eyes in all of English literature—those that Dekker describes as shining "as if this deity had with a look created a new world."

The first turn in the sequence comes with the next two sonnets, which are betrothal poems. One of them expresses a mood like that of Chaucer's Criseyde or of Elizabeth Barrett—a sense of shame at seeing her beloved yield to love for her. "For pure ashamed" Criseyde "gan in her head to pull" through the window, lest Troilus, passing by, should see her—so unworthy did she feel to arouse the love of so glittering a youth. And Elizabeth Barrett struggled against allowing Browning to lower himself, as it seemed to her, by giving his love to so poor an object as herself. It is characteristic of Millay that she does not pull in her head like Criseyde or nobly refuse the first offer of her happiness like Elizabeth Barrett. For, as she says, she is

> teased by shame and care
> That beauty should be brought to terms by me;
> Yet shamed the more that in my heart I know
> Cry as I may, I could not let you go.

It is a less noble mood than Elizabeth Barrett's, and I do not believe that it is a bit more sincere than hers. But it is undeniably more vigorous. And how convincing it is!

The other betrothal sonnet is a subtly feminized variant of Donne's *The Token*, in which he asked for a pledge of love rather than for a ring or a coral as a love token. Millay deprecates a wish for a pledge of any sort. Pledges of love are a trap, she says. They are like Renaissance jewels, so often ingeniously contrived to carry poison—jewels that carry the inscription

> *Semper fidelis*, where a hidden spring
> Kennels a drop of mischief for the brain.

Her love, on the contrary, shall be simple and untroubled about the morrow as the loves in Theocritean idylls, wherein a girl playfully pelts her favorite goatherd with small apples, or he proudly makes a present to her of ten large ones. Millay says:

> Love in the open hand, no thing but that,
> Ungemmed, unhidden, wishing not to hurt,
> As one should bring you cowslips in a hat
> Swung from the hand, or apples in her skirt
> I bring you, calling out as children do,
> "Look what I have!—And these are all for you."

As in most of her poetry, it is the contrast that gives this sonnet its living and earnest force. The lavishness

217

and duplicity of the Renaissance, suggested by the pearled casket filled with rubies and sapphires and subtle poisons, is set against the fresh air of Sicilian orchards and meadows, suggested by the cowslips and apples of the sestet. And there is another contrast. A very modern woman is uttering very emancipated speech here, and yet the tone of the speech recalls to the mind the legendary youth of the world. It is another instance of poetic irony.

Then comes the consummation of passion, in a sonnet which might be called a pagan Magnificat. In it there is the glory and defiance of accomplishment, as in the cry of Donne's (and after him Brooke's) lovers: "Who is so safe as we?" Yet Millay does not remind me of Donne here so much as of Fletcher. She is like the gaoler's daughter in *Two Noble Kinsmen*, who, after her long anxiety over her lover, burst out with the exultant cry of relief,

> Let all the dukes and all the devils roar!
> He is at liberty!

For in the same extremity of exultation Millay cries to heaven:

> Call out your golden hordes, the harm is done:
> Enraptured in his great embrace I lie!

Her lover becomes, to her enkindled imagination, Jove himself. And un-Vergilian as the ecstatic mood is, yet the conception of the sonnet comes from the *Aeneid*. It is the Jove of Vergil "with that look that calms the sky and quiets the tempest" whose likeness she expects to give to her son—that son who will never be frightened by display

> Of blackened moons or suns or the big sound
> Of sudden thunder on a silent day.

218

That, surely, is the same son who is addressed in the *Aeneid:*

> Nate, patris summi qui tela Typhoia temnis.

I have said that the sonnet is un-Vergilian in mood, but that is not true of the fine concluding couplet, which, in contrast with the delirious excitement of the opening lines, holds Vergil's mood of sad and noble serenity. The poet prophesies of her son,

> Pain and compassion shall he know, being mine,—
> Confusion never, that is half divine.

The next sonnet, the aubade, is far below this level. The shortness of a lover's night has been commented on by Ovid, by Chaucer, by Donne, and, of course, above all by Shakespeare in *Romeo and Juliet*. This is a good sonnet, but one would not care to place Millay's words besides Juliet's. And I, for one, do not like the sonnet after it, which tortures the same conceit that Donne used in *The Paradox*, in *A Nocturnal upon St. Lucy's Day*, and in *The Computation*. It is the conceit that, since the lover is dying of love now, he is forever secure from physical death. I hate that sort of tortured elaboration of a hyperbole, whether it be in Donne or in Millay. I much prefer honest old Thomas Middleton's straightforward expression of love's mood on too early rising:

> 'Tis even a second hell to part from pleasure
> When man has got a smack on't.

The following sonnet, the fifteenth, is the one poem that Millay has ever published that is not crystal clear. Or perhaps it is clear to other readers. But though I do not understand the logic of its conclusion, I admire the sonnet for its octave, with the beautiful

219

stir of all those *r*'s running through it, like the light morning stir of air through the Idalian groves of Venus. Vergil is very close to Millay's thought in this sonnet about Venus and Cupid. Very fine, I think, is her phrase "the inquiring dawn," rendering so briefly the feeling of Vergil's apostrophe, "O thou sun who bringest all deeds of the earth into daylight!"

In the sixteenth sonnet the consummated love is still in its first exultation, possessing her so utterly that it erases all her earlier prescience of its end. It controls even the irresponsible phantasms of dream. Not even in the depths of sleep is there, as yet, any cold ocean current of foreboding. Sleep can carry her only to Elysium, or to the windless flowery meadows where Chaucer met the "good women" of his dream; and there Millay greets the women loved by Jove and walks with them as their peer, since no honor of Olympus could dignify them more than to be loved by the man who has taken her.

But in the next sonnet the first tidal wall of passion crashes, and in the forlornness of recoil she finds that love holds

How sharp an anguish, even at the best!

The metaphor of the sonnet is as old as Aeschylus, who spoke of "love's flower that stings the heart," and I suppose that the mood of the woman is older, as like a shocked child she sobs that, had she known what this hurt would be, she would not have

so come running at the call
Of one who loves me little, if at all.

And now she is left at the mercy of the antagonism between the two sides of her nature. Now reciprocated passion has lost its first innocence of utter single-

heartedness, and one part of her must henceforth cold-
ly deprecate the irrational recklessness of the rest of
her. (How much of the poetry of our day is a debate
within the self!) In this nineteenth sonnet the quarrel
within herself is, true to human nature, projected as a
quarrel with a friend. The sonnet reminds us of Sidney, who in his *Astrophel and Stella* recounted an
argument with a friend who was pointing out the
perilous folly of his infatuation with Stella. Sidney
met his friend's reproofs with a good-natured acknowledgment of their reasonableness and his own
incorrigibility. He expressed ironical gratitude for the
advice:

> Sure you say well; your wisdom's golden mine
> Dig deep with learning's spade. Now tell me this,
> Hath this world aught so fair as Stella is?

But Millay lets her reproving friend's words sink
farther into her heart, deeper than humor. Yet the re-
proof has no more effect on her than on Sidney, for,
however tragic the consequences of her plight may
be, she feels as helpless to evade her fate as to evade
death itself. With prescient and disillusioned eyes she
must watch the course of her self-destruction.

And yet in the next sonnet (the twentieth) she
reaches, for the moment at least, a high and shining
peace with herself. She catches the conviction that
Plato expressed in his *Phaedrus*—that the lover is
really in love with abstract beauty, and that one must
never expect it to yield content and safety since ideal
beauty cannot love its imperfect human lover. It is the
same idea expressed in Christian terms by Spinoza:
"He who loves God rightly must not desire God to
love him in return." Millay sternly tells herself, in
this spirit:

Beauty, above all feathers that have flown,
Is free; you shall not hood her to your wrist

. . . .

She loves you not. She never heard of love.

Technically I admire this sonnet for its cleanness of execution, its articulateness of utterance, as in the distinction made between thinking and merely letting the mind "doze" upon a thought. It is the same distinction that T. S. Eliot makes between living belief and that which is "believed in memory only, reconsidered passion."

And still more I admire the sonnet for its solution of the problem of presenting all of an elaborate picture to the mind simultaneously, instead of bit by bit. In these days when *Gestalt* psychology is so popular, poets are very much concerned over the inevitable falsification of experience by its report in language. A report of an experience ought to come all at once, they feel, like the snapping-up of a window shade, revealing a varied landscape. But instead, in poetry, an experience or picture is presented to the mind bit by bit, detail after detail, until one has in the end not so much a vision as a catalogue. There must be some way, poets are telling themselves, of overcoming the difficulty that language is an utterance of one tiny part of an idea after another. They are trying to force poetry to enter the mind as a whole, not as a succession of parts. This was what Lessing, in the *Laocoön*, had said literature, as one of the temporal arts, could not do. This was what Gerard Manley Hopkins, fifty years ago, was determined to prove that it could do. The wish to present an idea so that it would, as Hopkins said, "explode" all at once in the reader's consciousness was what led him to juggle English gram-

222

mar and sentence order so shamelessly in his poetry. If the reader could be led to memorize the words of a poem before he understood them, then, Hopkins felt, he might latter experience the glory of sudden and startlingly complete illumination, which was to Hopkins the most poetic of all experiences. Ever since twentieth-century poets became aware of Hopkins, a good many of them have been struggling with his theory and method, with, to my mind, deplorable results. And though Millay is so out of sympathy with obscurantism, she too seems to have had Hopkins' method in mind as she made this twentieth sonnet. She has refused to jumble grammar; she has refused to be deliberately obscure or to hold back her meaning from the reader on a first perusal. And yet, in the second quatrain of this sonnet she achieves the same effect that Hopkins occasionally achieves, of exultant surprise:

> If, in the moonlight from the silent bough
> Suddenly with precision speak your name
> The nightingale. . . . .

When one reaches that word, "nightingale," suddenly the moonlight, the woodland, the articulate syllables issuing from the shadowed tree flower into unsuspected beauty. If Hopkins' influence always worked so musically and purely as in that clause, English and American literature would be in a better condition than it is in at present.

Now comes the next turn in the sequence, as the lovers are separated, and then recklessly rush together again under conditions of turbulence and danger. In the twenty-first sonnet the beloved one is gone from her; and her forlornness persists in her most satisfying sleep. Even her most wishful dreams are permeated by the sense of loss. Like the sixteenth and the thirty-third sonnets, this sonnet is pure dream. . . . . English poetry has never caught the quality of dream very well, except in Poe and Coleridge and in Elizabethan nightmares; and even in them the pictures are too elaborate to convince a psychologist. Uncompromising morning sunlight is likely to pour down on Chaucer in his dreams, and other medieval poets' dreams are such as no man ever dreamed on land or sea, I am fairly sure. Nineteenth-century French poetry, after Poe, reports dreams much better, for it is content with tenuous and shifting suggestions of ideas, relinquished before they enter the waking world by becoming clear.

In the twentieth century most writers are decidedly self-conscious about dreaming. Edith Sitwell catches the quality of dream marvelously in a few lines of her *Sleeping Beauty*, but most other English poets of today, for all their efforts, succeed no better in expressing dreams than their literary forbears did. In fact, I think they generally fail more completely than earlier English poets failed, because poets of today are either abashed or brazened by Freudian interpretations of dream. Millay, however, refuses to be either intimidated or coarsened by all the psychological dream books. If Freudian symbols appear in her dreams and the dreams are exquisitely lovely, she will present them as something exquisite, and not with the leer of someone showing an obscene post card. The result is the tenuous dream quality, as of "fairylands forlorn," in this twenty-first sonnet. Freud would probably recognize it as an authentic erotic dream, but that does not make it a whit less delicate in its loveliness:

224

To that pavilion the green sea in flood
   Curves in, and the slow dancers dance in foam;
I find again the pink camellia-bud
   On the wide step beside a silver comb. . . . .
But it is scentless; up the marble stair
I mount with pain, knowing you are not there.

Seldom have vowels and consonants constricted and loosened to the nuances of the mood more subtly than in that sonnet.

If that sonnet is not in the English tradition, the next one is extremely like Elizabethan poetry in its exasperation of thwarted and reckless passion. A scholar might think of it as a mosaic of the outcries against continence in Donne, Daniel, Shakespeare, Fletcher, and Ford, save that the headlong rush of determination through it makes "mosaic" an absurdly incongruous word to apply to it. It is fascinating to trace a parallel for almost every phrase of the sonnet in the poetry of the Elizabethans and of Ovid and Catullus, and then to read it again to catch that onrush of peculiarly Millayan vehemence, straight on to its determined close,

Before this moon shall darken, say of me,
She's in her grave, or where she wants to be.

As for its morals, it is a passionate subscription to the moral code of Santayana, who once declared, "It is the charm and safety of virtue that it is more natural than vice, but many moralists do their best to deprive it of this advantage."

Equally vehement is the twenty-fourth sonnet with its tremendous metaphor of a puny human being shaking disaster like a tree whose fruits one is determined to have. There is vehemence in the Elizabethan paradox of being "lulled by the uproar" as she waits for the end of the hurly-burly she has caused, when she will learn whether she is to be hell's mistress or her own. It is in keeping with the imperious tone of the whole sequence that she does not doubt that she will be mistress, even in hell. Nothing could be farther from the tone of most poetry of the late 1920's, in which poets were watching their dubious personalities drift apart like smoke.

The next sonnet continues to deal with that glorying in danger which was typical of Elizabethan men, but which they prohibited to women. If *Peril upon the Paths of This Desire* is not more beautiful than the earlier poetry that it answers, it is only because nothing could be more beautiful than Donne's sixteenth elegy, with its prohibition:

> By our first strange and fatal interview
> Thou shalt not love by ways so dangerous.

The more dangerous the ways, the greater her exultation in following them, Millay replies. To express the danger she uses the shadow imagery of Shakespeare's line,

> Love thrives not in the heart that shadows dreadeth;

and the fearful ecstasy of the reckless lover she symbolizes by her picture of a little girl abroad in a dark and dewy garden. One can feel the dew on those blackened roses, as one can feel the dew in the Elizabethan Davenant's poetry.

When the next sonnet appeared on the first page of Harriet Monroe's *Poetry*, its egotism annoyed many people very much. The statement that only women in past ages were worthy to stand beside Millay as lovers shocked most women, especially, with its arrogance. It would not have shocked the Elizabethans. Sidney,

Drayton, and Donne all disparaged their obtuse and weakly times, in which they alone, they declared, paid that worship to beauty that was paid to it in past ages. Despite the arrogance of this sonnet, the passion is convincing, the love which Millay says she carries "like a burning city" in her breast. (The Helen legend is not dead so long as such a simile can be made.) It is interesting to place the poem beside the conviction which a leading critic expressed in the year *Fatal Interview* appeared, that no one in our day is capable of feeling the passions that swept through the major poets of past times.

Then the love begins to root itself more tenaciously in the flesh and comes to seem more exclusively a physical thing. And at first this leads to a pagan exultation in passion recalling Catullus and Ovid. As Catullus adjured his lovers, "*Munere assidue valentem exercete iuventam*," so this poet counsels her lover to behave so that, when the last embers of their passionate nature are burnt out, their solace may be

> that it was not said
> When we were young and warm and in our prime,
> Upon our couch we lay as lie the dead,
> Sleeping away the unreturning time.

And then comes a reply to another argument like that in Donne's "Fatal Interview" elegy, which had held the warning:

> Thy (else almighty) beauty cannot move
> Rage from the seas, nor thy love teach them love,
> Nor tame wild Boreas' harshness.

In her reply Millay is most reasonable in her unreasonableness. Love, she admits, is not all of life. She agrees to Donne's reminders of the frightfulness of

227

overwhelming seas and winter storms upon the roof-less. There is much in life that she might some time hold so dear as to forfeit love, in extremity, for it, she admits. But then, after all the reasonable admissions are made, strangely potent and convincing is her stubborn conclusion:

It well may be. I do not think I would.

After all, there is nothing like a good old Anglo-Saxon understatement to convince one of reserve power.

With the thirty-first and thirty-second sonnets the love is at a standstill. The tide is full, and it must turn. One knows it because of the too extravagant claims for permanence that she is making for this same love which, before it had well commenced, she had prophesied would end "before the flickers mate." And then, in the thirty-third sonnet, comes the first foreshadowing of the end—not because of a quarrel, not because of any event of her waking hours, but because foreboding seems to be welling up out of the depths of her subconsciousness, in "sorrowful dreams remembered after waking."

Like any hero of Greek or Elizabethan tragedy, she will fight against necessity, however. In the next sonnet there is protest against putting fears into language, lest the power of the spoken word give them added force. Here a very modern pragmatic philosophy is expressed in medieval imagery. It is as if William James were speaking in terms of the quaint personifications that early English poets were so fond of. The genealogy and feudal rank of those enemies of love—Doubt, Time, Death, and Despair—are given with medieval exactitude. But the sonnet is not

slowed or weakened by this artifice. It is another of
the tremendously muscular sonnets, and it is filled,
moreover, with a zest for battle. It is odd but natural,
I suppose, that passionate pacifists should have a warlike temperament. This sonnet, like so many of her
poems, shows Millay violently excited by war imagery. Perhaps Freud would say that it is a compromise
with her conscious censor, however, that leads her
almost invariably to depict the glories of battle in
archaic terms, as here.

Another equally muscular sonnet is the thirty-sixth,
but here another protest against speaking out doubts
of continued love is expressed not through medieval
imagery, but through memories of the powerful winds
of the Maine seacoast and of the stubborn, strong
women whom Edna St. Vincent Millay knew in her
childhood, living the bleak lives of fishermen's wives
on the island of Matinicus. She writes of her New
England memories, however, as the Elizabethan,
John Webster, might have written of them, had he
known them. She reminds me, in her imagery, of
Webster's Vittoria, who had cried to her accusers,

> For your names
> Of whore and murderess, they proceed from you
> As if a man should spit against the wind;
> The filth returns in's face.

But the literary reminiscence does not weaken the
force of Millay's protest against her lover's doubts of
her. As they stand in the same wind which she knows
is beating against the strong bodies of those women on
the Maine coast, she cries,

> The wind of their endurance, driving south,
> Flattened your words against your speaking mouth.

With the thirty-eighth sonnet begins the final break between the lovers. That sonnet is modern both in idea and in expression, as it holds a protest against her lover's rationalizing his impulse to leave her. The thirty-ninth is all Elizabethan, however, with the fresh homeliness of George Peele in its comparisons. Peele had said of a girl, "She is to my age as smoke to the eyes, or as vinegar to the teeth." Millay's imagery is her own, but it comes from the same world. She says she knows her unwelcome kisses are

> sand against your mouth,
> Teeth in your palm and pennies on your eyes.

And also the feeling of *Two Noble Kinsmen* strangely permeates this sonnet, as it does so much of Millay's poetry. The "dim trotting shapes" that she fears if she is left to face old age alone have the same mysterious terror in them as the shapes that the gaoler's daughter fears surround her lover in the dark forest— "fell things, that have in them a sense to know a man unarmed, and can smell where resistance is."

In the fortieth sonnet Millay is cursing heaven and earth and hell in considerable detail, not forgetting even "all the children getting dressed for school." One can hear the voice timbre in those curses. They are as human and convincing as Troilus' equally scattered curses when he lost Criseyde. They prove, as Shakespeare observed, that

> True grief is fond and testy as a child.

Such mixed and homely human moods are a relief after the too angelic endurance of heartbreak to which poetry became accustomed in the nineteenth century.

But the first violent despair and determination to

end all are not the worst of the suffering. There follow the days of sick suspense even after hope is gone, the unwelcome and inevitable protraction of love's death agony, filling one with horrified impatience for the end. The ugliness and pitiableness of the last state threaten to cancel the beauty of all that went before, for the passion is now like a desperately wounded bird, and the poet groans,

> O ailing Love, compose your struggling wing!
> Confess you mortal; be content to die.
> How better dead, than be this awkward thing
> Dragging in dust its feathers of the sky,
> Hitching, and rearing, plunging beak to loam,
> Upturned, disheveled . . . .

At long last there comes finality in the separation. And then there follows that always unexpected intolerableness of loud, insistent, meaningless everyday life and hackneyed people beating in upon one's exhaustion and deranging

> A will too sick to battle for repose.

And still, gradually, in not the least poetic part of the sequence, there comes the quietude of resignation and retrospection, reaching an almost ineffable mood of exaltation in the final poem. In one of the most exquisite sonnets in English poetry the poet turns, from the hot personal grief that she has been expressing, to meditation of almost classic objectivity. It is clear enough, however, that the poem is an allegory of this love whose course she has described; it is an expression of resignation to death, which will bring peace after heartbreak.

The sonnet is addressed to Endymion, and it is

reminiscent not of the Endymion of Keats or of Lyly, but of Theocritus. "Blessed, I think, is the lot of him that sleeps, and tosses not, nor turns, even Endymion," Theocritus said in one of his idylls. In this mood of Theocritus, Millay offers her pity not to Endymion, but to the moon, who has not the privilege of dying of a mortal love.

It is almost as astounding to have written a fresh sonnet to the moon as to have written a fresh sonnet about starry eyes. After the classical poets, after the Elizabethans, after Keats, it would seem effrontery to attempt a poem on that subject. Twentieth-century poets have revived a fashion of writing of the moon as insane, to be sure, but they have relied upon the ugliness of modern psychopathic description to redeem the new poetry from pale plagiarism. Such a hideously demented moon one finds in T. S. Eliot and in Evelyn Scott, for instance. But Millay's moon is mad as a goddess might become mad, with no loss of divine grace. What future generations will think of this sonnet, I cannot guess, but I can read it beside any of the other poems that have been written about the moon and like it best of all. The eerie quality of cloud-dappled moonlight on a windy night by the sea is evoked here so magically that one is scarcely aware that words are the source of the vision, and the picture of the wavering, distracted moonlight is so shot through with the tragic mood of heartbreak that it seems unthinkable that the feeling could have been expressed in other terms. And there can be no more intensely poetic contrast anywhere in literature than in the phrase fusing the climax of frantic human passion with the inhuman and intangible essence of light, which has been all poets' most persistent symbol of ideality. Thus the poet says that Endymion clasped his love

> And deep into her crystal body poured
> The hot and sorrowful sweetness of the dust.

The sonnet is a triumphant close for a sequence in whose course Millay has (whether consciously or unsciously I do not know) challenged comparison with much of the greatest poetry that has ever been written.

XI

WINE FROM THESE GRAPES
In a Time of Foreboding

FASHIONS are fickle and verse is vertiginous nowadays. During the early 1930's it has been the fashion to write poetry in the compressed telegraphic esperanto that was forced upon Russian poets by a paper shortage and was then imitated by communist poets and their admirers everywhere, especially in England and America. Just before the Russian influence it was the fashion to string together excerpts from the classics to make a satirical commentary on our times. A few years earlier the most fashionable poets were moaning and groaning in the latest jazz rhythms and slang. Before that they were jotting down unpunctuated ejaculations of drunken exultation; and before that they were artificially isolating single sensations in seventeen-syllabled "hokkus" or five-lined poems of free verse. Scarcely one in a hundred poets has been immune from the torturing self-doubt that seems to have instigated this headlong rush from one style to another.

During these dizzy years Millay's style has changed a little, but only as an orchestra changes if it is gradually augmented by new instruments and becomes capable, through long practice, of bravura development of its old style. Millay's fundamental simplicity and clarity remain unchanged. If her 1934 volume had been published anonymously, few readers would have failed, I suppose, to recognize the poet who wrote

Renascence, more than twenty years before. She uses the same simple Elizabethan New England speech as when she was eighteen. The first glance at the opening poem in *Wine from These Grapes* reveals the homeliness and purity of her speech still:

> Earth cannot count the sons she bore;
>   The wounded lynx, the wounded man
> Come trailing blood unto her door;
>   She shelters both as best she can.

No less than when she was eighteen, she feels a child-like animistic sympathy with natural forces and growths; she sees

> the great lightning, plunging by,
> Look sidewise with a golden eye;

she sees earth's envelope of air as

> Whirling Aeolus on his awful wheel;

and she sees the aged and decaying tree

> Crawl in beside the root to sleep.

She has the same muscularity, the same intense awareness of tactual sensation as when she was in her teens; she still conceives of man as a feeler and a struggler:

> him, him bereaven
> Of all save the heart's knocking and to feel
> The air upon his face, not the great heel
> Of headless Force into the dust has driven.

And she is still hungry for the meaning of the world; she is still reaching out for simplicity and synthesis in human life, though less hopefully than at first, for she is becoming convinced that

> Man, by all the wheels of heaven unscored,
>   Man, the stout ego, the exuberant mind
> No edge could cleave, no acid could consume,
>   Being split along the vein by his own kind
> Gives over, rolls upon the palm abhorred,
> Is set in brass on the swart thumb of Doom.

Yet despite the fundamental oneness of her latest volume and her first, there are traces of the changing times on her poetry. She has assimilated the most recent developments of scientific experiment and theory. For instance, she refers to the indeterminism of the movements of electrons, translating this indeterminism into poetry by calling the atom an "ambiguous room." It is impossible, she says,

> To bind to truce in this ambiguous room
> The planets of the atoms as they ply.

And new theories of psychology she has assimilated also. No longer, as in one of her earliest poems, does she hold to Wordsworth's doctrine that a child possesses fading memories of his pre-existence in an "imperial palace." Rather (with irony in her phrasing so closely paralleling Wordsworth's) she now says the child slowly

> Forgets the *watery darkness* whence he came.[1]

And though she seldom speaks of the mechanics of our age, yet more poetically than the young "machinist" group of poets she refers to aviation, speaking

> Of Man, who when his destiny was high
> Strode like the sun into the middle sky
> And shone an hour, and who so bright as he,
> And like the sun went down into the sea,[2]
> Leaving no spark to be remembered by.

And she hits off our world of bond issues and formulas, of purses and print, of "painted nails and shaven arm-

---

[1] The italics are mine.

[2] The cadence of this line shows how Coleridge's *Ancient Mariner* still haunts her memory, no less than when she wrote *Renascence*.

236

pits." She speaks of chemical manufactures, of explosives made from "the bewildered ammonia and the distracted cellulose." And she imitates, in the *Apostrophe to Man*, the dry and staccato speech of the big-business man, intent upon increasing his fortune by a second World War. In a few strokes she has drawn a sharp picture of our world of the 1930's. Yet she has kept these shifting superficialities of human life in their proper subordinate place.

The chief technical change in her poetry has been a steady development in the direction of a rhymed free verse. During the vogue of free verse, from 1912 to 1922, Millay did not use it at all. She never subscribed to the naïve theory that absolute prosodic anarchy would result in dropping into magnificent rhythms by accident. Instead, she has worked toward her own distinctive free verse through modulations of ballad meter, of iambic pentameter, and of the Pindaric ode. In her first volumes she revealed more variety in simple ballad meter than most of her contemporaries were revealing in all the license of free verse. It is amazing how many changes she rings on ballad meter by subtle variations of rhyming, by deferred or hastened accent, by shifted caesuras.

From the time she was a child Millay has been fond of setting two accents together, not as a spondee, but as two feet, and out of that simple trick of *Mother Goose* have developed the most distinctive qualities of her prosody. Later, her study of Old English for *The King's Henchman* taught her to take liberties in grouping unstressed syllables together; and the result has been her discovery of a big, pounding line, already much imitated, and as expressive of our century as the tight decasyllables of Pope are of the eighteenth. Old

237

English freedom and force of accent, in a longer and more harmonious line than the Old English one, seem to express perfectly our nervous and noisy and yet spacious and aspiring time. Archibald MacLeish is her most inspired follower in using this new, freely accented line, with strong stresses like a double pillar in the center. It is a powerful line, and the two poets make a tremendous and exciting new music with it.

It is interesting to watch Millay's growing freedom in the handling of pentameter, in particular. A line about the skylark,

> And that high wing, untouchable, untainted,

is characteristic of her, for though it is possible to scan it as regular iambic pentameter, all its pulsing music is ruined by so doing. Rather, the first four syllables make three feet, the fifth foot is amphibrachic, and the fourth foot is one for which conventional prosody has no name. With the accents thus distributed,

> And thát high wíng, untóuchable, untaínted,

one feels her skylark actually soaring and sallying up into the sky. And then, of course, there are little sub-accents on the two *un* syllables. Millay's poetry really needs a whole new system of prosody, taking account of major and minor accents, of retarded and accelerated syllables, and of long and short pauses. A further liberty with pentameter is in the lines,

> Nów goes únder the sún, and I watch it go únder.
> Farewéll, sweét líght, greát wónder,

wherein each line has five accents, although the first has thirteen syllables and the second only seven. But

238

the slow musing on each syllable in the second line
makes it as long in time as the other line.

Sometimes Millay gives an effect of spaciousness to
pentameter by a double stress before a pause, as in

On the wíde heáth, at évening óvertáken.

Something of the same effect of space is in the first
part of another line,

Dówn, dówn, dówn, into the dárkness of the gráve,

in contrast with the second half of the line, wherein
the clusters of many unaccented syllables give an
effect of fumbling bewilderment. But she gets many
different effects with clusters of unaccented syllables.
With the many *f*'s and *r*'s and *th*'s a fine feeling of
fluffiness is given to one line by the many unaccented
syllables;

Cómfort, sófter than the feáthers of its breást,

sounds as soft as the bird's downy breast feels. In
another line,

I stánd, remémbering the íslands and the seá's lóst soúnd,

the three unstressed syllables before and after the
stressed *isl* isolate that syllable as the island is isolated in the sea, and the three strong stresses together
at the close of the line suggest the strong pounding of
the tide. One of the biggest lines which yet keeps the
effect of being pentameter is

O Ápril, full of blóod, full of breáth, have mércy upón us,

where almost every foot is a full phrase, set off by
caesuras.

From such practices Millay goes on in her latest
volume to break away from pentameter entirely whenever she wishes, and to write great cadenza-like lines.

An extreme example is in *Conscientious Objector*, a poem
in which the sound imitates the clatter of a horse's
hoofs on a barn floor. The line,

> He is in haste; he has business in Cuba; business in the
>   Balkans; many calls to make this morning. . . . .

not only echoes clattering hoofs but catches the ugly
rat-tat-tat so characteristic of the impatient speech of
an "executive." The alliteration of *h* and *b* and *m*, of
course, gives form to the intentionally bizarre line.
Another extreme line, totally different in effect, imitates the smooth, ever recurrent lurch of ocean tide
lifting a swimmer:

> Under his weightless body, aware of the wide morning,
>   aware of the gull on the red buoy bedaubed with
>   guano, aware of his sharp cry. . . . .

In this line the five alliterated *w*'s hold the thirty-
three syllables together, but the form of the line is
given by the paired stresses "wide morn," "red
buoy," and "sharp cry," suggesting the lurch at the
crests of the tidal waves. In striking contrast with
the floating leisureliness of this line is the constriction
of the closely rhymed lines that follow in the next
stanza:

> Painfully, under the pressure that obtains
> At the sea's bottom, crushing my lungs and my brains. . . . .

If one sets that heroic couplet beside any one by Pope
or Dryden, one sees the means by which Millay has
achieved the effect of struggle and burden; the obtru-
sive consonants, the syncopated accents, the crowded
syllables are potent.

But Millay's versatility leads her not only to
crowded or lengthened lines but to shortened ones

also, even to single-syllabled ones. In the poem *In the Grave No Flower* the short lines fall heavily as clods:

> Here dock and tare.
> But there
> No flower.

Then the lines swell to greater length as she describes the mingled weeds and flowers of this world, working up to an outburst of vexation over the viciously spreading dandelions:

> here
> Dandelions,—and the wind
> Will blow them everywhere. . . . .

But then comes the sudden chilling turn of mood, which is so characteristic of Millay—a turn, in this instance, from irritation to hopeless love of the stubborn bright flowers, shining against her black despair. The wind will blow them everywhere, she suddenly realizes,

> Save there;
> There
> No flower.

And so the poem returns, at its close, to the toneless, clodlike weight of the short lines.

Despite all her virtuosity in unusual rhythms, however, it is still true that Millay's loveliest rhythms are the most regular ones, lifted to distinction by one can scarcely say what refinements of sound and silences. There is *Sappho Crosses the Dark River into Hades*. For pure and muted music one must make a very long search through the anthologies before finding anything equal to its simple octosyllables. In the phrases she has put on Sappho's lips Millay has not been unaware that Sappho was the most euphonious singer of all time, that she was πάρθενον αδύφωνον, the "sweet-voiced maiden." And so, as Sappho begins to speak here, the exquisitely spaced caesuras and the *r*'s and *d*'s of the first line, making the sound of a dipping and dripping oar—

> Charon, indeed, your dreaded oar . . . .

lead into a poem whose sound throughout is the silver echo of a sound, as if Sappho has already taken on the shadowy quality of the "pale city" they approach. To compare it with the things of this world, her voice has the innocent inconsequence of faraway sounds as one floats up to them from the deep sleep that follows relief from physical agony. The careful understatement of all the words, the light, oarlike beat of the rhythm, note on note, give Sappho's story of her so recent anguish and self-destruction the dream quality of something that happened long ago—πάλαι πότα, as Sappho herself said. Surely Sappho speaks with her own voice here.

Perhaps Millay's achievement in her latest volume is comparable to Sappho's as represented in this poem. She has reached a certain distance from her own pain and egotism. Not always, to be sure. *Apostrophe to Man* is raw; it is gory and brutal in its rage against her own sensibility. But most of the poems show that she has traveled a long way since she wrote some of the poems of her girlhood. Her first volume of lyrics revealed a violent contrast of moods. The childlike faith and serenity of *Renascence* were set against *Interim*, expressing utter abandon to human tragedy as in her total inexperience she imagined it must be. With Elizabethan extravagance she invented an agony remindful of Middleton's tirade:

WINE FROM THESE GRAPES

'Tis an affliction
Of greater weight than youth was made to bear,
As if a punishment of after-life
Were fallen upon man here; so new it is
To flesh and blood, so strange, so unsupportable,
A torment even mistook, as if a body
Whose death were drowning, must needs suffer it
In scalding oil. . . . .

In the next volume of lyrics actual grief has reached
her, and the tone is very different. But the volume is
made up entirely of variations on the theme of despair.
In the *Harp-Weaver* volume her mood has become more
complex. Joy and pain have become subtly interfused
in her life, and every poem in the volume reveals a
tempered mood. In *The Buck in the Snow* and still more
in *Wine from These Grapes* the intense egotism of her
moods is becoming transcended. She is becoming, as
she travels up the long and steep hill-slope of poetry,
not less herself, but more a human being, and from
personal agony she is climbing to the bleak grandeur
of our mortal infelicity. All her troubles and joys she
sees as those of the strange earth-dweller, man:

Man, with his singular laughter, his droll tears,
His engines and his conscience and his art.

Man is becoming a simple and a piteous being to
her. He is the "breather" and the "dust." And pitying herself in him she has begun to achieve a poetry of
communism—very different from the polemic communistic verse that is so prevalent just at present, but
not the less communal or poetic for that. The common
fate of man is coming to be her own deepest sorrow;
and her own death is scarcely distinguishable for her
from the extinction which she so deeply fears for the

243

race. She imagines a human skull on the insensible
earth, long after men have disappeared, and she muses:

> Heavy with music once this windy shell,
> Heavy with knowledge of the clustered stars;
> The one-time tenant of this draughty hall
> Himself, in learned pamphlet did foretell,
> After some aeons of study jarred by wars,
> This toothy gourd, this head emptied of all.

Is it her own skull she is thinking of, or that of her
enemy? The question no longer makes sense, for the
two are at one now. It is merely a skull of man, and
mankind has become to her an individual being, like
a character in a Dostoevski novel, a being who loves
and fears and hates everything, and is monstrous and
pitiable in his tragedy. Her genius for simplification
has made all mankind as real and as individual to her
as such a character. This, in spirit, is truly communal
poetry.

Millay's poetry is not utterly alone in this achievement of a cosmic simplicity. At a time when people
feel a common danger, an intense feeling of unity always arises among them. And now, in a time of wars
and rumors of wars, a time of foreboding for all mankind, the part of the human race that counts most,
the keenly thinking and feeling minority, has a
stronger feeling of unity than ever before, it seems to
me. Regardless of the field of research or of endeavor,
regardless of nationality or of class, all have become
her-buende, dwellers in the here-and-now, faced with
the problem of survival. And the poets' task, in such
a time, must be to sum up the poetic insight of all
the ages and determine the agreement and disagree-
ment of the intuitions of men in different times. All
the history of the world appears to be focused in the

present, and the direness of our need to understand it gives back to poetry a power of achieving synthesis and simplicity—that simplicity which only a few years ago it seemed so impossible to attain in our complex age without general beliefs.

If there are not many poets who are achieving this simplicity, that is natural enough, I suppose, and merely means that now, as always, there are not many living poets. At one level it seems as if our age were lavishly rich in poets: poets with sensuous impressibility and verbal cleverness and generous sentiments and erudition. But when it comes to philosophical significance, to awareness of a cosmos, there are today, as in other days, very few poets. There is Robinson Jeffers, who in a very few short lyrics, though never in his terrible long poems, it seems to me (unless conceivably in *At the Fall of an Age*) almost reaches cosmic expression. There is Archibald MacLeish, who is able to think of the human race in relation to the world-whole, and who writes, in *Men*,

> Our history is grave, noble, and tragic.
> We trusted the look of the sun on the green leaves,
> We built our towns of stone with enduring monuments. . . . .

There is George Dillon, who has written a few lines more beautifully philosophic than any by these other men. But Dillon's poetry holds the pallor of a moony reflection from Millay; in fact, it is the pallor of his poetry that gives it its delicate distinction. Reading his *Address to the Doomed* beside Millay's *Epitaph for the Race of Man* (first published in 1928) fades it. It is like hanging Whistler's "Trafalgar Square" beside El Greco's "Toledo." Dillon's poetry has breadth and fine gravity, but it is crepuscular. I admire it, but I somehow do not admire it enough. Other poets have

tried for this high philosophical simplicity: Hart
Crane, Mark Van Doren, Roy Campbell, John Mase-
field, Stephen Spender, W. H. Auden, C. Day Lewis.
. . . . But trying hasn't much to do with the matter.
If it had, Ezra Pound would have achieved philosophic
breadth and unity in the terrific clutter of excerpts
from historical documents that make up his *Cantos*.
T. S. Eliot tried, it seems, for such a philosophical
synthesis in his *Waste Land*, and it may well be that
the future will pronounce his synthesis a triumphant
one, but so far his fate has been to be admired most by
readers whose minds are most chaotic. If not he, then
Jeffers or MacLeish or Millay seems destined to be
the great philosophic poet of out time. Jeffers is often
merely nauseated and nauseating; MacLeish is sometimes obscure and uncertain of his direction—neither
reaches the verbal distinction of Millay, but there is
as compelling a sense of reserve power in them as in
Millay. All three sometimes afford one a momentary
glimpse of the stern and magnificent Alpine summits
of existence. Who knows what any one of them may
yet do? . . . . And on the other hand, of course, there
is the possibility that our generation will not have
its great philosophic poet. Perhaps we shall all merely
survive our common danger and settle down to being
comfortably Dickensian little individuals again. But
whatever our fate, we shall at least have had *Epitaph
for the Race of Man*. And not in a great many years, it
seems to me, has any English poem come so close to
greatness.

One secret of its fineness, as in *Fatal Interview*, is the
wide range of integrated learning which Millay brings
to it. She does not go scrambling through past history
gathering grist to her mill; as she comes to this poem

she *is* the past. She feels as men in other days would have felt under our catastrophes; she is Elizabethan, Chaucerian, Anglo-Saxon, Vergilian, and Sapphic, without being eclectic—ugly word! For she is always herself, an earth-dweller, at home in all the centuries. She might say even more truly now than when she wrote the war sonnet of her girlhood that all the past has brought her soul and personality into existence:

> Not in this chamber only at my birth—
> When the long hours of that mysterious night
> Were over, and the morning was in sight—
> I cried, but in strange places, steppe and firth
> I have not seen, through alien grief and mirth;
> And never shall one room contain me quite
> Who in so many rooms first saw the light,
> Child of all mothers, native of the earth.

If any poet has impressed *Epitaph for the Race of Man* more than another, it is, perhaps, and unexpectedly, Ovid. Ovid, too, wrote of a world emptied of its people, a world where a deep silence filled the desolated lands, as Millay writes of the time when

> Earth will have come upon a stiller day.

And Ovid, as well as Millay, contrasted care-worn men with the boyish gods who wear "golden curls outflung about their childish foreheads." And he wrote of a deluge so great that the farmer plied the oar where he had plowed, and brushed the keel of his boat over his vineyard tops, much as Millay sees man

> leaning on his single oar
> Above his garden faintly glimmering yet.

And Ovid made the king of the gods wish to cut the warfaring nature out of the bodies of men lest the untainted part also draw infection, just as Millay dreams

247

that man might have cut his warlike instincts out of himself:

> Would he had whittled treason from his side
> In his stout youth, and bled his body whole!

In fact, in its finished simplicity and purity of expression Millay's *Epitaph* might make another chapter of Ovid's *Metamorphoses;* and it is this high simplicity, as of ancient legends, posed against the bitterness of her mood and the staggering hugeness and complexity of her theme, that gives Millay's style the irony wherein lies much of its effectiveness.

Also the larger and graver style of the *Aeneid* is not without its impress on the *Epitaph*. Vergil's description of the fall of Priam's palace towers and of the sea tide sweeping away the ruins is in the key of Millay's last sonnet, foretelling the washing of the Atlantic waves among the fallen towers of New York. And in the sonnets wherein she shows the noble side of man's nature, his fortitude and cheer under natural disasters, one is continually reminded of the spirit of Aeneas' buffeted associates on their long pilgrimage to Italy, as they build their bonfires on one shore after another, and start "joyfully" onward once more after they are forced to give up their settlement in Crete. Millay's schoolgirl memories of Vergil[3] fuse with her experience of newspaper headlines that scream out the cataclysms of our day, and the strange blending results in some of the most moving of the sonnets in *Epitaph for the Race of Man*.

What is the philosophy expressed in *Epitaph for the*

[3] I do not mean to suggest that she has ever ceased to read Vergil. She still makes closer companions of the Latin poets than of any modern ones. But it is one's extremely youthful literary impressions that have deepest effect on one's writing.

Race of Man? It is a philosophy of a horribly unconscious fate driving all the starry host of heaven; "the
great heel of headless Force" is all that Millay can see
in the universe as a whole. It is a philosophy of earth
as an anomaly in the black and fiery universe, of earth
as a green homeland and an almost sentient being,
mother of all comforts and all manifold delights. It is
a philosophy of man as pure miracle in a universe of
nightmare unconsciousness, of man as an earth-child
bringing earth to true sentience, of man marvelously
capable of seeing and feeling, capable of conceiving
beauty and grandeur, capable even, were it not for
some nightmare trick of unconscious fate, of actually
achieving grandeur, but doomed, through the fear and
greed that accompany his sentience, to destroy himself, and so blot out all intellectual meaning from the
cosmos.

Millay's conviction that a soulless doom rules the
astronomical universe has come upon her gradually.
Her *Renascence* volume showed her holding a childlike
faith in God. Vassar tried to foster this religious
belief, but her nightmares there revealed that it was
already gone. In her dreams she felt that the vast
tides of the heavens were too much for any God to
control. And after the *Renascence* volume God fades
entirely out of her poetry. But astronomy remains.
Though she feared the unconscious starry courses, she
was fascinated by them; and she has learned much
more of them than most poets know. "Propping a
mattress on the turning sphere" she has gazed through
the great telescopes, and learned the names of stars
unknown to poetry heretofore. In the eighteenth and
nineteenth centuries poets knew the names of two or
three planets and constellations, but Venus and Mars,

Orion and the Pleiades come surprisingly close to exhausting the names of heavenly bodies in poetry up until the World War. Possibly Alfred Noyes, in his versified astronomy, helped to bring poets to a keener awareness of the sky depths, some years before Eddington and Jeans revealed to the general public the unimaginable fiery whirlpools there. At any rate, Frost and Fletcher and Aiken and Millay began to write a new kind of starry poetry. Like very few poets of the past, Aiken and Millay not only know the earth is rolling through space, but as poets they feel it doing so; they not only know of the vast abysses between the spiral nebulae, but they tremble and shrink from them. But Millay, though she shudders from this inhuman starry monster with its writhing movement, knows that it is foolish to fear it, for its remoteness has nothing to do with us or our immediate fate. She says:

> Now for the void sets forth, and farther still,
> The questioning mind of Man . . . . that by and by
> From the void's rim returns with swooning eye,
> Having seen himself into the maelstrom spill.
> Blench not, O race of Adam, lest you find
>   In the sun's bubbling bowl anonymous death,
> Or lost in whistling space without a mind
>   To monstrous Nothing yield your little breath.
> You shall achieve destruction where you stand
> In intimate conflict, at your brother's hand.

Her comfort, out under the heavens, is in the astronomical lies that greet the eye there. The fictions of the constellations are a kind of human fairy tale written across the heavens, a fairy tale of beneficence, of "radiant potentates bringing winter and summer unto mankind," as Aeschylus called the constellations long ago. And though knowledge of the true astro-

nomical spaces sometimes gives Millay a ghastly sense
of the unreality in these legends, so much so that,
remembering Hesiod's belief that the star Sirius
brings harvest heat to the wheatfields, she is only the
more aware of the terrible infinities of the skies, and
can write, ironically, of nothingness being

> Less than the heat
> Of the *farthest* star
> To the ripening wheat,

—yet, in spite of all this, she still loves the humanized
figures in the sky: Orion and the Pleiades, the Centaur
and the Cross, Aldebaran who "drives his wedge into
the western hill," and Capella "with her golden
kids." She loves these constellations chiefly, it appears, because the sight of them seems to bind all
mankind together. The sight of the Centaur binds
together the prehistoric man and the jungle-dweller of
today who, fearing the prowling tiger in the night, is
cheered by the sinking constellation that tells him
the sun is on its way,

> The sun, far off but marching, bringing light.

And the sight of Capella binds together the workman
of today and the workman under the Pharaohs, who
on his homeward way used to observe that

> The risen She-Goat, showing blue and red,
> Climbed the clear dusk, and three stars followed her.

Thus arbitrarily pricking out the constellations
from the welter of the trillions of suns suits Millay's
philosophy. She is still a pragmatist at heart, convinced as truly as William James and C. S. Pierce ever
were, that the all-inclusive wholeness of the universe
is a mere mess, that disorder is the original state of

things, and that all order is a selective order, an
achievement:

> Draw from the shapeless moment
> Such pattern as you can

Millay says as her (so far) final word on the design of
the universe.

Nor will she allow herself to be cowed by the al-
most-infinitude of this welter. Earth with its mankind may be a diamond that

> Is set in brass on the swart thumb of Doom,

but that does not mean that Millay will cringe before
this unconscious Doom. Her egotism asserts itself as
proudly as the independence of Shelley's Prometheus.
In spirit she addresses Doom as Prometheus did, as

> Monarch of Gods and Daemons, and of all spirits
> But One.

Unlike Margaret Fuller, Millay will not "accept the
universe" except piecemeal. She proudly "lets" this
and that exist with her approval. This "let" con-
struction has been one of the idiosyncrasies of her
sentences throughout her life. No doubt she has no
more to do with the existence of the things that she
regally "lets" exist than Chanticleer has to do with
the sun rising, but she cannot help that. What she
can help, and does help, is giving her approval and
sanction to anything in the universe that does not
satisfy her notion of fitness:

> I know, but I am not resigned, and I do *not* approve,

she says of universal human mortality in *Dirge without
Music;* and, though Doom may smash her and all mankind under his swart thumb, he cannot make her
change that dictum. And if she herself is actually no

individual being, but only a dizzy electron in the callous thumb tip of Doom, if her words are only part of a hollow and idiotic soliloquy that Doom is making to himself—what then? The defiant words are, she feels, a good thing to say and a true thing to say and a chastening thing to say, and she will still say them, and say them with gusto. That is her egotistical spirit; and as for me, in our intimidated and spiritless day, I glory in her spunk.

And this spirit saves her from Wordsworthian romanticism when she turns to the little earth, which she loves. This lonely and lovely emerald island in the universe, this bringer-forth of thought and beauty and ecstasy, it would be so easy to worship as faultless. And yet groveling on its bosom in infantile and undiscriminating love is not the way to realize the spiritual independence that we have almost achieved by growing out of it.

Millay is not a Wordsworthian; she does not see the earth as wise and divinely beneficent. On the other hand, she is not a Thomas-Hardyan; she does not see it (as Hardy did in certain moods) spitefully and meanly malevolent. She sees the earth as a being of impulses much like her own, mostly free and generous and eager ones, but sometimes wilful and hateful ones. Aldous Huxley has said that Wordsworth would never have been a Wordsworthian if he had lived in the tropics and seen Nature in her ill-behavior. Millay, on the other hand, takes full account of these bad moods. She shows the tropical jungle allowing man only a brief interval of content between the terrors of the night and the torrid heat of the day. His happy hour is that in which he lies "serene and undevoured." And she shows earth in cataclysmic quaking, making man "grin with terror" as his house slides from view. And she shows the horror of volcanic eruption, with earth

Rolling its pitchy lake of scalding stone

after fleeing man. And she takes account of floods and of fires and of lightning, "the golden fang of furious heaven."

Her fear of these things saves her from building up a pompous philosophical system of nature-worship, and most fortunately. For a poet ceases to be a poet the minute his philosophical schemes exceed the evidence of his poetic experience. He must ride on the pity and terror and joy and pain of his experience of life, and not apply his emotions to things too big to be proved by them. Millay remains always (well, nearly always) a poet because her philosophy always remains frankly the expression of a mood. She hates the world today and loves it tomorrow, but never without keeping the sense of time and of personality, the sense that it is her world of the present moment that she is judging, and that world alone.

But in spite of its occasional bad moods, her earth is usually a bounteous, beneficent earth, with great cleansing winds sweeping through it and free ocean tides. Sometimes, in moods in which she is most fond of it, it is like a middle-aged woman a bit run down at heel, an earth of shabby cattails and wizened apples and bedraggled birds and unfertile, weed-grown acres. Often it is a bleak and rocky earth that she loves; and she is not alone in this. One of the most striking resemblances in the nature poetry of twentieth-century poets is their love of earth in cold and barren moods. Poets so unlike as Elinor Wylie and

Robinson Jeffers share this feeling. They love earth when it seems in a state of endurance; there seems to be an assurance of permanence and of courage in it.

And Millay does not romanticize earth by giving it a human consciousness, as Wordsworth so nearly did. Her feeling seems to be that of the philosopher Whitehead, who is convinced that human thought and a green hill are one order of being, and who yet does not conceive of the green hill ruminating in a rational fashion. Whitehead and Santayana and Jeans—in fact, most of the philosophic writers of today who are influencing poets—think of the earth as holding only a vague potentiality of consciousness, which reaches actuality in the little human creatures on its surface. And so Millay says to earth:

> But no, you have not learned in all these years
> To tell the leopard and the newt apart.

Pitifully inadequate as any individual's human consciousness is, it is all the synthesis that the complex earth is capable of. Under the metaphor of the leaf and the tree, Millay muses to this effect about earth and a single human being:

> The fluttering thoughts a leaf can think,
> That hears the wind and waits its turn,
> Have taught it all a tree can learn.

And if this in certain moods is disquieting, still the unconsciousness of earth that is almost consciousness is often its greatest comfort and charm to a high-strung and nerve-racked human being. The truest nature poem of our century—truest to the moods and convictions of our century, I mean—is, in my opinion, Millay's *The Return*, in which she reveals the restful comfort for a man in this kindly indifference of earth:

255

Earth does not understand her child,
  Who from the loud gregarious town
Returns, depleted and defiled,
  To the still woods, to fling him down.
      . . . .
Who, marked for failure, dulled by grief,
  Has traded in his wife and friend
For this warm ledge, this alder leaf:
  Comfort that does not comprehend.

And in the earth nature of human sorrows Millay finds a comfort, a kind of peace. As Dante, at the beginning of the *Purgatorio*, washed the grime of hell from his face with the dew of earth, to which he was newly returned, so this poet, too, seems to find earth dew cooling and cleansing to her feverish and egotistical spirit. Because she loves the earth so much, the sorrows that grow out of it seem, somehow, strangely endurable.

Life lasts but a very little while. Tomorrow the individual will die, and day after tomorrow the race. And is this all there is to it? Millay seems to think so; but after all she is not sure. In *From a Train Window*, she looks out at a little country graveyard, where the self-sown trees of the region are growing among the graves, and where the old headstones are tilting back toward the earth, looking already much like the natural stones about them. And she tells herself,

Precious
In the early light, reassuring
Is the grave-scarred hillside.
As if after all, the earth might know what it is about.

Being a poet, she hungers for earth as roots do, and her hunger is satisfied by all her senses as directly. Possibly—barely possibly—death that she so abhors may be a satisfaction of a deeper hunger for the earth.

Her poem *Spring in the Garden* suggests as much. But if there is some physical immortality for man in the vegetative and mineral life of the globe, it is the only immortality that she can believe in. History has taught her the irony of other dreams of immortality. She says of the mummied kings of Egypt:

> Their will was law; their will was not to die;
> And so they had their way; or nearly so.

And yet because she is herself possessed of all the unreasonable human instincts that she may smile at, she too must have her poet's dream of individual immortality. Art alone seems to her a survival and a victor over time, at least so long as humanity may endure. Therefore, it is necessary for her dream that men will survive the frenzy of self-destruction which seems about to overtake them and that they will exist upon the globe ten thousand years from now. If they do exist then, they will be—however different in their social and political customs, however exalted or degraded—still susceptible to poetry, she is sure; for, being human, they will still know aspiration and aching disappointment. And so she addresses such a man standing in his apple orchard—a seedling of the same old *apulder* of Old English times—a man beset in the moonlight by his lost dreams:

> . . . .
> Things you could not spare
>   And live, or so you thought, yet these
> All gone, and you still there,
>
> A man no longer what he was,
>   Nor yet the thing he'd planned,
> The chilly apple from the grass
>   Warmed by your living hand—

I think you will have need of tears;
    I think they will not flow;
Supposing in ten thousand years
    Men ache, as they do now.

She does not hope that he will phrase his grief in her words—she does not think that she has this hope—and yet the deep subconscious undercurrent is a cry for her own immortality. It is Sappho's "Men, I think, will remember us hereafter."

But this is only a dream. What is not a dream to her is the survival of poetry throughout the few moments of one's own existence, here and now. Her "soul's chastity" still lies in her devotion to poetry, which gives her life its only shape and meaning. The lower our logical conception of what the human mind is may fall, the taller and the more radiantly the miracle of poetry and music lifts itself. The miracle of a small song played on a Chinese flute by an ill-smelling and oppressed boatman was for a time, she says, all she had to preserve her faith and joy in human nature. And her satisfaction in her own nature comes from her undeviating devotion to this poetic beauty—a beauty indifferent and unconscious as earth itself. She counsels herself:

From cool and aimless Beauty
    Your bread and comfort take,
Beauty, that made no promise,
    And has no word to break:

Have eyes for Beauty only,
    That has no eyes for you;
Follow her struck pavilion;
    Halt with her retinue.

For years she has renewed this decidation: in *Cherish You Then the Hope*, in *The Poet and His Book*, in *Bluebeard*, *Dragonfly*, *The Cameo*, *Lethe*, *Life Were Thy Pains*,

On Thought in Harness, Above These Cares, and *My Spirit Sore from Marching.*

In the fickle chaos of a lifetime the strange charm of the poetic memory is to her, as to Proust, that it cannot be lost. If the surface of the mind forgets, the impression only sinks the deeper, and forms the hard jewel of poetic remembrance. This is the theme of *The Cameo:*

> From the action of tears and the action of sorrow forever
> secure,
> White, against a ruddy cliff you stand,
> Chalcedony on sard.

And this is also the theme of *Lethe:*

> In these cool waves
> What can be lost?—
> Only the sorry cost
> Of the lovely thing, ah, never the thing itself.
> Immerse the dream.
> Drench the kiss:
> Dip the song in the stream.

The crystallization of the myriad curiosities of sensation, of agonies and joys, of hates and loves into a deeply satisfying poetic empathy within a man's heart during his little span of life—this is for Millay the kernel of pure good in the universe. And despite the deeply tragic tone of her latest volume, this still seems to be, for her, enough. To ask for more than felicity would be stupid. That a man emerging from the unconscious cosmos should be, in sensibility and apprehension, how like a god, even though it be but for a little while, is an incomparable boon. It makes this tragic and sorrowful earth life, which is all we know and all we any longer believe in, inexpressibly precious— not less precious, to Millay, at least,

> Than that sweet heaven our fathers hoped to gain.

INDEX

INDEX

INDEX

265

EDNA ST. VINCENT MILLAY

Troilus and Criseyde, 83
Two Noble Kinsmen, 38, 75, 84, 218, 230
Tzara, 95

Untermeyer, Louis, 12, 72, 76

Valéry, Paul, 103, 139
Van Doren, Mark, 246
Vanzetti, Bartolomeo, 176, 177, 178, 181, 183, 184, 201
Vassar College, 14, 26, 28, 59, 64, 249
Vaughan, Henry, 185
Vergil, x, 14, 15, 108, 111, 181, 192, 203, 219, 220, 247, 248
Verlaine, Paul, 201
Vicar of Wakefield, The, 108

Wagner, Richard, 8
Waste Land, The, 78, 93, 106, 108, 112, 114, 119, 150, 153, 246
Watson, John Broadus, 124, 127, 146

Webster, John, vii, 35, 36, 45, 57, 83, 84, 85, 86, 87, 90, 93, 97, 118, 214, 229
Welch, Marie de L., 142, 187, 191
Wheelock, John Hall, 12
Whistler, James McNeill, 119, 143, 245
White Devil, The, 36, 39, 87, 97
Whitehead, Alfred North, 255
Whitman, Walt, 112
Wild Swans, 190, 191
Wilde, Oscar, 7, 71
Wine from These Grapes, xi, 181, 235, 243
Woodberry, George, 12
Wordsworth, William, 6, 10, 126, 144, 236, 253, 255
Wylie, Elinor, 46, 60, 61, 110, 129, 139, 144, 189, 205, 254

Yeats, William Butler, 102, 115, 155, 156